Fireworks® 4 For Dummies®

Cheat Sheet

D1101757

Tools Used to Edit Objects and Make Selections

	Pointer tool
	Select Behind tool
	Subselection tool
	Marquee tool
	Oval Marquee tool
	Lasso tool
	Polygon Lasso tool
	Magic Wand tool
	Rubber Stamp tool
	Scale tool
	Skew tool
	Distort tool
	Freeform tool
	Redraw Path tool
	Reshape Area tool
	Paint Bucket tool
	Eyedropper tool
	Eraser tool (bitmap mode)
	Eraser tool (vector mode)

Tools Used to Create Objects

	Line tool
	Pen tool
	Rectangle tool
	Rounded Rectangle tool
	Ellipse tool
	Polygon tool
	Pencil tool
	Brush tool
	Text tool

For Dummies®: Bestselling Book Series for Beginners

Fireworks® 4 For Dummies®

Cheat Sheet

File Menu Keyboard Shortcuts

Command	Windows	Macintosh
New	Ctrl + N	Command + N
Open	Ctrl + O	Command + O
Close	Ctrl + W	Command + W
Save	Ctrl + S	Command + S
Import	Ctrl + R	Command + R
Export	Ctrl + Shift + R	Command + Shift + R

Edit Menu Keyboard Shortcuts

Command	Windows	Macintosh
Undo	Ctrl + Z	Command + Z
Redo	Ctrl + Y	Command + Y
Cut	Ctrl + X	Command + X
Copy	Ctrl + C	Command + C
Paste	Ctrl + V	Command + V
Select All	Ctrl + A	Command + A
Deselect	Ctrl + D	Command + D

Insert Menu Keyboard Shortcuts

Command	Windows	Macintosh
New Symbol	Ctrl + F8	Command + F8
Convert to Symbol	F8	F8
Hotspot	Ctrl + Shift + U	Command + Shift + U
Image	Ctrl + R	Command + R
Slice	Alt + Shift + U	Option + Shift + U

Hungry Minds™

For Dummies®: Bestselling Book Series for Beginners

TM

...FOR DUMMIES

BESTSELLING BOOK SERIES

References for the Rest of Us!®

Are you intimidated and confused by computers? Do you find that traditional manuals are overloaded with technical details you'll never use? Do your friends and family always call you to fix simple problems on their PCs? Then the For Dummies® computer book series from Hungry Minds, Inc. is for you.

For Dummies books are written for those frustrated computer users who know they aren't really dumb but find that PC hardware, software, and indeed the unique vocabulary of computing make them feel helpless. For Dummies books use a lighthearted approach, a down-to-earth style, and even cartoons and humorous icons to dispel computer novices' fears and build their confidence. Lighthearted but not lightweight, these books are a perfect survival guide for anyone forced to use a computer.

> "*I like my copy so much I told friends; now they bought copies.*"
> — Irene C., Orwell, Ohio

> "*Quick, concise, nontechnical, and humorous.*"
> — Jay A., Elburn, Illinois

> "*Thanks, I needed this book. Now I can sleep at night.*"
> — Robin F., British Columbia, Canada

Already, millions of satisfied readers agree. They have made For Dummies books the #1 introductory level computer book series and have written asking for more. So, if you're looking for the most fun and easy way to learn about computers, look to For Dummies books to give you a helping hand.

Hungry Minds™

Fireworks 4®

FOR

DUMMIES®

by Doug Sahlin

Hungry Minds™

HUNGRY MINDS, INC.

New York, NY ◆ Cleveland, OH ◆ Indianapolis, IN

Fireworks® 4 For Dummies®

Published by
Hungry Minds, Inc.
909 Third Avenue
New York, NY 10022
www.hungryminds.com
www.dummies.com

Library of Congress Control Number: 00-110829

ISBN: 0-7645-0804-0

Printed in the United States of America

10 9 8 7 6 5 4 3 2 1

1B/QY/QT/QR/IN

Distributed in the United States by Hungry Minds, Inc.

Distributed by CDG Books Canada Inc. for Canada; by Transworld Publishers Limited in the United Kingdom; by IDG Norge Books for Norway; by IDG Sweden Books for Sweden; by IDG Books Australia Publishing Corporation Pty. Ltd. for Australia and New Zealand; by TransQuest Publishers Pte Ltd. for Singapore, Malaysia, Thailand, Indonesia, and Hong Kong; by Gotop Information Inc. for Taiwan; by ICG Muse, Inc. for Japan; by Intersoft for South Africa; by Eyrolles for France; by International Thomson Publishing for Germany, Austria and Switzerland; by Distribuidora Cuspide for Argentina; by LR International for Brazil; by Galileo Libros for Chile; by Ediciones ZETA S.C.R. Ltda. for Peru; by WS Computer Publishing Corporation, Inc., for the Philippines; by Contemporanea de Ediciones for Venezuela; by Express Computer Distributors for the Caribbean and West Indies; by Micronesia Media Distributor, Inc. for Micronesia; by Chips Computadoras S.A. de C.V. for Mexico; by Editorial Norma de Panama S.A. for Panama; by American Bookshops for Finland.

For general information on Hungry Minds' products and services please contact our Customer Care Department within the U.S. at 800-762-2974, outside the U.S. at 317-572-3993 or fax 317-572-4002.

For sales inquiries and reseller information, including discounts, premium and bulk quantity sales, and foreign-language translations, please contact our Customer Care Department at 800-434-3422, fax 317-572-4002, or write to Hungry Minds, Inc., Attn: Customer Care Department, 10475 Crosspoint Boulevard, Indianapolis, IN 46256.

For information on licensing foreign or domestic rights, please contact our Sub-Rights Customer Care Department at 650-653-7098.

For information on using Hungry Minds' products and services in the classroom or for ordering examination copies, please contact our Educational Sales Department at 800-434-2086 or fax 317-572-4005.

Please contact our Public Relations Department at 212-884-5163 for press review copies or 212-884-5000 for author interviews and other publicity information or fax 212-884-5400.

For authorization to photocopy items for corporate, personal, or educational use, please contact Copyright Clearance Center, 222 Rosewood Drive, Danvers, MA 01923, or fax 978-750-4470.

Hungry Minds˜ is a trademark of Hungry Minds, Inc.

About the Author

Doug Sahlin is a writer, digital artist, and Web site designer living in Central Florida. He is the author of the *Carrara 1 Bible* and *Carrara 1 For Dummies,* both published by Hungry Minds, Inc. He is also the author of *Flash 5 Virtual Classroom*. In addition, he has authored online courses and written numerous articles and tutorials about 2-D and 3-D graphics programs. He uses Dreamweaver, Flash, and Fireworks to create Web sites for his clients.

Dedication

This book is dedicated to my family, friends, and mentors.

Author's Acknowledgments

I would like to thank Mike Roney, Senior Acquisitions Editor at Hungry Minds, for making this book possible. Many thanks to the talented Andrea Boucher, the book's Project Editor, for providing editorial guidance and reminding me that I ain't a spring chicken anymore. Thanks to Technical Editor Marisa Bozza for her attention to detail while reviewing the text. Thanks to my friends, family, and fellow authors for being a never-ending source of encouragement, inspiration, and support. Special thanks to everyone at Macromedia, especially the members of the Fireworks team.

Publisher's Acknowledgments

We're proud of this book; please send us your comments through our Online Registration Form located at www.dummies.com.

Some of the people who helped bring this book to market include the following:

Acquisitions, Editorial, and Media Development

Project Editor: Andrea C. Boucher

Acquisitions Editor: Michael L. Roney

Technical Editor: Marisa Bozza, Macromedia Fireworks

Editorial Manager, Freelance: Constance Carlisle

Media Development Manager: Laura Carpenter

Media Development Supervisor: Richard Graves

Editorial Assistants: Amanda Foxworth, Jean Rogers

Production

Project Coordinator: Bill Ramsey

Layout and Graphics: Amy Adrian, Gabriele McCann, Jacque Schneider Julie Trippetti, Jeremey Unger

Proofreaders: Laura Albert Sally Burton, David Faust, Andy Hollandbeck, Nancy Price, Charles Spencer York Production Services, Inc.

Indexer: York Production Services, Inc.

General and Administrative

Hungry Minds, Inc.: John Kilcullen, CEO; Bill Barry, President and COO; John Ball, Executive VP, Operations & Administration; John Harris, CFO

Hungry Minds Technology Publishing Group: Richard Swadley, Senior Vice President and Publisher; Mary Bednarek, Vice President and Publisher, Networking and Certification; Walter R. Bruce III, Vice President and Publisher, General User and Design Professional; Joseph Wikert, Vice President and Publisher, Programming; Mary C. Corder, Editorial Director, Branded Technology Editorial; Andy Cummings, Publishing Director, General User and Design Professional; Barry Pruett, Publishing Director, Visual

Hungry Minds Manufacturing: Ivor Parker, Vice President, Manufacturing

Hungry Minds Marketing: John Helmus, Assistant Vice President, Director of Marketing

Hungry Minds Online Management: Brenda McLaughlin, Executive Vice President, Chief Internet Officer

Hungry Minds Production for Branded Press: Debbie Stailey, Production Director

Hungry Minds Sales: Roland Elgey, Senior Vice President, Sales and Marketing; Michael Violano, Vice President, International Sales and Sub Rights

◆

The publisher would like to give special thanks to Patrick J. McGovern, without whom this book would not have been possible.

◆

Contents at a Glance

Cartoons at a Glance

By Rich Tennant

"Mary-Jo, come here quick! Look at this special effect I learned with the new Fireworks software."

page 7

"Well, it's not quite done. I've animated the gurgling spit-sink and the rotating Novocaine syringe, but I still have to add the high speed whining drill audio track."

page 211

"Jeez—that's impressive! Let's see that airbrush effect again."

page 299

"Why don't you try blurring the brimstone and then putting a nice glow effect around the hellfire."

page 103

Cartoon Information:
Fax: 978-546-7747
E-Mail: richtennant@the5thwave.com
World Wide Web: www.the5thwave.com

Table of Contents

Introduction

•••

*A*pplications that create content for Web sites can be pretty daunting to work with. There's so much to do and often so little time to do it. When you're under the gun to come up with a first-class Web page, you have to create graphics, animations, navigation menus, and of course there's the HTML code that makes the whole thing appear pixel perfect in a Web browser. If you've ever had a good look at the code that needs to be generated to create the simplest of Web pages, it's enough to make you swear off the Internet.

If you're thinking of buying Fireworks 4 or already own a copy of the program, you'll be relieved to know that this program goes a long way towards making the process of creating graphics and HTML pages for Web sites much easier. With Fireworks 4, you spend more time putting your creative mind to work creating Web site artwork rather than wracking your brain to remember the right bit of code to make a rollover button. When you create items like a rollover button in Fireworks, the program applies the right behavior and HTML code to make the button strut its stuff on a Web page.

Who Should Buy This Book

If you bought a copy of Fireworks 4 or took a look at it in the comfort of your favorite computer retailer's air-conditioned showroom and freaked out when you saw all the menu commands and panels and tools and toolbars, you've got the right book in your hands. Whether you're a newcomer to Web graphics programs or a seasoned pro, you can quickly come up to speed with the new and improved features of Fireworks 4. Find a nice spot for this book alongside your computer and use it as a handy reference guide. Read the book until the pages are folded, spindled, and mutilated worse than the Lotto card you've been playing for the last five years. You can use this book in one of two ways:

✔ When you need the lowdown on a particular feature, task, or tool, refer to the index, which will lead you to concise, bite-size chunks of Fireworks know-how.

✔ If you know nothing about Fireworks 4, read the book from cover to cover to find out how to use Fireworks most used features.

I've waded through enough applications manuals to work myself into a pair of tri-focals. Along the way I found out that the people who write applications manuals are awfully proud of their vocabulary and do their best to show off their techno-geek vocabulary. Reading techno-geek is about as exciting as watching a shuffleboard tournament. Rest assured, I don't resort to techno-geek if there's a way to explain it in good old everyday English. I dole out the information in easy to digest slices, like that pineapple you buy that comes in a can.

Stuff You Oughta Know

Before you can be-bop your way into Fireworks and start creating Web graphics and Web pages and other Web related stuff, it's time to take a quick inventory. You should have the majority of the following to get up and running.

- ✔ You should either have a copy of Fireworks 4 or plan to buy one in the near future.

- ✔ You know that Fireworks 4 is an application to create Web graphics and Web pages, not a guide to the most powerful and colorful Fourth of July incendiary devices. If the latter is your goal, kindly put this book back on the shelf and check with your bookseller.

- ✔ You have a basic knowledge of Web pages and the elements used to create them.

- ✔ You have an HTML editor such as Macromedia Dreamweaver. This is not essential as Fireworks does a bang-up job of generating HTML code. If, however, you plan on incorporating your Fireworks documents with other HTML documents, an HTML editor of some sort is essential.

- ✔ You have a basic knowledge of computer graphics and know a pixel from a pixie. This is not essential, but it sure helps.

- ✔ You have a basic knowledge of vector objects and how they are created. I show you how to create vector objects in the book, but a basic knowledge of the techniques involved will get you up and running quicker.

To use Fireworks effectively, you need a system with the following minimum requirements:

- ✔ If you're using Fireworks on a Windows based machine, you need an Intel Pentium (Pentium II is recommended) processor with a Windows 95, 98, 2000, ME or NT operating system. Your machine should have a hard drive with a minimum available storage capacity of 80 MB, 64 MB of available RAM and a minimum display of 640 x 480 with 256 colors (1024 x 768 display with millions of colors is recommended).

- ✔ If you're using Fireworks on a Macintosh based machine, it should have a Power Macintosh Processor (G3 or higher is recommended) using the Mac OS 8.6 of 9.XX. Your machine should have 64 MB of available RAM with 80 MB of available hard disk storage.

How This Book Is Organized

I've laid out the book so you can use it as a whole or read it in sections. The book is broken down into four parts, each one consisting of chapters of related material, all of which contain material that is designed to inform and maybe put a grin on your face at the same time. Each chapter is broken down into sections, which are further broken down into paragraphs, which are further broken down into sentences, which are then broken down into words, which, as you may remember from grade school, are comprised of consonants and all the vowels I bought from Vanna.

Part 1: Fireworks: A Graphic Design Program, Not a 4th of July Sparkler

Fireworks 4 is a major revision of an existing program. The program has lots of new bells and whistles, but to begin understanding the program, you've got to start somewhere. In the case of this book, your first helping of Fireworks is served up in Part I. If you're new to Fireworks and Web design in general, I suggest you begin at the beginning and read the book word for word. If you're a Fireworks veteran, browse through Part I and read what you need.

In Part I, I give you the tour of the interface and introduce you to some basic Fireworks concepts. I show you how to use the tools to create neat little shapes, introduce you to bitmap images, and also show you how to use color for the Web.

Part II: Creating Complex Graphics for Fun and Profit

If a Web site doesn't have graphics, it looks pretty bland. If you want your Web pages to attract visitors and attract attention, good-looking graphics are a must. Most Web pages are a combination of vector objects and bitmap images.

In Part II, I show you how to create complex vector objects and how to add solid color or gradients to them. I also show you how to modify these graphics and apply effects to them to make them special (everyone likes special effects). Last but not least, I show you how to optimize the images you create for export in the optimal amount of space, one chapter.

Part III: Making Fireworks Even Hotter: Creating Animations and Dynamic Web Elements

Animations look pretty spiffy on a Web site. They draw the viewer's attention and can be used as eye candy or as advertising banners. In this section, I show you how to create animations and add interactivity to your designs with behaviors. Behaviors don't correct a Fireworks document's bad manners; they create a lot of neat effects like teaching a button to roll over (or more precisely, to change images on a multi-state rollover button). I also show you how to create hotspots, which do something special when the exported document is viewed in a Web browser.

Part IV: The Part of Tens

Each chapter in the Part of Tens consists of ten what nots or why nots that show you how to do something special with Fireworks. I devote one of the chapters in this section to showing you how to do things to streamline your workflow. In another chapter I show you ten cool Fireworks tricks and tips. And last but not least I show you twelve (I know. I did the math, but felt you needed to see all twelve.) Web sites that have Fireworks resources or HTML resources.

Icons Used In This Book

Throughout the book you'll see little icons in the margin. These icons are your signposts to tasty tidbits of Fireworks information. The following icons are used in this book:

Whenever you see this icon, you'll find out something that comes in handy in your Fireworks projects. The tips help you be more efficient with Fireworks, and when you become more efficient, people stand up and take notice. And if you're using Fireworks at work, the added efficiency may spring you up to the next rung on the ladder. (And even if it doesn't, at least you'll know how to create a ladder in Fireworks.)

Wherever you see this icon you're being alerted to a potential problem area. The contents of this warning may have come about as a result of someone else finding out the hard way that something doesn't work. If you decide to ignore the sage wisdom attached to this icon and go boldly where other Fireworks designers have crashed and burned before, I won't be there to say I told you so, but remember: I did tell you so.

This icon alerts you to some useful Fireworks info or perhaps a different way to achieve the same result. It may also be a reminder of something I've already shown you how to do. Whenever you see this icon get a piece of string or some used dental floss and tie it — but not so tightly as to impede your circulation — around one of your fingers. Then when you see the string you'll remember the Remember icon and with any luck at all, remember the bit of info attached to it.

 If there's just no way around the techno-geek speak, I at least give you fair warning by attaching this icon to tech-heavy text.

 When you see this icon, you'll find a link to another chapter that presents additional information related to the topic at hand. I've tried to make each chapter as self-sufficient as possible, but Fireworks has a lot of bells and whistles that are used with many different aspects of the program. To present the information again when needed would create a book the size of the New York City telephone directory, a tome you'd be afraid to hold, let alone read.

Where to Go From Here

Fireworks creates images for the Web par excellence and can create a full-fledged HTML document for Web page with all the interactivity the Internet allows. In this book I show you how to use Fireworks' most popular features to design images and pages for the Web. If, however, after reading this book you decide you've got to know every Fireworks nook and cranny, pick up a copy of *Fireworks 4 Bible* (published by Hungry Minds, Inc.) by Joe Lowery and Simon White. If you want to learn more about HTML publishing, pick up one of this fine books (also published by Hungry Minds, Inc.):

- *HTML 4 For Dummies,* 3rd Edition, by Ed Tittle and Natanya Pitts
- *HTML 4.01 Weekend Crash Course* by Greg M. Perry
- *Master Visually HTML 4 and XHTML1* by Kelly Murdock
- *Creating Cool HTML Web Pages* by Dave Taylor
- *Dreamweaver 4 Bible* by Joe Lowery
- *Dreamweaver UltraDev 4 Bible* by Joe Lowery
- *Dreamweaver 4 For Dummies* by Janine Warner and Paul Vachier
- *XHTML in Plain English* by Sandra Eddy
- *XHTML Master Reference* by Heather Williamson

Part I

Fireworks: A Graphic Design Program, Not a 4th of July Sparkler

The 5th Wave By Rich Tennant

"Mary-Jo, come here quick! Look at this special effect I learned with the new Fireworks software."

In this part . . .

Okay, yesterday you didn't know a GIF from a TIFF from your boss's dog named Biff. And now you've got a picture of Biff, which your boss wants you to scan and put up on the Internet as the corporate mascot. And he's given you this gaily-colored box with something named Fireworks 4 inside to do the work with. After loading the program into your computer and looking at all the program's menus, icons, and toolbars, you decided discretion was the better part of valor and rushed out to pick up a copy of this book. Now that you have the book in your hands, you've wisely decided to begin at the beginning — which I would personally like to thank you for because the beginning of this book took a considerable amount of time to write — and find out what all the cute little icons, panels, and toolbars are used for.

In this part of the book, I show you how to get around in Fireworks, giving you a detailed tour of the workspace. After you're familiar with the location of everything, I show you how to create objects and work with color. If you've never worked with color for the Web or dabbled with vector objects, this part of the book brings you up to speed on both counts. If you've never used Fireworks before, you probably want to read every precious word that I have carefully chosen for this section. If, however, you're a Fireworks veteran and need to come up to speed with the new features, pick and choose what you need and mosey on over to Part II.

Chapter 1

Fireworks: A Web Designer's Best Friend

In This Chapter

▶ Understanding what Fireworks does

▶ Living a day in the life of a Web designer

Y ou're sitting in your little cubicle, safely tucked away, cleaning up loose ends as the clock ticks ever so slowly towards quitting time. As you're jotting down your to-do list for tomorrow, you hear it: the dreaded slam of a solid wooden door that you know only too well. And then you hear the sound of shoes squeaking on a highly polished floor as your boss winds his way through the cubicles. The sound gets closer and you think, "No way is he headed for my little cubbyhole. Overtime is out of the question — I've got laundry to do, kids to take to the softball game, and . . ." Your boss appears, smiling, holding a brightly colored box, which is deposited on your desk. "Fireworks" it says on the label, and you think, "Oh neat, we're gonna have fireworks at the company picnic." But your boss explains that there will be no company picnic this year. The marketing mavens have decided to use the budget for the picnic to create a Web site instead. And your boss explains that you've been assigned the task of creating the Web site with the software in the brightly colored box on your desk. Before you can even think of a logical rebuttal, your boss turns on his heels and is winding his way back to the safety of an overstuffed high-backed leather chair, doing whatever bosses do in their high-backed overstuffed leather chairs. So with great trepidation, you carefully peel the shrink-wrap off the box and wonder: "What the heck is Fireworks, anyway?"

What Is Fireworks, Anyway?

First and foremost, Fireworks is a graphics program. You use it to create graphics for the Web. If you've done any surfing on the Web, you know that the Internet is more than just pretty pictures. You have many types of graphics (also called *images*) on the Web. Some are indeed pretty pictures, while others are company logos or buttons or arrows or frames or things called *Animated GIFs,* which move about the Web page. (GIF is pronounced *jiff,* by the way.)

One thing you'll be happy to find out is that Fireworks does all the tough stuff. You don't have to know much about HTML (*HyperText Markup Language* for the techno-geek), which is a good thing, because HTML ain't easy to learn. All you need to do is create the artwork; when you export the document, Fireworks creates the HTML. It's just that simple. Figure 1-1 shows a Fireworks image ready to be exported for use as a Web page.

And after you use Fireworks to create all of these images, you then use Fireworks to optimize graphic objects for the Web. Okay, you're thinking: "Why do I need to optimize a graphic for the Web?" Well, if you've ever been to a Web page that takes three forevers (three forevers is the equivalent of a zillion New York minutes) to download, you've visited a Web site that didn't use optimized graphics. Fireworks gives you the tools to optimize graphics, and even tells you how long they'll take to download from the Internet. Such a deal.

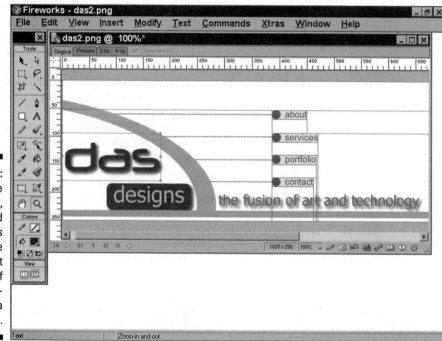

Figure 1-1:
You create
the artwork,
and
Fireworks
does the
grunt
work of
transform-
ing it into a
Web page.

When you create images for Web pages, one of your biggest concerns is *bandwidth* (the amount of data that can be downloaded per second at a given Internet connection speed). When a Web page exceeds a user's available bandwidth, it's kinda like trying to pour a jug of water through a small straw — it just trickles out. Downloading images from the Internet can be like that. If you're downloading a large image file, things progress rather slowly. So your job as an intrepid Web developer is to create the skinniest image file possible. And Fireworks makes child's play of this.

Creating a Fireworks Document

So then, you use Fireworks to create stuff like images, animations, and pages for the Web. If you're wondering how to do it, then you're in the right place. The chapters of this book tell you everything you need to know to successfully create images for the Web and export them in formats that download quickly. You can also choose to *export* (save an image in a particular format) your Fireworks artwork with an HTML document that will assemble all of your artwork nicely and neatly in a Web browser.

A typical Fireworks project involves a few stages. In the long list that follows, I show you a typical day in the life of a Fireworks Web designer, which gives you an overview of how the program dovetails together to take an artistic vision from your mind's eye and transform it into something you can share with the millions of people who surf the Internet. I include a cross-reference in each bullet to the chapter(s) that cover the details of the topic at hand.

✔ **Beginning the project:** When you, your client, or your boss gets the notion to put some images on the Internet, it's time to call Fireworks in to the rescue. You begin a Fireworks project by creating a document. The document is like an artist's canvas; in fact, in Fireworks it actually is called a *canvas*. The canvas is where you get expressive and create objects with the Fireworks drawing tools. Everything you create on the canvas can be moved at will while you're creating the project. Figure 1-2 shows a document in the Fireworks workspace. I show you how to create a new document in Chapter 2.

I know, you're looking at Figure 1-2 and wondering what the heck all the stuff is on the canvas. Well, you've got your Toolbox, some panels, and a lot of menus. You use the Toolbox to create and modify objects for your documents. You use the panels to modify other attributes such as an object's color, outline, and opacity. Panels and menus are used for other things as well. I show you how to use the panels and menus throughout the book as the need arises. Some of the more esoteric (read: fancy-schmancy) tools and panels are covered in the later chapters of this book where I show you how to apply effects to objects and optimize objects for export. I show you how to navigate around the Fireworks workspace in Chapter 2.

Toolbox   Canvas   Panels

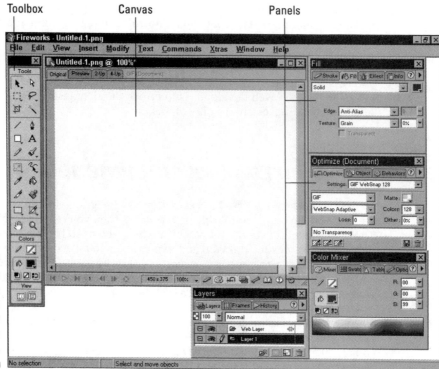

Figure 1-2:
You begin a
Fireworks
project by
creating a
document.

✔ **Bitmap versus vector objects:** You can create all of your artwork within Fireworks, import it, or combine your original artwork with imported images. The choice is yours because you are the creator. In Fireworks you use two different types of images: bitmaps and vector objects:

- *Bitmaps* are photo-realistic images, such as photographs of people and places and spaceships and things. You can import bitmap images into Fireworks and then modify them for use on your Web pages. *Bitmap* is a generic name for images created from pixels. *Pixels* are not the little sparkles that follow a fairy's wand through the air (although you could create a reasonable facsimile in Fireworks); they're little dots of color that are blended together to create an image. Bitmap images are resolution dependent, which means you can't blow 'em up without distorting them. I show you how to import and edit bitmap images in Chapter 4.

- *Vector objects* are images you create with the Toolbox drawing tools and are great for things like backdrops for text or button shapes. You can import vector objects created in other programs as well. Vector objects are comprised of lines (also known as *paths*) and solid shapes, which when enlarged do not distort because they are redrawn using mathematics. It all adds up. Trust me. I show you how to create vector objects in Chapter 3; how to modify the line of the image (called the *stroke*) in Chapter 7; and how to add a fill and color in Chapter 8.

You can mix and match bitmap images with vector objects in Fireworks, sort of like a family meal in a Chinese restaurant: one bitmap from folder A, one vector object from folder B, one bitmap from Folder C and an order of Dim Sum on the side in case you get hungry when you're creating all this wonderful artwork.

✔ **Modifying artwork:** As you create and import objects in Fireworks, you need to position them on the canvas. You also need the ability to resize and otherwise modify the artwork to create a finished product for the Web. You modify the objects with tools from the Toolbox and with menu commands. You can modify both vector objects and bitmap images in Fireworks. I show you how to modify vector objects in Chapters 9 and 10. Many of the techniques presented in these chapters are used on bitmap images as well.

✔ **Organizing artwork:** Fireworks gives you the capability of creating sophisticated artwork for your Web designs. However, with this sophistication also comes the possibility for chaos. As you create more objects for a document, the canvas becomes cluttered and things may become difficult to select, let alone find. Fortunately, the makers of Fireworks have supplied you with the tools you need to bring order to the chaos. You can group items to make them behave as a single unit, organize objects by segregating them on layers, or combine grouping and layers when you've got a lot of objects to deal with. I show you how to organize your artwork in Chapter 10.

✔ **Getting the message across:** Creating artwork for your Web pages is all well and good, but at some point in time you're actually going to have to get a message across with the written word. Fireworks gives you a Text tool, backed with a powerful Text Editor that lets you create anything from plain-Jane text to razzle-dazzle text. I show you how to create and edit text for your documents in Chapter 6.

✔ **Using symbols and instances:** You can also create reusable artwork known as *symbols*. When you create a symbol, it's stored in the document Library. Whenever you take a symbol from the Library and use it in a document, Fireworks creates a copy of the original, which is known as an *instance*. I show you how to create symbols and work with the document Library in Chapter 13.

✔ **Putting the sizzle in your Fireworks artwork:** To make your Web designs stand out, you can apply effects to the artwork you create. You can create special effects like beveled buttons, glowing text, or artwork that appears to float off the canvas, just to name a few. I show you how to create special effects in Chapter 11. In Chapters 19 and 20, I show you how to combine effects to create some unique elements for your Fireworks documents.

✔ **Animating your artwork:** Remember the flipbooks you used to buy when you were a kid? (Well, I still buy them, but then again, I'm very easily amused.) If you look at a flipbook one page at a time, you see a still image of something like a cartoon character or a monster. As you look at the pages one by one, the character is in a slightly different pose or position on each page. Run your thumb across the pages and you see something like a cartoon character or monsters moving. You animate your Fireworks artwork in much the same way. But instead of creating objects in different positions on consecutive pages, you create frames and then modify some characteristic of an object on each frame. When the frames play in succession, the illusion of motion occurs. I show you how to animate your artwork in Chapter 14. Chapter 15 is devoted to creating animations for the Web.

✔ **Getting interactive for the Web:** Most of the documents you create in Fireworks will end up as or in Web pages. When you put stuff up on the Internet, you need menus — and I don't mean the kind you order food from. On Web pages, *menus* are used to navigate from one Web page to another. Menus for Web pages can be comprised of buttons or text, or they can take the form of pop-up menus. You can create all of these without knowing how to program JavaScript. (And if you've ever had a good look at JavaScript, you know how much fun it *isn't.*) I show you how to get interactive for the Web in Chapter 16 and 17.

✔ **Optimizing your artwork:** After you create, import, and modify the artwork for your Web images, you're almost home free. Before you can export your artwork for a Web page, you've got to optimize it. By *optimizing,* I mean choosing an image format for the artwork so that it downloads quickly into a user's Web browser. Huh? I know. Creating the artwork should be enough work for one day. Fortunately, Fireworks makes it easy to optimize your artwork. You can use the Optimize panel to manually optimize your artwork or let the Fireworks Export Wizard do it for you. I give you the lowdown on optimizing artwork in Chapter 12. I show you how to use the Export Wizard in Chapter 18.

✔ **Exporting your artwork for the Web:** Fireworks is for the artistically inclined who want to strut their stuff on the Internet or take advantage of their artistic endowment to showcase their client's services or products on the Web. The bane of every artistically inclined person — or at least 85 percent of the artistically inclined persons I've run across — has been writing the HTML code that's needed to display their talent on the Web. Well, rest easy, artistic one; when you export a Fireworks document, Fireworks exports your artwork, optimized to perfection, and if you choose, Fireworks also writes the code. When people visit a Web site you create with Fireworks, they think you're an HTML genius, when in reality all you do is make the image look good and then let Fireworks generate the HTML when you export the document. I show you how to export Fireworks documents in Chapter 18.

Figure 1-3 shows a Web page that Fireworks — with a little help from yours truly — built as viewed in a Netscape Web browser.

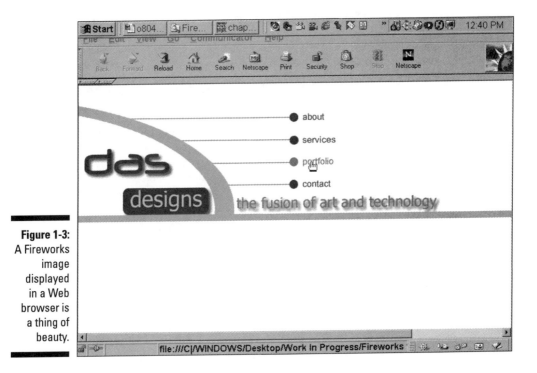

Figure 1-3:
A Fireworks image displayed in a Web browser is a thing of beauty.

Chapter 2

Finding Your Way in Fireworks

· ·

· ·

*W*hen you get a hankering to create an image or Web page, or one of your clients throws cold hard cash in your face because he or she has a hankering for an image or a Web page, it's time to call in Fireworks. But before you can put the sizzle in a Web page, you need to know how to create a project and find your way around the wild and wooly kingdom of Fireworks. So roll up your sleeves 'cause I'm going to show you how to get around in Fireworks.

Creating a Document

A typical Fireworks project ends up on the Internet, as either an image that will be part of a Web page or as a fully contained Web page with buttons, rollovers, images, and most of the other neat things that people look at when they go to Web sites. But to begin a project, you first need to create a document.

Before you rush headlong into a project, a little thought is in order. If you're creating a full-blown Web page with a menu, header, and a splash image (a *splash image* is a large image that visually introduces the Web page and occupies much of the page), how large will the page be? The average desktop size these days is 800 pixels x 600 pixels. To create an image that fills an 800 x 600 browser, you need a canvas size of 760 x 420 pixels. If all you're creating is an image for a Web page, you need to consider the other elements that will be part of the Web page. For instance, if you're creating a menu that's 100 pixels wide to be displayed alongside an image, don't create an image so large it exceeds the width of the browser. (But if you do, you can change it. Fireworks is very flexible.)

Creating a document involves a couple of steps, so sit back and relax while I show you how it's done. To create a document:

1. **Choose File⇨New.**

   Fireworks opens the New Document dialog box.

2. **Accept the default Width setting or double-click the number currently listed in the field to select it.**

   Fireworks highlights the current width.

3. **Enter a new value for the Width.**

   Fireworks displays the new value in the Width field.

4. **Accept the current Height setting or double-click the setting to enter a new value.**

   Fireworks displays the chosen setting in the Height field.

5. **Enter a new value for the Height.**

   Fireworks displays the new value in the Height field.

6. **The default unit of measure for a Fireworks document is pixels. To select another unit of measure, click the triangle at the end of the Width section and select an option from the menu. You can choose from Pixels, Inches, or Centimeters. Repeat for the Height section.**

   Fireworks displays the selected units of measurement to the right of the Width and Height windows.

7. **In the Canvas color section, select an option. Choose from White, Transparent, or Custom.**

   If you choose transparent and export the document in the GIF format, the background image or background color of the Web page the document is displayed on shows through blank areas of the canvas. If you choose Custom, you choose a color from the palette, something I show you how to do in the next section.

8. **Click OK to create the new document.**

   Fireworks creates a canvas the size and color you specified.

The next step is to set the document size and resolution, which I cover in the following section.

Creating a Custom Canvas Color

The default color for a Fireworks document is white, which is good for a number of things, like bread and delivery vans. It's also good for certain Web pages, especially those that are lean on images and heavy on text. However, if you're going to create a true masterpiece, you need a little color to spice things up.

To create a custom color for your new Fireworks document:

1. **Choose File⇨New.**

   Fireworks opens the New Document dialog box.

2. **In the Canvas Size section, enter values for the document's Width, Height, and Resolution.**

   Fireworks displays the chosen values in the Width, Height, and Resolution fields.

3. **In the Canvas Color section, choose Custom.**

4. **Click the Canvas Color swatch.**

   Your cursor becomes an eyedropper, and the color palette is displayed, as shown in Figure 2-1.

   You can also choose a color by clicking the small rainbow-colored button in the upper right-hand corner and choosing a color from the system color picker. Note that this color may or may not conform to the Web-safe palette.

5. **Drag your cursor through the color palette.**

   As you drag over a color, a large window at the top left corner of the palette displays the color.

6. **Click to select the desired color.**

   The Canvas Color swatch displays the selected color.

7. **Click OK to create a new document with the chosen color.**

   Fireworks creates a blank canvas of the specified size and background color.

Whenever you click a color swatch, the eyedropper appears, and you can sample a color from anywhere within the workspace by moving your cursor over an object or image and then clicking. This technique comes in handy when you need to create a background that's the same mustard yellow as your client's logo.

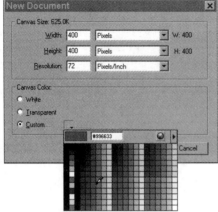

Figure 2-1:
Select a
color from
this palette
to create a
canvas with
a custom
color.

Perusing the Panels

When you create a new document, Fireworks places the canvas in the work-space, which probably looks pretty cluttered, what with all those doohickeys scattered around the canvas. For a first-time Fireworks user the *interface* (the menus, panels, toolbars, and canvas you use to create the document) can seem quite daunting — I know it did when I first launched the program. You'll be happy to know (or even relieved, as it was in my case) that you can change way the interface is arranged to suit your needs.

The first and most obvious things you notice in Fireworks are the panels. *Panels* are those square windows floating about the interface that look like homeless index cards. Each panel is actually a group of tabs. Behind each tab you find a series of associated menus or windows that you use to modify objects that you create or import. When you launch Fireworks for the first time, the panels are neatly laid out on the right side of the workspace. For the life of me, I can never figure out why they're called panels; they look more like tabbed index cards to me. Figure 2-2 shows panels in all their glory.

Panels are very useful critters when you're actually using them to modify an object in your document. But at times they just get in the way. You can hide panels or move them anywhere within the interface. And if you don't like the way they're arranged, you can customize the layout to suit your working pref-erence. (See the following sections for more on arranging panels.)

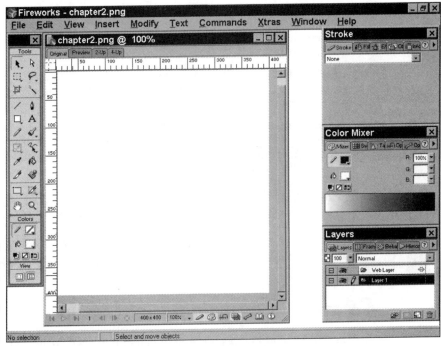

Figure 2-2:
The panels
are coming!
The panels
are coming!

Now you see 'em, now you don't: Hiding panels and other tricks

With a large canvas and an interface full of panels, things can get mighty confusing. And if you suffer from interface claustrophobia like I do, you're going to feel a little hemmed in. Well luckily, you can do almost anything with panels, short of send them to the Laundromat for cleaning. Here are some of the neat things you can do with panels:

- ✔ **To move a panel group:** Click its title bar and drag it to a new location. Release the mouse button when the panel is in its new location.

- ✔ **To coliapse a panel group**: Double-click its title bar.

- ✔ **To expand a collapsed panel group:** Double-click its title bar.

- ✔ **To hide a panel group:** Click the Close button in the upper right-hand corner (Windows) or upper left-hand corner (Macintosh).

- ✔ **To dock one panel group to another:** Click a panel's title bar and drag it to the bottom of a collapsed or open panel group. When the panel is close enough, it feels the magnetic attraction of its kin and locks into place. (When you *dock* one panel to another, you're temporarily aligning them to each other. This alignment is lost when you select one of the docked panels and move it to a different location. Panels of a feather do not stick together.)

- ✔ **To separate a panel from its group:** Click its tab and drag it from the group. Although the panel won't be happy with this turn of events, the panel is just a victim of circumstance and stays wherever you drop it.

- ✔ **To combine one panel with another group:** Click the panel's tab to select it and then drag it by the scruff of the tab. As you drag the panel, a rectangular bounding box signifies its current position. Drop it on top of another group to add it to that group.

To quickly hide all displayed panels, press the Tab key on your keyboard. Press it again to reveal the same set of panels previously displayed.

You can add only one panel at a time to an existing panel group. You cannot drag an entire panel group by its title bar and drop it into another group.

Creating a custom panel layout

After you work in Fireworks for a bit, you'll find yourself using certain panels more than others. You'll also find yourself using certain panels at certain stages in a project. For example, when you're creating objects, you'll use the panels related to color choices, tool options, and object information. After you've created the objects and are finalizing the project for the Internet, you use panels that relate to image optimization, creating links, and assigning behaviors to objects like buttons. To get Fireworks to perform as efficiently as you do, you can create panel groups, arrange them to suit your needs, and then save them as a custom layout.

To create a custom panel layout:

1. **Close any panels that you don't want included in the layout.**

   The panels you close go bye-bye.

2. **To create a custom panel group, click a panel's tab and then drag it away from its parent group. Click the tab of another panel you want to add to the custom group and drag it on top of the first panel in the custom group you are creating. Continue adding panels as needed.**

   The panels become accustomed to their new surroundings.

3. **Collapse each panel.**

   The panels become a mere figment of their former selves. Note that when you open the saved panel layout, the panels appear non-collapsed in full display mode. Collapsing the panels makes it a bit easier to organize them prior to saving the layout.

4. **Dock the collapsed panels to each other.**

   The interface looks much neater, thanks to your good housekeeping. (And if you skipped the part where I discuss how to dock panels, take a look at the preceding section.)

5. **Choose Commands⇨Panel Layout.**

   The JavaScript dialog box appears.

6. **Enter a name for the layout and click OK.**

   Fireworks saves the layout to your hard drive for future use and the layout is added to the Panel Layout Sets submenu.

To use a saved custom panel layout, choose Command⇨Panel Layout Sets and choose a panel from the submenu.

To delete a saved panel, use your computer's operating system to locate the Panel Layout Sets directory, which is a subdirectory of the Commands directory, which is a subdirectory of the Configuration directory, which is a subdirectory of the Fireworks 4 directory. Whew, that's a lot of directories.

Opening panels

You use panels to change certain characteristics of objects in your Fireworks document such as the object's *stroke* (Fireworks speak for line or outline), *fill* (a shape's color), and size among other things. Other panels are used to optimize images and change the options of a tool. You use panels to do many different things throughout the course of a Fireworks project. Stay tuned for updates in future chapters.

Panels are kept in groups according to what they do, kind of like employees in a big company where they keep the guys in sales separated from the guys in production. Talk about your oil and water. Fortunately for you, getting a panel to do something is much easier than getting work done in a major corporation. (I show you how to use panels throughout the book. But before you can get a panel to do something, you've got to open it.)

To open a panel:

1. **Choose Window and select a panel from the menu.**

   The panel appears, along with its group buddies, ready to do its thing to an object on your canvas.

2. **To choose a different panel from the group you just opened, click the panel's tab.**

   The panel you select becomes the active panel.

3. **To open up another panel group simultaneously, choose Window and select another panel from the menu.**

   You can use as many panels as needed to modify your objects.

Exploring the Toolbox

On the left-hand side of the interface, away from everything else on the interface, lies this innocuous looking tall and narrow toolbar with a lot of buttons. Even though it doesn't have a handle, it's called the Toolbox, because it's full of icons, and when clicked, the Toolbox gives you a tool to work with. You use the Toolbox to create and edit items on the canvas, select already-created objects, and add hotspots (*hotspots* are interactive areas that respond to a user's mouse when the exported document is viewed in a Web browser) to your documents without causing an uprising, as well as change your point of view of the canvas. Versatile Toolbox that. And of course, the obligatory eraser is also present in case you make a mistake. But you don't make mistakes, do you?

The Toolbox is your friend, so please give it some attention. In spite of the fact that you can't create much without it, the Toolbox feels neglected and outnumbered by all the panels floating about the workspace. Figure 2-3 shows the Toolbox and its tools. (If you're wondering how to use all of those cute little icons to actually do stuff, I show you how to use each tool in appropriate sections that are tastefully sprinkled about the book for your reading and entertainment pleasure.)

Figure 2-3:
You use the
Toolbox to
create and
edit things.

The Toolbox floats about the Fireworks workspace. You can close the Toolbox, but you can't dock it. The Toolbox is just a rambling kind of toolbar. To move the Toolbox to a different location, click just above its title, drag it across the workspace, and then release the mouse button when you've got the Toolbox where you want it.

Using a tool

You choose a tool from the Toolbox when you decide to create or edit something on the canvas.

Some of the tool buttons actually expand to reveal more tools. These expandable gems can be identified by a little triangle in the button's lower right-hand corner.

To use a tool:

1. **Click a tool to select it.**

   The tool's button depresses when selected.

2. **Move your mouse over the canvas.**

   The cursor icon changes to reflect the tool selected.

3. **Use the selected tool to create or modify an object.**

Some of the tools in the Toolbox are actually tool groups. Tool groups are like Swiss Army Knives; they've got all manner of doohickeys to play with.

To expand a tool group:

1. **Click the triangle in the tool group button's lower right-hand corner.**

   The group's button expands horizontally to display the other tools in the group, as shown in Figure 2-4.

2. **With the mouse button still depressed, drag horizontally.**

   A tool's button becomes depressed as you drag the mouse over it.

3. **Release the mouse button when your cursor is over the desired tool.**

   The selected tool proudly displays itself on the toolbox.

4. **Use the newly selected tool on the canvas to create or modify an object.**

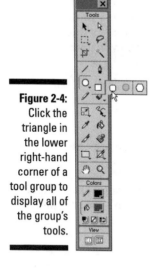

Figure 2-4:
Click the triangle in the lower right-hand corner of a tool group to display all of the group's tools.

Exploring a tool's options

Some tools have options; other tools don't. Options modify the way a tool performs, like moving the thumbwheel on a crescent wrench to expand its jaws. A casual glance at the Toolbox won't give you a clue as to whether a tool's got options or not. The only way to display and change a tool's options is to use the Options panel. (Remember panels? There's a whole section in this chapter about 'em.)

To display a tool's options:

1. **Double-click the tool.**

   The Options panel opens and displays the tool's options. If the selected tool has options, you see one or more of the following:

   • Text fields with a triangle that open a menu

   • Sliders to adjust a tool's parameters

   • A combination thereof

   If a tool has no options, the Options panel still pops up — the panels can't help it — and displays a cheerful little message that says `No options`.

2. **Adjust the tool's options to the desired settings.**

   The selected settings are applied to the tool the next time the tool is used (and each subsequent time) until you change the options. Figure 2-5 displays the Options available for the Polygon tool.

Figure 2-5:
Changing
a tool's
options
affects
the way it
performs.

Windows only: Floating a toolbar

Note to readers using Fireworks with the Macintosh platform: This
section applies only to readers who use Fireworks with the Windows
operating system.

If you use the Windows operating system, you have two Windows-only toolbars at your disposal:

- ✔ **Main:** Performs various sundry functions such as creating a new document, saving a document, opening an existing document, importing and
  exporting, and undoing and redoing, as well as cutting, copying, and
  pasting.
- ✔ **Modify:** Used to group and ungroup objects, join objects together, arrange
  the stacking order of objects on the canvas, align objects to one another,
  and transform the position of objects without using a compass.

To display your Windows-only toolbars:

1. **Choose Window⇨Toolbars.**

   A submenu makes a hasty appearance, stage right.

2. **Choose Main or Modify.**

   The toolbar of your choice joins the fray.

To move a toolbar, click its title bar and drag it to a new position.

To dock a toolbar:

1. **Click the toolbar's title bar and drag it towards the top, bottom, or
   left-hand side of the interface.**

   As you drag the toolbar, a gray bounding box appears, showing you the
   toolbar's current position. When it approaches a position where it can be
   docked to the interface, the bounding box gets shorter (when the toolbar
   can be docked to the top or bottom of the interface) or becomes vertical
   (when the toolbar can be docked to the left-hand side of the interface).

2. **Release the mouse button.**

Fireworks docks the toolbar.

To undock a toolbar, click an open spot on the toolbar and drag it away from its docking point.

Using the Canvas, a Multi-Tabbed Wonder

The canvas is where it all happens. The *canvas* is where you duke it out with the tools and create the image which, when displayed on the Internet, will catapult you to fame, or at the very least, earn you a paycheck from your boss or client.

The area surrounding the canvas is called the *document window.* At the top of the document window, the title of the project is displayed. Notice there are three tabs to the right of the document's title: Preview, 2-Up, and 4-Up. These tabs are used for previewing the document in various modes. The Preview tab is used to display the document with the currently selected optimization settings. The 2-Up and 4-Up tabs are used to display the document with optimization settings applied while at the same time comparing it to the original. To display the canvas in a different mode, click a tab. Figure 2-6 shows a document displayed in the 4-Up mode. Notice the dialog at the bottom of each window, which shows the Optimize settings chosen for each window, as well as the file size and download time.

I show you how to optimize your artwork in Chapter 12.

Using the Launcher bar

At the very bottom right-hand corner of the document window are eight gaily-colored buttons that look like window dressing, but they're not. They're used to launch frequently used panels. Hmm, guess that's why they call it the *Launcher bar.*

To launch a panel from the Launcher bar:

1. **Move your cursor over the buttons.**

Tooltips appear, signifying which panel opens when the button is clicked. If a panel is already open, the tooltip reads Hide followed by the panel's name.

2. **Click the desired button to show or hide a panel.**

   The panel appears or disappears.

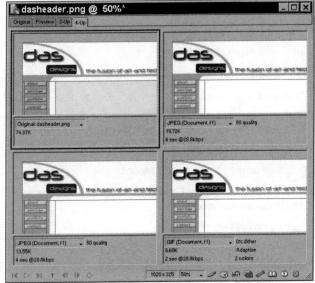

Figure 2-6:
The 4-Up
mode is
used to
display the
document
with
different
optimization
settings.

The Grid: Your guiding lines

When you create a Fireworks document you're working with a lot of stuff —
images, objects, buttons, and text, to name a few. As you get more and more
stuff on the canvas, it becomes harder and harder to bring order to the chaos.
Keeping track of everything is one challenge, and precise placement of objects
is yet another. Fortunately, you can turn on a grid that displays in front of the
objects on your canvas. You use the grid for aligning purposes. The grid has a
magnetic personality — even when it isn't displayed, objects snap to it.

To view the grid:

1. **Choose View⇨Grid**

   The grid appears and it looks like someone's thrown a piece of transparent graph paper over the canvas.

2. **Choose View⇨Grid⇨Snap to Grid.**

   The Snap to Grid option is enabled by default of the program designers,
   but you can toggle this snapping option on and off. If you see a checkmark to the left of Snap to Grid menu command when you choose it,
   snapping is enabled. Invoking the command turns snapping off and the
   grid loses its magnetic personality.

If don't like the way the grid looks — the lines are too hard to see or they're spaced too close or too far apart — you can easily change the appearance of the grid by editing it.

To edit the grid:

1. **Choose View⇨Grid⇨Edit Grid.**

   Fireworks opens the Edit Grid dialog box.

2. **To change the color of the grid lines, click the Color swatch.**

   Fireworks opens a color palette and your cursor becomes an eyedropper.

3. **Click a color to select it.**

   Fireworks displays the selected color in the Color display window. When you select a color for the grid, select one that contrasts well with the canvas color to make the grid be easier to see.

4. **The next two options, Show Grid and Snap to Grid, function identically to their menu counterparts.**

   Click an option to select it.

5. **To change the grid spacing width, click the triangle to the right of the width field (the horizontal double-headed arrow) and drag the slider to select the spacing. To change the height of the grid spaces, click the triangle to the right of the height field (the vertical double-headed arrow) and drag the slider to select a spacing value.**

   This setting determines how far apart Fireworks draws the grid lines. The values are in pixels.

6. **Click OK to apply the new settings.**

   Fireworks displays the grid with the settings you specified.

Measuring up with rulers

If you have a grid displayed, the grid ought to measure up. You can do this by activating rulers. You use rulers to place items with mathematical precision (no slide rule needed). To view the rulers:

1. **Choose View⇨Rulers.**

   Vertical and horizontal rulers decorate the top and left side of the workspace. Rulers are always measured in pixels, regardless of the unit of measurement you select when you create the document. The default zero point of each ruler is the top left-hand corner of the canvas, and all measuring begins from that point. For example, if you have a 400 pixel x 400 pixel canvas, the center of the canvas is at 200 on each ruler. Some people prefer to measure from the center of the canvas out.

2. **To change the zero point of the each ruler, click the crosshair where the vertical and horizontal rulers meet and then drag to create a new zero point for each ruler.**

   As you drag, the crosshair follows the cursor. Use the vertical and horizontal rulers as guides when moving the cross hair. For example, if you want the vertical and horizontal zero point of the ruler to be in the center of a 400 x 400 pixel canvas, line the cross hair up with the 200 mark on both the vertical and horizontal rulers. When you release the mouse button, the zero point for both rulers will be at the center of the canvas.

3. **Release the mouse button when the crosshair is at the desired position.**

   Fireworks changes each ruler to reflect the new zero position.

To change the rulers back to their default settings, double-click the cross hair where the rulers meet. Figure 2-7 shows a document with the grid and rulers activated. The rulers are at their default setting.

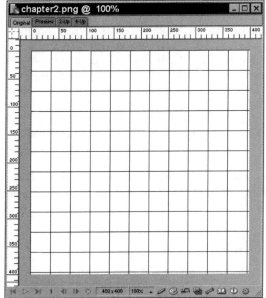

Figure 2-7: Use the grid and rulers to get things on the canvas to measure up.

Creating guides

The Fireworks grid is a very useful tool for aligning objects on canvas, but sometimes you need your own guides. For example, if you're creating a menu on the left-hand side of the canvas, you don't need to see all of the lines on the grid; you need just one guide for the left-hand boundary of the menu. Sometimes less is more.

To create guides:

1. **Choose View⇨Rulers.**

   A vertical and horizontal ruler appear.

2. **To create a vertical guide, click the vertical ruler and drag right.**

   As you drag, a green line appears showing you the current position of the guide. Use the horizontal ruler to accurately position the guide.

3. **When the guide is in the desired position, release the mouse button.**

4. **To create a horizontal guide, click the horizontal ruler and drag down.**

   Once again, the green line appears as you move the guide into position. Use the vertical ruler as a positioning guide.

5. **Release the mouse button when the guide is in the desired position.**

   After you have the guides positioned, you can lock them to prevent inadvertently moving them while editing other objects on the canvas.

6. **To lock guides in place, choose View⇨Guides⇨Lock Guides.**

   Any guides on the canvas are locked in their current positions.

By default, objects snap to guides. To disable snapping, choose View⇨Guides⇨ Snap to Guides. Invoke the command again to reactivate snapping.

If you use guides with the snapping option enabled, choose View⇨Grid⇨ Snap to Grid to turn off snapping to the grid. If you have both options enabled (Snap to Guides *and* Snap to Grid), it will be difficult to tell whether Fireworks is snapping an object to the grid or one of your carefully placed guides.

After you have guides set up, you can edit them. You can move any guide (provided it's unlocked), change the color of guides, or erase guides.

To move guides:

1. **Move your mouse towards an unlocked guide.**

   When you can latch onto a guide and move it, the cursor changes to two vertical lines with arrows (vertical guide) or two horizontal lines with arrows (horizontal guide).

2. **When the cursor changes, click the guide and drag it to a new position.**

   The green line moves with the mouse, signifying its new position.

3. **Release the mouse button when the guide is where you want it. Repeat for any additional guides you want to reposition.**

4. **When you have all your guides in position, choose View⇨Guides⇨ Lock Guides.**

You'll find that using guides is much easier if a guide's color contrasts the canvas color. If you've chosen green for a canvas color, the default guide color of green will make the guide very difficult to see. You can change the color of guides by editing them.

To edit guides:

1. **Choose View⇨Guides⇨Edit Guides.**

2. **To change the color of all guides used in the document, click the color swatch.**

   The cursor turns into an eyedropper and the color palette appears.

3. **Click a color in the palette to select it.**

   The new color is displayed in the color swatch window. If the selected color is not a good contrast to the canvas color, choose a different color that is.

4. **The next three options in the dialog box, Show Guides, Snap to Guides and Lock Guides, function identically to the menu commands of the same name. Click an option to select it.**

5. **Click OK to apply the changes.**

   All guides in the document are updated to reflect the changes you applied.

Changing your point of view

When you really get the knack of working with Fireworks, you'll find yourself creating documents of increasing complexity. When you create these increasingly complex documents, you'll often have more than one document open at the same time, and your workspace can get very crowded. You can solve this dilemma by changing your view using the Zoom and Hand tools.

The Zoom tool

 You use the Zoom tool (it looks like a magnifying glass) to zoom in and out on parts of your canvas.

To zoom in:

1. **Select the Zoom tool from the Toolbox and move your cursor over the canvas.**

   The cursor changes into a magnifying glass with a plus sign (+) in it.

  2. Click the canvas to zoom to the next level of magnification.

    The canvas is magnified. You can also use the Zoom tool to magnify a specific object, or part of the canvas.

  3. To zoom in on a specific object, move your cursor to the top and left of the object you want to zoom in on; then click and drag down and to the right.

    As you drag, a rectangular bounding box appears, signifying the size of the area you're selecting.

  4. Release the mouse button when the area you want to zoom in on is surrounded by the rectangle.

    The object is magnified.

To zoom out:

  1. Select the magnifying tool and hold down the Alt (Windows) or Option (Macintosh) key.

    The cursor becomes a magnifying glass with a minus sign (–) in it.

  2. Click the canvas to zoom out to the next lowest level of magnification.

    The magnification of the canvas is decreased.

 You can also change the magnification of the canvas by choosing a preset level of magnification. On the bottom of the document window, you find a number followed by a percent sign (%). Click the number and choose a level of magnification from the pop-up menu.

The Hand tool

The Hand tool gives you a helping hand by enabling you to *pan* (move) the document left, right, up, or down. You use the Hand tool when the document is magnified and the canvas is bigger than the document window. If the total document is displayed, the Hand tool has no effect.

To pan the canvas:

  1. From the Toolbox, select the Hand tool (it looks like a hand) and move your cursor over the canvas.

    The cursor changes into a hand.

  2. Drag right, left, up, or down to change your view of the canvas.

    The position of the canvas in the document window changes as you drag.

  3. Release the mouse button when the desired portion of the canvas is displayed.

To momentarily activate the Hand tool, press the spacebar. With the spacebar depressed, pan the canvas to the desired position. Release the spacebar to reactivate the tool last used.

Saving a Document

When you save a document in Fireworks native format (.png, pronounced *ping*), all the elements you used to create it are saved and can be edited the next time you open the document, which is a tremendous advantage if after exporting the finished document you decide to change your mind, or if your client has the gall to question your artistic judgment.

To save a document:

1. **Choose File➪Save.**

   The Save As dialog box appears.

2. **Enter a name for the document and then select a file folder where you want to store the document.**

3. **Click Save.**

   Fireworks saves the document and all the elements used to create it.

You typically finish a Fireworks project by exporting a document for use on the Internet. I show you how to export the finished product in Chapter 18.

Making Changes to an Existing Document

Things change, and Web pages change, too. After you export a Fireworks document and upload it to the Web, you may need to change images or buttons, or update links. If you saved the original document, you can apply changes to it rather than creating a new document from scratch.

To open an existing document:

1. **Choose File➪Open.**

   Fireworks displays the Open dialog box.

2. **Locate the file you want to open and click Open.**

   The saved file is opened and ready for editing.

You can open more than one document at a time by selecting the first document and then selecting a second document while holding down the Shift key.

The following two sections tell you how to modify your existing document now that you have it open.

Modifying canvas size

You can modify a document's size at any time by using a menu command. Use this option when you need more room to add more items to a document, like additional buttons or a navigation menu.

To modify a document's size:

1. **Choose Modify⇨Canvas Size.**

   The Canvas Size dialog box appears.

2. **In the New Size section, double-click the current width (the field to the right of the horizontal double-headed arrow) value.**

   The width is selected.

3. **Enter a value for the new width.**

4. **Double-click the current height (the field to the right of the vertical double headed arrow) value.**

   The current height value is selected.

5. **Enter a new value for the canvas height.**

6. **In the Anchor section, click a button to select an alignment option.**

   When you resize a canvas, Fireworks aligns all objects to the center of the document by default. You use the buttons in the Anchor section to change this alignment. The button's icon and position tell you how that button will align the objects.

7. **Click OK to apply the changes.**

   Fireworks resizes the canvas to the specified size and anchors all objects to the specified position.

Modifying canvas color

You can modify the canvas color whenever needed by using a menu command. You modify the color of the canvas when the images used to create the document change and just don't look good against the current color.

To change canvas color:

1. **Choose Modify⇨Canvas Color.**

   The Canvas Color dialog box appears.

2. **Choose an option.**

   If you choose transparent, when the document is used as part of a Web page, the page's background color or tiling background image appear through blank areas of the canvas.

   If you choose an opaque color for the canvas and then change it to transparent, you will need to change the optimization settings for the document in order for the background to be transparent when the document is exported. I show you how to optimize your artwork in Chapter 12.

3. **If you choose Custom, click the color swatch.**

   Your cursor becomes an eyedropper and the color palette appears.

4. **Click a color to select it.**

   The selected color is displayed in the color swatch.

5. **Click OK.**

   The canvas looks absolutely mah-velous in its new color.

Chapter 3

Creating Shapes

• •

In This Chapter

▶ Creating shapes

▶ Drawing lines

▶ Creating paths

• •

The Toolbox is a many splendored thing. And one of the many splendors that you find there are tools that you use to create shapes. Some of the shapes, like polygons and stars, are very chic, while other shapes such as the oval and rectangle, are ho-hum. And then you have your useful-but-boring shapes like the basic line.

Shapes are the basis for many things in a Fireworks project. You use them as window dressing, background for text objects, and as the basis for navigation buttons. In this chapter I show you how to create your basic shapes. The more esoteric stuff is sprinkled throughout the rest of the book.

Creating Shapely (Or Not-So-Shapely) Shapes

A shape is a shape and a thing of beauty is a joy forever. With Fireworks, you get the best of both worlds. When you create a shape you choose a tool, and then assign an outline color and a color for the shape. You can create shapes with no outlines, just a solid mass of color, or shapes without a basic color and just an outline. The choice is yours because it's your artistic vision and it's your program and that's the name of that tune, Charlie Brown. Figure 3-1 is your road map to finding the shape tools in the Toolbox.

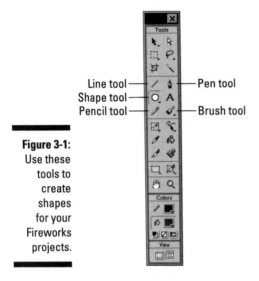

Line tool —
Shape tool —
Pencil tool —

— Pen tool
— Brush tool

Figure 3-1:
Use these
tools to
create
shapes
for your
Fireworks
projects.

Introducing strokes and fills

When you create a line or an outline in Fireworks, it is called a *stroke*. A stroke can be defined as the characteristic of a line or outline including things like color and the type of line (dotted, dashed, solid, and so on). Basic shapes like the line, or a path drawn with the Pen, Pencil, or Brush tools, have only a stroke.

You can modify the way a stroke looks using the Stroke panel, a technique I show you in Chapter 7.

When you create a basic shape like an oval and you want it to be solid instead of just an outline, you assign a fill to it. Fills can get pretty fancy; I show you how to create these fancy fills in Chapter 8.

To select a basic stroke color and fill color for an object, use the Colors section of the Toolbox. The Colors section of the Toolbox (shown in Figure 3-2) has buttons for selecting stroke color (the pencil) and one for selecting fill color (the paint bucket). To the right of the Stroke Color button is the Stroke Color well, which is a small window displaying the currently selected stroke color. To the right of the Fill Color button is the Fill Color well. At the bottom of the section are three buttons. You use the first button to change the stroke and fill colors to their default color, which are — yawn — black and white. You use the second button to assign no color to either a stroke or a fill. You use the third button to swap the stroke and fill colors.

To assign a stroke color to an object:

1. Select one of the drawing tools.

2. **In the Colors section of the Toolbox, click the Stroke Color button that looks like a pencil.**

3. **Click the Stroke Color well.**

   The cursor becomes an eyedropper and the color palette opens.

4. **Click a color in the palette to select it.**

   The selected color is displayed in the Stroke Color well and will be applied to the stroke you create with the selected tool.

Whenever you open the color palette, you see a button that looks like miniature color wheel. Click the button to open the system color picker. You can then choose a color other than those available from the Fireworks color palette.

To assign a fill color to an object:

1. **Select one of the drawing tools.**

2. **In the Colors section of the Toolbox, click the Fill Color button that looks like a paint bucket.**

3. **Click the Fill Color well.**

   The cursor becomes an eyedropper and the color palette makes a colorful appearance.

4. **Click a color to select it.**

   The color you selected is displayed in the Fill Color well and is used to fill the object you create.

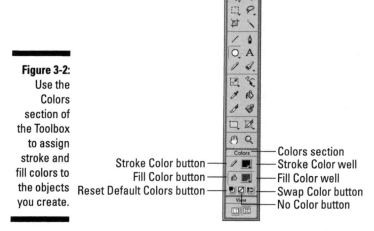

Figure 3-2:
Use the Colors section of the Toolbox to assign stroke and fill colors to the objects you create.

Stroke Color button
Fill Color button
Reset Default Colors button

Colors section
Stroke Color well
Fill Color well
Swap Color button
No Color button

To create an object with no stroke:

1. **In the Colors section of the Toolbox, click the Stroke Color button.**
2. **Click the No Color button.**

   When the object is created, it will have no outline.

To create an object with no fill:

1. **In the Colors section of the Toolbox, click the Fill Color button.**
2. **Click the No Color button.**

   When the object is created, it will have no fill.

Creating rectangles

Rectangles are the essence of geometric rigidity. After all, they have 90-degree corners and sometimes they're even square. How droll. But you can use rectangles for many things in Fireworks, like backdrops for text objects.

To create a rectangle:

1. **Select the Rectangle tool.**

   The Rectangle tool is the default tool displayed on the fifth button on the left-hand side of the toolbox.

2. **Assign a stroke and fill color for the rectangle.**
3. **Click the spot on the canvas where you want the rectangle to start and then drag down and across.**

   A bounding box appears as you drag, showing you the outline of the shape.

4. **When the rectangle is the desired size, release the mouse button.**

   Fireworks draws the rectangle on the canvas using the specified stroke and fill colors.

Hold down the Shift key while using one of the tools to create a shape and Fireworks will constrain the shape to equal width and height dimensions. You'll create a square if you're using one of the rectangle tools, a circle if you're using the Ellipse tool, or a polygon or star with equal width and height dimensions if you're using the Polygon tool.

Creating rounded rectangles

Rounded rectangles have corners that are curved and are OSHA-approved because they aren't sharp. You use rounded rectangles for many things in Fireworks; for example, they make excellent shapes for buttons. To create a rounded rectangle:

1. **Click the triangle at the lower right corner of the fifth button in the left column of the toolbox to expand the tool group; then select the Rounded Rectangle tool.**

   The Rounded Rectangle tool becomes the currently selected shape tool.

2. **Click the spot on the canvas where you want the rectangle to begin and then drag down and across to define the size of the rectangle.**

   As you drag, a rectangular bounding box appears, giving you a preview of the rectangle's size as you create it.

3. **When the rectangle is the size you want it, release the mouse.**

   Fireworks draws a rounded rectangle on the canvas, but it isn't as round as you want it yet.

4. **Choose Window⇨Object.**

   The Object panel opens, as shown in Figure 3-3.

5. **The default roundness is 30. Click the triangle to the right of the Roundness field to adjust it.**

   A slider appears.

6. **Drag the slider to specify how round the corners will be.**

   Or you can enter a value between 0 and 100 in the Roundness field. After you release the slider, Fireworks adjusts the round corners of the rectangle. To create rounder corners, repeat Step 5.

To create the ever-present pill shape that is all the vogue for Web site buttons, select the Rounded Rectangle tool and in the Options panel, drag the slider to a value of 100, creating a rounded rectangle that is long and short. Voilà, instant pill.

Creating ovals

Ovals are the essence of geometric rotundity. You can make ovals that are short and squat like eggs or perfectly round like a big rubber ball. You use the Ellipse tool to create oval shapes.

To create an oval:

1. **Click the triangle in the lower right hand corner of the fifth button on the left-hand side of the Toolbox and select the Ellipse tool from the expanded group.**

   The Ellipse tool becomes the currently selected shape tool.

2. **In the Colors section of the Toolbox, select a stroke and fill color for the oval.**

3. **Click a spot on the canvas where you want the top of the oval to be and then drag down and across the canvas.**

   An outline of the oval follows your cursor, giving you a preview of what the finished shape will look like.

4. **When the oval is the shape and dimension you want, release the mouse button.**

   Fireworks draws an oval.

Figure 3-3:
You specify
the corner
radius of a
rounded
rectangle by
dragging
this slider in
the Object
panel.

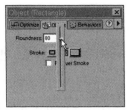

Creating polygons

Polygons are multi-sided shapes. You can use Polygons to add interesting shapes to your projects or as the basis for buttons or hotspots. To create a Polygon:

1. **Click the triangle in the lower right corner of the fifth button on the left side of the Toolbox. When the tool group expands, select the Polygon tool.**

   The Polygon tool appears on the group's button.

2. **Double-click the tool.**

   The Options panel opens, as shown in Figure 3-4.

3. **Click the triangle to the right of the Shape field and select Polygon from the menu.**

4. **Click the triangle to the right of the Sides field.**

   A slider appears.

5. **Drag the slider to specify the number of sides the polygon has.**

   The field displays the number of sides the polygon has when it is drawn. Don't go overboard on the number of sides. A polygon with a lot of sides bears a striking resemblance to a circle.

6. **Click the spot on the canvas where you want the center of the polygon to be and then drag.**

   As you drag, Fireworks creates a preview of the shape. Rotate the mouse as you drag and the preview will rotate with it, revealing the exact orientation of the object.

7. **Release the mouse button when you're satisfied with the size and orientation of the polygon.**

   Fireworks draws the polygon to your specifications.

Figure 3-4:
You use the Options panel to specify how many sides a polygon has.

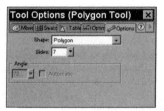

Creating stars

If you want Web site visitors to see stars before their eyes, you can do it in Fireworks. The Polygon tool does double duty. You use it to create stars with a little help from the Options panel.

To create stars:

1. **Click the triangle in the lower right corner of the fifth button on the left-hand side of the Toolbox. After the group expands, select the Polygon tool.**

   The Polygon tool asserts itself and is displayed on the button.

2. **Double-click the tool.**

   The Options panel opens.

3. **Click the triangle to the right of the Shape field and select Star from the menu.**

4. **Click the triangle to the right of the Sides field.**

   A slider appears.

5. **Drag the slider to specify the number of sides the star will have.**

6. **In the Angle section:**

   Leave the default Automatic option checked if you want Fireworks to compute the angle based on the number of sides you specify.

   If you want to specify the angle of each of the star's arms yourself, deselect this option and then click the triangle to the right of the Angle field and drag the slider to specify the angle. Small angles create long pointy arms; large angles create short blunt arms. Figure 3-5 shows two variations of the same star created by varying the angle.

7. **Click the point on the canvas where you want the center of the star to be and then drag outward.**

   Fireworks creates a preview of the shape as you drag. Rotate the mouse to rotate the orientation of the star.

8. **When the star is of the size and orientation you want, release the mouse key.**

   A star is born.

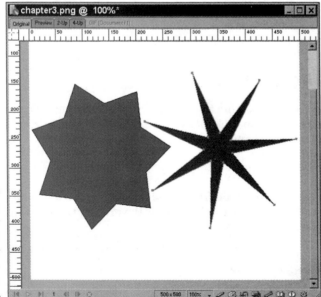

Figure 3-5:
You got your
pointy stars
and your
not-so-
pointy stars.

Drawing Lines

Lines. They're the shortest distance between two points if I remember my geometry correctly. In Fireworks you've got four tools for creating lines: the Line tool, the Brush tool, the Pencil tool, and the Pen tool. The Pen tool is a specialized critter; so specialized they got a special place for him on the interface. In fact, the Pen tool is so important, it's got a special section in this chapter, too.

Drawing arrow-straight lines with the Line tool

Lines are used to accentuate the positive — and sometimes the negative, but that's an equine of a different hue. Use lines to draw attention to items in your Fireworks projects, such as text.

To create a line:

1. **Select the Line tool.**

2. **In the Colors section, click the Stroke Color button and then click the Stroke Color well and select a color for the line.**

   The selected color graces the stroke color well.

3. **Click the point on the canvas where you want the line to start and drag in the direction you want the line to go.**

   As you drag the tool across the canvas, Fireworks creates a preview of the line.

4. **When the line is the length and orientation you want, release the mouse button.**

   Fireworks draws an arrow-straight line on canvas.

Hold down the Shift key and drag the Line tool down to constrain the line to vertical; right to constrain the line to horizontal; diagonal to constrain the line to a 45-degree angle.

Scribbling with the Pencil tool

You use the Pencil tool to create a one-pixel path (a *path* is a series of connected points.) After the path is drawn, if you want to change it, you can modify it via the Stroke panel while it's selected. To create a line with the Pencil tool:

1. **Select the Pencil tool.**

2. **In the Colors Section, click the Stroke Color button, click the Stroke Color well, and then select a color from the palette.**

   The color is displayed in the Stroke Color well and will be applied to the line you draw.

3. **Click where you want the line to begin and drag.**

   Fireworks creates the line as you draw. To constrain the tool to a straight line, hold down the Shift key while dragging.

4. **When the line is the length you want, release the mouse button.**

   Fireworks draws the line and dares you to cross it.

Painting with the Brush tool

You use the Brush tool to create freeform splashes of color on the canvas. You can modify the tool's stroke to mimic an airbrush, felt tip marker, or a watercolor brush, among other effects (I show you how to modify stroke attributes in Chapter 7). When you use the Brush tool, you are actually creating a path. A *path* is a collection of points that Fireworks automatically generates as you drag the tool across the canvas. You can modify the location of points with the Subselect tool, which I show you how to use in Chapter 10.

To use the Brush tool:

1. **Select the Brush tool.**

2. **In the Colors Section of the Toolbox, click the Stroke Color well and select a color from the palette.**

   The color is displayed in the Stroke Color well and will be applied to your brush stroke.

3. **Drag the tool over the canvas to paint a brush stroke.**

   As you paint, Fireworks displays your artistry.

4. **When the brush stroke is the shape you want, release the mouse button.**

   Congratulations, maestro — you've just painted on a Fireworks canvas.

Plotting a path with the Pen tool

When you use the Brush or Pencil tool, Fireworks generates the points, which are connected to become a path. The Pen tool however, gives you point-to-point control when creating a shape. With the Pen tool, you click where you want to add a point to the path. You decide whether the point will be a corner point or a curve point. The line between two points is known as a *path segment* or *line segment.*

When Fireworks connects two corner points, a straight line results. When Fireworks connects a corner and a curved point, a curve is created between the two points. Curve points have handles, which you can modify with the Subselect tool. You can also use the Subselect tool to change the position of a point. I show you how to modify a path with the Subselect tool in Chapter 10.

Creating straight lines with the Pen tool

Figure 3-6 shows a path with three points. Notice that the path segments between interconnecting points are arrow straight. To create straight path segments with the Pen tool:

Figure 3-6:
A straight line is the shortest distance from point to point.

 1. **Select the Pen tool.**

As you place the tool over the canvas, the cursor becomes a pen nib, like the ones attached to fountain pens that leak all over your shirt or blouse when you put them back in your pocket with the cap off.

2. **Click the spot on the canvas where you want the straight line to begin.**

A point appears on the canvas looking quite bored and lonely.

3. **Click a spot on the canvas where you want the first line segment to end.**

Fireworks connects the two points to create a straight-line segment.

4. **Add additional points as needed to complete the path.**

Fireworks connects the dots, er, I mean points.

5. **Double-click the point where you want the path to end.**

Fireworks creates the last line segment and the Pen tool is ready to create another path.

Creating curves with the Pen tool

Curves are things of beauty. For one thing, they look great on foreign sports cars. You can create curvy things of beauty — curved path segments — with the Pen tool. Figure 3-7 shows a path with three points. The middle point is a curve point. Notice the two handles sprouting from the middle point. When you draw a curve point, Fireworks creates two handles that you can tug with the Subselect tool to make the curved segment curvier, or straighter. To create a path with curve points:

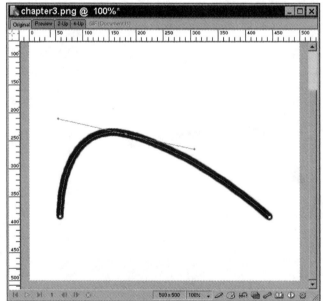

Figure 3-7:
This is not the shortest path between points.

1. **Select the Pen tool.**

As you move the cursor over the canvas, it becomes a pen nib.

2. **Click a spot on the canvas where you want the first point of the segment to begin.**

Fireworks adds a spot to the canvas and your Dalmatian does a quick inventory to make sure all its spots are intact.

3. **Move to the spot where you want the curve point and then click while dragging your mouse to create it.**

   As you drag two handles appear. Continue dragging until the curve segment is to your liking.

4. **Click and drag a spot on the canvas to create another curve point, or click to create a corner point or double-click to create the final point of the path.**

   Fireworks adds another segment to your path.

Closing a path (making ends meet)

You also use the Pen tool to create closed path. A *closed path* is where all the points are connected (see Figure 3-8). The closed path can be unfilled to create an outline or filled to create a solid shape. To create a closed path:

Figure 3-8:
Close the path to create an outline or solid shape with the Pen tool.

 1. **Select the Pen tool.**

2. **In the Colors section of the Toolbox, click the Stroke Color well and select a color from the palette.**

   If you want the closed path to be a solid shape, click the Fill Color well and select a color from the palette. To create a solid filled shape with no outline, click the No Color button for the stroke color.

   The selected colors are displayed in the Stroke and Fill Color wells.

2. **Move your mouse over the canvas and click the spot where you want the closed path to begin.**

   As you inch your mouse over the canvas, the cursor changes into a pen nib. Notice that the Fill Color well displays the no color symbol. This will change when you close the path.

3. **Add additional curve or corner points to define the shape of the path.**

   Fireworks connects the points to make path segments.

4. **To close the path move your cursor over the first point you created and click.**

   Fireworks closes the path. If you selected a fill color, it is applied to the shape.

Chapter 4

Fun with Pixels 101: Editing Images

*T*he Internet is a colorful place. Almost every Web site you visit these days has one or more images on each page. Creating vector objects in Fireworks is a flash. (*Vector objects* are shapes that you create using mathematical formulas to define the object's shape.) Just use one of the tools to create a shape or draw one with the Brush, Pen, or Pencil tools (see Chapter 3 for more on these tools). On top of that, there's the Text tool when you just gotta say it with words (see Chapter 6 for more on the text tool). But sometimes you need more than just shapes and words. Sometimes you need pretty pictures to spice up a Web page using pixel-based images. In this chapter I show you how to import and use bitmap images in your Fireworks documents.

Using Bitmap Images

Bitmap is a generic term for any pixel-based image. Don't confuse bitmap as it's being used here with the Windows-based .bmp image format, which is also referred to as bitmap. I know. It's confusing. Wouldn't it be lovely if all the techno-geeks who create the names for things-you-use-with-computers sat down in one room and agreed on a standard nomenclature? Okay, I'm off my soapbox now.

Pixels are little dots of color that when combined create the final image. After you have an image into Fireworks, you can modify the image — and the pixels that make it up — eight ways to Sunday to create the look you're after. You can resize the images, apply special effects to them, select part of the image with a mask and toss the rest, and on and on. In fact you can modify pixels so much, their own parents won't recognize them.

Importing images into a document

After you decide to grace your Fireworks document with an image, you need to import it. If the image you want to import needs a little pixel RX, not to worry. After the image is in your document, you can perform all manner of pixel magic with Fireworks image editing tools.

To import an image:

1. **Choose File➪Import.**

   Fireworks opens the Import dialog box as shown in Figure 4-1.

2. **Navigate to the folder the file you want to import is stored in and then click Open to import the file.**

3. **Move your cursor over the canvas.**

   The cursor changes into two small lines intersecting at a 90-degree angle. This icon represents the top left-hand corner of the image.

4. **Move your cursor to the spot where you want the top left corner of the image to appear and click.**

   Fireworks places the image on the canvas.

You can resize an image when importing it. After selecting the image file, click and drag to proportionately size the image while importing it. Be careful not to exceed the original size of the image or the image will be distorted when Fireworks redraws the pixels.

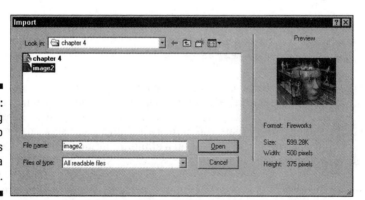

Figure 4-1:
Importing images into Fireworks is not a taxing task.

Scanning images into Fireworks

If you work-for-hire and your customers give you their latest snaps from GlamorPusses-R-Us, you can bypass your photo-editing program and scan the image right into Fireworks. Most scanning utilities have methods for *cropping* (selecting a portion of an image) images before the image is scanned into a program.

To scan an image into Fireworks:

1. **Choose File⇨Twain Select.**

   Where Fireworks is concerned, Twain is not the last name of a famous American author (actually Twain is a pseudonym for the author's real last name, Clemens); in this case, *Twain* is a gizmo used to get an image out of your scanner. If you've got a scanner, Fireworks detects all Twains associated with it.

2. **Select a Twain.**

3. **Choose File⇨Twain Acquire.**

   Fireworks hooks up with you scanner and the Twain dialog box appears.

4. **Follow the dialog box's prompts to complete the scan.**

   The image appears in Fireworks as a new .png document. You are now free to modify the image with the image editing tools, which I show you how to use in the upcoming section "Editing Images."

5. **Choose File⇨Save.**

   The Save As dialog box opens.

6. **Select the folder you want to save the image in.**

7. **Enter a name for the file in the File Name field and then click Save.**

   Fireworks saves the file for posterity or until the next time your computer crashes and wipes out your hard drive.

Editing Images

When you get an image into Fireworks, you can edit it. If the image is part of a document, you can edit it as a bitmap by entering bitmap mode. (To enter bitmap mode, double-click an image inside a Fireworks document.) If the image is all by its lonesome, it's already in bitmap mode by default. You can tell when an image in a document is in bitmap mode because it's surrounded by a chic blue-and-black striped border, shown in Figure 4-2.

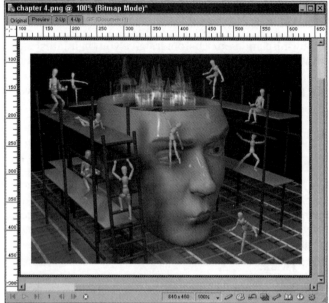

Figure 4-2:
To edit or
not to edit?
The answer
is to edit
because
this image is
in bitmap
mode.

Modifying image size

If you import an image into a document, the size remains the same (unless you sized the image while importing it) but can be modified using the Transform command. You can modify the size and resolution of any image you scan or open in Fireworks by using a menu command.

Please note that this command does not apply to individual bitmaps within a Fireworks document. When you choose this command, you resize the entire document. To resize an individual bitmap in a document, refer to the "Cropping a bitmap in a document" section.

To modify the size of an image:

1. **Choose Modify⇨Image Size.**

   Fireworks displays the Image Size dialog box.

   By default, Fireworks resizes the image proportionately. In other words, when you enter a new width, Fireworks does the math and enters the proper height value to keep height and width proportionate. Unless for some ghastly reason you want to distort an image, leave the Constrain Proportions option enabled.

2. **In the Pixel Dimensions section, double-click the current width value to select it and then enter a new value.**

The entered value appears in the width field. Fireworks automatically supplies the height value (or vice-versa if you decide to be unique and enter the height value first).

3. **To change the resolution of the image, enter a value in the Resolution field.**

4. **Click OK to apply the changes.**

   Fireworks resizes and resamples the image.

To resize an image for a printer, deselect the Constrain Proportions option and modify either the width or the height in the Print Size section of the Image Size dialog box, or you can enter the resolution of your printer in the Resolution field. When you change a value in one of the three fields, Fireworks does the math and resizes the image to the proper size and resolution.

When you resize an image, Fireworks *resamples* it. When an image is resampled, pixels are redrawn to give the image the same relative appearance at its new size. This is generally not a problem when you are downsizing an image, but when you enlarge an image, Fireworks must redraw pixels to a larger size than the original. Something is almost always lost in the translation. If you go over the top while increasing an image's size the results can be quite literally gruesome.

Cropping documents

You crop a document when you don't want all of it. Cropping is like when you take a pair of scissors and cut out the image of your ex-significant other from a photo. The document you crop can be a solitary bitmap image or a complete Fireworks document with objects and bitmaps. With Fireworks you can crop only a rectangular selection. But don't worry if you have images where you need to get precise and remove irregular sections of an image. Fireworks has a tool for that, which I show you how to use in the upcoming section "Cropping a bitmap in a document." To crop a document:

1. **Select the Crop tool from the Toolbox.**

2. **Move your cursor over the canvas.**

3. **Click the spot that will be the top corner of the cropped document and then drag down and across.**

   As you drag, a bounding box appears, giving you a preview of what will be left after you crop the document.

4. **When the bounding box surrounds the part of the document that you want left after the operation, release the mouse button.**

   The bounding box has eight handles, as shown in Figure 4-3.

- The handles at the corners of the box are used to resize the entire bounding box. Hold down the Shift key as you drag one of these handles, and the box resizes proportionately.

- The handles at the middle of the bounding box's top and bottom are used to change its height.

- The handles on the middle of the left and right side of the bounding box are used to change its width.

To move the bounding box, click its center and drag.

5. **When the bounding box is positioned correctly and is the shape and size you want, move your cursor towards the center of the box and then double-click.**

    After you double-click, Fireworks crops the document as you specified and the pixels outside of the bounding box go to that great pixel recycling center in the sky.

Cropping a bitmap in a document

If you have a bitmap within a document and want to crop it, don't use the Crop tool. You'll end up shrinking the whole document and lose whatever is outside the Crop tool's bounding box. To crop a selected bitmap within a document, you use the Pointer tool and a menu command.

To crop a selected bitmap in a document:

1. **Select the bitmap with the Pointer tool.**

    A bounding box surrounds the bitmap.

2. **Choose Edit⇨Crop Selected Bitmap.**

    A bounding box with eight handles surrounds the bitmap (see Figure 4-4).

3. **Drag the handles to size the bounding box and move the bounding box to enclose the part of the image that you want to be left after cropping.**

    - Use the handles in the middle of the top and bottom of the bounding box to change the bounding box's height.

    - Use the handles on the corners to change the size of the box.

    - Hold down the Shift key while dragging one of the handles to resize the box proportionately.

    - Use the handles in the middle of the right and left hand sides of the box to change its width.

    - Click in the center of the bounding box and drag to move the entire box.

4. **When you've sized and positioned the bounding box as desired, double-click in the center of it.**

   The pixels surrounding the bounding box vanish.

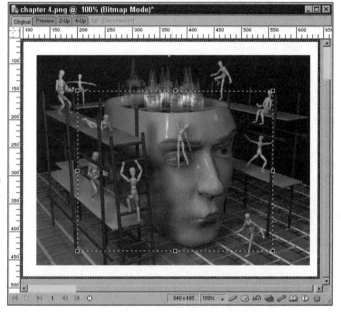

Figure 4-3: Use the Crop to remove unwanted parts of a document.

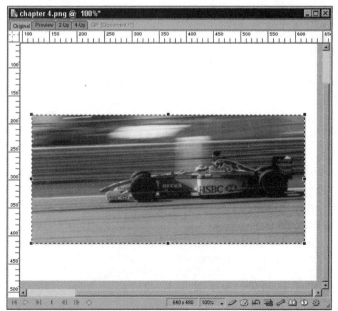

Figure 4-4: You use the Crop Selected Bitmap command to crop a bitmap inside a document.

Creating Selections

Selections — you make them every day. Which tie goes with this shirt? Which dessert topping goes with pralines? Which wine goes with tortellini? Well, in Fireworks you make selections, too; in fact, you create them. You can select all pixels of one color, you can select part of an image, or you can select a circle full of pixels or a rectangle full of pixels. And after you create the selection, you can use it or lose it.

To use a selection, you can select it (is that redundant?) and move it to another part of the document. Or you can apply one of the *filters* (image-editing tools to modify the way an image looks) from the Xtras section of the menu and the filter applies only to the selection of pixels that you selected with one of the selection tools.

The following sections cover the selection tools at your disposal.

Pixel roundup at the bitmap corral: Using the Lasso tool

To create an irregular selection from a bitmap, use the Lasso tool to round up the pixels you want. You can use the Lasso tool like a lariat and draw the pixels in, or you can use the Lasso tool in the polygon mode and create a point-by-point selection. To create a free-form selection with the Lasso tool:

1. **Select the Lasso tool (it looks like a lariat) from the Toolbox.**

2. **Double-click the tool to open the Options panel.**

   The Options panel appears.

3. **Click the triangle to the right of the Edge field to reveal a drop-down menu.**

   Now you've done it. You've selected a tool that has options and you must make a decision. Okay, here's a helping hand.

   - Choose **Hard** and the selection is hard-edged with no blending of adjacent pixels.

   - Choose **Anti-Alias** and Fireworks blends the edge of the selection with neighboring pixels to smooth it.

   - Choose **Feathered** and then click the triangle to the right of the field and drag the slider to specify a number. This number is how many pixels Fireworks uses to *feather* (smooth) the edge of the selection. Try it. You'll be tickled pink.

4. Drag the tool over the area you want to select.

What looks to be an army of marching ants defines your selection, as shown in Figure 4-5.

Figure 4-5:
You use the Lasso tool to round up pixels, pardner.

If you want to have more control when creating a selection, use the Polygon Lasso tool. With the Polygon Lasso tool, you define a selection by clicking various points on the object you want to select. Point-by-point control gives you better control over the selection process (and that's the whole point).

To create a selection with the Polygon Lasso tool:

1. Select the Polygon Lasso tool.

2. Double-click the tool to open the Options panel.

Use the Options panel to specify how Fireworks blends the edge of the selection with adjacent pixels.

3. Click the triangle to the right of the Edge field and choose an option from the drop-down menu.

- Choose **Hard** and the selection you create has a hard edge.

- Choose **Anti-Alias** to blend the selection you create with the neighboring pixels.

- Choose **Feather** and Fireworks feathers (smooths) the selection by the number of pixels you specify.

4. **Click a spot on the bitmap image to define the first point of the selection.**

5. **Drag the tool towards where you want the second point of the selection.**

   As you drag the tool, Fireworks creates a line, which gives you a preview of Point A to Point B.

6. **Click to define the second point of the selection.**

   Fireworks connects the points.

7. **Continue adding points as needed.**

8. **Double-click to close the selection.**

   A pesky army of marching ants defines the boundary of the selection.

Waving the Magic Wand

You use the Magic Wand tool to select pixels with similar colors. This tool is very useful if you import an image of someone against a solid color background and you want to select the background and delete it. Select the tool, click the background, and after it's selected, delete it. All you're left with is the person's picture with no background. To create a selection with the Magic Wand tool:

1. **Select the Magic Wand tool.**

2. **Double-click the tool to open the Options panel.**

   The Options panel appears and is at your beck and call.

3. **Click the triangle to the right of the Tolerance field and drag the slider to set this option.**

   Specify a low number and when you use the tool, Fireworks creates a selection of pixels that are close in hue to the pixel you click with the tool. Specify a high value, and Fireworks selects pixels that aren't as close to the hue to the pixel you clicked, which creates a larger selection.

4. **Click the triangle to the right of the Edge field and select an option from the menu.**

   • Choose **Hard** for a hard-edged selection with no blending of adjacent pixels.

   • Choose **Anti-Alias** to blend the edge of the selection you create with the adjacent pixels.

   • Choose **Feather** to feather (smooth) the edge of the selection by the number of pixels you specify.

5. Click a spot in the image with the color you want to select.

Fireworks defines the selection, as shown in Figure 4-6.

Figure 4-6:
You use the
Magic
Wand tool
to create a
selection of
like-colored
pixels.

Creating rectangular selections

Sometimes you just need to modify a nice regular area of a bitmap image, say a rectangle. To create this rectangular selection you use — bright lights and fanfare please — the Marquee tool. To create a selection with the Marquee tool:

1. Select the Marquee tool.

2. Double-click the tool to open the Options menu.

The Options menu makes its grand entrance.

3. Click the triangle to the right of the Style field.

Feeling very much in vogue, the Style menu displays its styles.

4. Choose one of the following Style options:

- Choose **Normal** to create a free-form selection without restrictions, except of course the restriction of the document size.

- Choose **Fixed Ratio** to create a selection with a fixed ratio. The default ratio is 1 to 2, which means you'll create a selection twice as high as it is wide. To change the ratio, enter new values in the width (the horizontal double-headed arrow icon) field or height (the vertical double-headed arrow icon) field.

- Choose **Fixed Size** to create a selection with a fixed size. The default size is 64 pixels by 64 pixels. To change either dimension, double-click it and enter a new value.

5. **Click the triangle to the right of the Edge menu**.

   Surprise, surprise, another drop-down menu.

6. **Select an Edge option from the following:**

   - Choose **Hard** and Fireworks gives a hard edge to the selection with no blending of adjacent pixels.

   - Choose **Anti-Alias** and Fireworks blends the edge of the selection you create with its neighboring pixels.

   - Choose **Feather** and light as a feather, Fireworks smooths the edge of the selection you create with its neighboring pixels by the width you specify.

7. **Drag the tool over the bitmap to create the selection.**

   Fireworks creates a rectangular selection that you can use to further modify the bitmap.

8. **You can fine-tune the positioning of the rectangular selection by clicking inside and then dragging it.**

Creating oval selections

You use the Oval Marquee tool to create an oval section. Oval selections are just the thing for creating special effects around an angelic — or not so angelic, as the case may be — face. To create an oval selection:

1. **Select the Oval Marquee tool.**

   The Oval Marquee tool is on the *flyout* (a button with a group of tools that expands when clicked) of the second tool button on the left side of the Toolbox.

2. **Double-click the tool to reveal the Options panel.**

   Yup, this tool's got 'em too.

3. **Click the triangle to the right of the Style field.**

   The available styles are displayed on a drop-down menu.

4. **Choose one of the following styles:**

   - Choose **Normal** to create a free-form oval selection.

- Choose **Fixed Ratio** to create an oval selection with a fixed ratio of width to height. The default ratio is 1 to 2, which gives you an oval twice as tall as it is wide. To change the ratio, double-click a value to select it and then enter a new value.

- Choose **Fixed Size** to create an oval selection with fixed dimension width and height dimensions. The default dimension is 64 pixels by 64 pixels. To change either dimension, double-click a value to select it and then enter a new value in the field.

5. **Click the triangle to the right of the Edge field.**

   Oh my, another drop-down menu.

6. **Choose one of the following Edge options:**

   - Choose **Hard** to create selection with a hard edge and no blending of the pixels that live next door to the soon-to-be-created selection.

   - Choose **Anti-Alias** and old Aunty Alias creates a nice blend between the selection's pixels and those that reside nearby.

   - Choose **Feather** to create a selection with a feathered edge of the width that you specify with the slider.

7. **Drag the tool across the bitmap to create the oval selection.**

   An ovoid army of marching ants designates the position of the selection.

Modifying selections

After you create a selection with any of the tools, you can modify it to your heart's content, or at least to the extent that Fireworks lets you modify it. Here are some of the modifications you can make:

✔ To add to a selection, hold down the Shift key while creating a selection with any of the selection tools. Now you've got two areas surrounded by marching ants.

✔ To select the inverse of a selection, choose Modify➪Marquee➪Select Inverse. The area surrounding the selection you created is now selected. You invert a selection when you want to apply an effect outside of the area you originally selected, for example, the area around an oval selection surrounding a person's face.

✔ There are other commands that you can apply to a selection. You'll find them by choosing Modify➪Marquee and then choosing a command from the submenu. The commands are fairly self-explanatory, and I know you need to feed the cat, so I won't take up your time by launching into a long-verbose-rhetorical-discussion of same said commands that you can figure out on your own.

Cloning Images with the Rubber Stamp Tool

Have you ever wished you could create two or more of yourself to take care of business? Well, you can do it virtually in Fireworks with the Rubber Stamp tool. You use the Rubber Stamp tool to touch up photos by picking up an area of color and applying it to a crack or flaw in the photograph. The Rubber Stamp tool is also great for removing crow's feet and applying a virtual face-lift. You can even use the tool to copy one part of a photograph, such as an eye, to another spot in the document. Such fun!

To use the Rubber Stamp tool:

1. **Select the Rubber Stamp tool in the Toolbox.**

2. **Double-click the tool to open the Options panel.**

   The options panel appears.

3. **Click the triangle to the right of the Source field and choose from:**

   - **Fixed:** Locks the Rubber Stamp tool's source pointer (a hollow blue circle) to a specific area of the image so you can clone it over and over and over again. The two pointers move together until you release the mouse button. The source pointer then returns to the area of the image you initially clicked with the tool. This option works great for creating a document full of eyes.

   - **Aligned:** Aligns the source pointer with the tool so you can clone pixels from different areas of the image. Play the song "Me and My Shadow" when using the tool in this mode.

4. **Click the triangle to the right of the Sample field and choose from:**

   - **Image:** Lets you clone pixels from the selected image only.

   - **Documents:** Lets you clone pixels from anywhere on the canvas.

5. **Drag the slider to the right of the Stamp window to control the softness of the tool's edge.**

   Drag the slider down for a harsh edge; up for a smooth edge.

6. **Drag the slider to the right of the Stamp Size window to set the size of the area the tool will clone pixels from.**

   For those of you who just gotta know, the Stamp Size is in pixels.

7. **Click a spot on the bitmap to define the location of the source pointer.**

   Fireworks creates a hollow blue circle where you clicked.

8. **Move the tool away from the spot you just clicked.**

As you move the tool, the hollow circle remains stationary. A rubber stamp icon appears showing you how far away from the source the cloned pixels will be painted.

9. **When the distance between the source and place you want the clone to begin is what you want, click the mouse button; then drag the tool to start cloning.**

   Figure 4-7 shows the Rubber Stamp tool at work, doing its part to stamp out bitmap monotony.

10. **To reset the source pointer (the hollow blue circle) hold down the Alt key (Windows) or Option key (Macintosh) while clicking the Rubber Stamp tool's button in the toolbox.**

   The source pointer and clone pointer are realigned.

Figure 4-7:
The Rubber
Stamp tool
clones
pixels
without
resorting to
biology.

Using the Eraser Tool

To err is human, but to create a major league foul-up requires a computer. Fireworks can't help you with glitches of the digital kind, but you can use the Eraser tool to soak up pixels painted in error or in the white-hot heat of creative passion or any combination thereof. The Eraser tool has a split personality: When you're in bitmap mode, it looks like an eraser; when you aren't in bitmap mode, the tool looks like a knife. I show you how to use the tool's alter ego in Chapter 10.

To erase pixels:

1. **Select the Eraser tool in the Toolbox.**

2. **Double-click the tool to open the Options panel.**

   The Option panel opens. Please note that the options you choose here are for erasing bitmap images and have no effect whatsoever when using the Eraser tool on vector-based images. See Chapter 10 for how to use the Eraser tool on vector objects.

3. **The Erase To field sets the color of the eraser, or more accurately, the color that replaces the pixels that are erased. Click the triangle to the right of the Erase To field and choose one of the following:**

   • Choose **Transparent** and in the area where you erase, the pixels become transparent if the canvas color of your document is transparent. If you selected a color for the canvas, erased pixels will be replaced by that color.

   • Choose **Fill Color** and the pixels you erase are replaced by the currently selected fill color.

   • Choose **Stroke Color** and when you drag the eraser over pixels, they are replaced by the currently selected stroke color.

   • Choose **Canvas Color** and you erase pixels down to the base canvas color.

4. **Click the slider to the right of the Edge Softness window to determine what the edge of the area you erase looks like.**

   Drag the slider down for a hard edge and up for a softer edge.

5. **Click the slider to the right of the Eraser Size window and drag up to make the eraser bigger (for really big mistakes) or down to create an itsy-bitsy-teeny-weeny eraser (but without the yellow polka-dots).**

6. **Click the Round Eraser button to make the eraser tip round, or click the Square Eraser button for a square eraser tip.**

   It is no reflection on your personality if you choose a square eraser tip.

7. **Drag the tool across the area you want to erase.**

   The pixels you erase are replaced with the color you specified in the Options panel.

Creating Special Effects

Your garden-variety 3 x 5 photo-quickie snapshots can be folded, spindled, and mutilated beyond recognition in the hands of an infant. Bitmap images can't be folded, spindled, or mutilated; however, they can be modified to achieve some pretty neat effects. So to create your own brand of eye candy, read on.

Merging images

You merge bitmap images together when you're creating a photo collage in Fireworks. Merging the images prevents you from messing up your artistic arrangement of images with an errant mouse click. To merge two or more bitmaps together as one:

1. Select the bitmaps you want to merge together.

Click the first bitmap to select it; then hold down the Shift key and click additional bitmaps to add them to the selection.

2. Choose Modify⇨Convert to Bitmap.

Fireworks converts the images you selected to a single bitmap. A blue bounding box surrounds the newly created bitmap, and you can now select and edit it as a single bitmap image. If there were any blank areas between bitmaps when you merged them, the canvas color or objects behind the bitmap show through.

Figure 4-8 shows four individual images that were combined to create one bitmap.

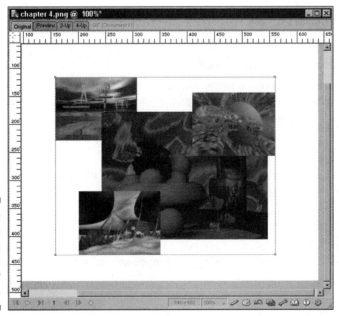

Figure 4-8: Where there were once many, there is now only one.

You can also use the Convert to Bitmap command to convert vector and text objects into bitmaps.

Masking bitmap images

A mask is a window to something underneath. The Lone Ranger's mask showed only his eyes. You create an object using the shape tools and then use it as a *mask* to reveal a part of a bitmap. For example, create a star and then use it as a mask over a bitmap, and it looks like you cut a photograph into the shape of a star.

To mask a bitmap image:

1. **Create a document and import a bitmap image.**

   Any bitmap image will do. For the purpose of this exercise, import a bitmap of your mother-in-law.

2. **Use one of the shape tools to create an object.**

3. **Align the shape over the top of the bitmap.**

   Don't be too concerned with aligning the object exactly. If the mask doesn't line up exactly the way you want, you can edit the results.

4. **Select the object that will mask the bitmap and then choose Edit⇨Cut.**

   The shape is gone, but not forgotten.

5. **Select the bitmap.**

   A blue bounding box surrounds the bitmap.

6. **Choose Edit⇨Paste as Mask.**

   Quicker than you can say, "Hi, ho Silver. Away!" the image is masked by the shape. A red bounding box surrounds the masked image letting you know it is masked.

7. **If the image isn't positioned correctly inside the mask, double-click it until the red bounding box becomes blue.**

8. **Drag the blue crosshair in the center of the image to move the image within the mask.**

9. **When the image is in the position you want, click anywhere outside of the mask.**

   The red bounding box once again appears around the masked image, and you can move the image and mask as one. Figure 4-9 shows a shape masked to an image.

I show you how to create great special effects in Chapter 11.

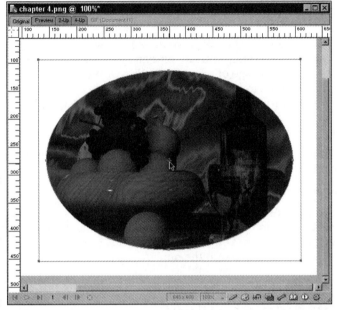

Figure 4-9:
Create special effects by applying a mask to a bitmap.

Fun with Filters

You find Fireworks filters in the Xtras menu (read all about it). You've got lots of filters to choose from — filters that adjust color, blur bitmaps, sharpen bitmaps, and more. You can localize the effect of any filter by creating a selection of pixels. If you just jumped straight to this section when you saw the word, "Fun," read the earlier sections in this chapter on creating selections where I show you how to create selections of pixels.

In this section I show you how to use a couple of the more popular filters. If you have the time, I urge you to explore all the filters.

You can also apply filters through the Effects panel. When you apply filters through the Effects panel, they can be edited after you apply them or disabled if you don't like the way they make your document look. I show you how to use the Effects panel in Chapter 11.

Inverting a bitmap's color

You invert a bitmap's color to convert an image into something that looks like a photographic negative. To invert a bitmap's colors, select the bitmap and then choose Xtras⇨Adjust Color⇨Invert.

Blurring an image

I know what you're thinking: Why would anyone want to blur a perfectly good bitmap? Well for one thing, you can blur an image to simulate motion. For example, to blur an image of a car, select the car using the Lasso tool and then apply the blur. Fireworks blurs only the selected pixels, in this case the car, and the background is crystal clear. To blur a bitmap:

1. **Select the bitmap you want to blur.**

2. **To blur a portion of the bitmap, use one of the selection tools to create a selection.**

3. **Choose Xtras⇨Blur.**

   Fireworks blurs the image. To gain more control over the blur, choose Xtras⇨Gaussian Blur. When you choose Gaussian Blur, the Gaussian Blur dialog box appears. You drag a slider inside the dialog box to control the amount of blur applied to the object.

Sharpening an image

If a client supplies you with an image that's blurry, or you scan an image into Fireworks and it isn't very sharp, you can sharpen a blurry image with the Sharpen commands. I warn you this is not a cure-all for a bad photograph, but it helps you in cases where the image is just a tad fuzzy.

To sharpen a bitmap:

1. **Select the bitmap that you want to sharpen.**

2. **Choose Xtras⇨Sharpen⇨Sharpen.**

   Fireworks sharpens the image. If the image still isn't sharp enough, Fireworks has a second line of defense.

3. **To apply further sharpening choose Xtras⇨Sharpen⇨Sharpen More.**

Chapter 5

Working with Color

*T*he Internet is a very colorful place. Web pages everywhere are brimming in yellows and greens and reds and blues. And it's a good thing the Internet has color, because an Internet without color would be, well black and white. And you know how dreary that can be — with the notable exception of some films from the 40s and 50s.

Color on the Internet is more than just choosing a pretty color and running with it. What looks like a lovely shade of lavender on your monitor may end up looking like a hideous shade of chartreuse or worse yet, salmon in someone else's Web browser. Fortunately, Fireworks knows all about sizzling colors that work well on the Web. In this chapter I show you how to work with color that is safe in any browser.

Using Web-Safe Color for the Web

Most monitors support millions of colors; however, sticking with Web-safe colors when creating objects for your Web pages is a good idea. *Web-safe colors* are colors that look pretty much identical on both Macintosh and Windows platforms.

The Web-safe color palette is comprised of 216 colors and is the default Fireworks palette. Unless you load a different palette, whenever you click a color well in the Colors section of the Toolbox, the Web-safe palette appears. As long as you choose a color from this palette, you have chosen a color that is safe in any browser at any speed. Figure 5-1 shows the Fireworks Web-safe

216 color palette. (The figure shows the hexadecimal color value, too, which I tell you about in the section "Matching a known color using hexadecimal colors." Say that five times fast.)

You can't use Web-safe color with bitmaps (unless you export them in the GIF format). Bitmaps are generally photographic images with millions of colors. And when I went to school, a million wasn't anywhere close to 216. You can use this Web-safe palette to create all the other elements for your Web pages such as text objects, animated banners, and buttons. If you don't go over the top and select every color in the Web-safe palette, you can export your document with less than 216 colors and create a smaller file size.

Figure 5-1:
You use the
Web-safe
color palette
when you
want to be
sure a color
displays
properly on
a Macintosh
and
Windows
OS.

Hexadecimal color value

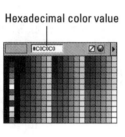

Creating Rainbow Colors with the Color Mixer Panel

If you want to become adventurous, throw caution to the wind and hope it doesn't turn right back around and slap you in the face, you can create your own colors with the Color Mixer panel. These colors will work just fine in most browsers, and there hasn't been a single recorded case of monitor failure when they don't display properly.

The sole purpose of the Color Mixer panel is to mix colors. (Yep, I guess that's why they call it the Color Mixer panel.) You mix a color by dipping your cursor into the color bar. The color bar is displayed at the bottom of the Color Mixer panel.

To create a color:

1. **Click anywhere in the workspace to deselect the currently selected shape.**

   If you neglect this step, Fireworks applies the color you mix to the currently selected object. Of course, if that's what you want to do, disregard this step.

2. **Choose Window➪Color Mixer.**

   The Color Mixer panel makes a colorful appearance (see Figure 5-2). Notice the two color wells to the left of the panel. These wells are the same wells that you find in the toolbox, except that they're in a different place. The well to the right of the pencil icon is the Stroke Color well whose cohort in crime, the Fill Color well, resides to the right of the paint bucket icon.

3. **To create a stroke color, click the Stroke Color Well button that looks like a pencil, and then move the mouse towards the color bar at the bottom of the panel.**

   The cursor becomes an eyedropper.

4. **Click the mouse button and drag the cursor through the color bar.**

   As you drag, the color the cursor is over is displayed in the stroke color well.

5. **When the desired color is displayed in the color well, release the mouse button.**

   The color you selected is on display — until you select a different color — in the Color Mixer panel's Stroke Color well and also shows up in the Stroke Color well in the Colors section of the Toolbox.

6. **To create a fill color, click the Fill Color Well button that looks like a paint bucket and then move the mouse towards the color bar. When the cursor changes into an eyedropper, click the mouse button and drag to select a color.**

   As you drag, the color value that the cursor is over is displayed in the Fill Color well.

7. **When you see the color you want, release the mouse button.**

   The selected color is displayed in the Fill Color well on both the Mixer panel and the Colors section of the toolbar.

When you mix up a stroke and fill color with the Color Mixer panel, you can apply it only to vector objects you create with the drawing tools or text that you convert into an editable object.

Stroke Color well

Fill Color well

Figure 5-2:
You use
the Color
Mixer panel
to mix up a
custom
color.

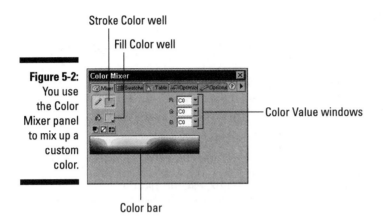

Color Value windows

Color bar

Using Color Models

All of these color models are really just different ways of saying the same thing, although each model does have a particular use for a printer or cartographer or some other "er." The following sections detail the various models.

Matching a known color using hexadecimal colors

The Hexadecimal Color Model is a universal way of expressing colors. Web designers use the hexadecimal system to match a color exactly to a known value. When you see color expressed in *hex* (short for hexadecimal), it is expressed as a combination of six integers and/or letters. You don't need to memorize which letters and which digits make up a color — Fireworks handles that for you. But if you're interested, jet black in hexadecimal is expressed as #000000 and snow white is expressed as #FFFFFF.

If the color you're trying to match is represented in hexadecimal format, do this:

1. **In the Colors section of the Toolbox, click the Stroke Color button (the pencil) to match the known color to the stroke, or the Fill Color button to match the known color to the fill.**

2. **Click the color well for the button you clicked in Step 1.**

   Fireworks displays the color palette.

3. **Double-click the value listed in the field to the right of the color displayed at the top left corner of the palette window.**

   The current value is selected.

4. Enter the known Hexadecimal value and press Enter (Windows) or Return (Mac).

You can enter the letters in lower case. You do not need to include the # sign before the color value. Fireworks automatically adds it and capitalizes the letters for you. Capital, isn't it?

The color representing the value you entered is displayed in the appropriate color well.

Matching RGB colors

The RGB Color Model creates a color by mixing values of Red (R), Green (G), and Blue (B). Each color can have a value from 0 (unsaturated) to 255 (fully saturated). In the RGB model, white has a value of 255, 255, 255 and black has a value of 0,0,0.

To match a stroke or fill color to a known color noted in the RGB Color Model:

1. Choose Window⇨Color Mixer.

The Color Mixer panel makes a flashy entrance.

2. Click the triangle at the upper-right corner of the panel.

A menu pops up, as shown in Figure 5-3.

3. Select RGB from the menu.

4. Click the Stroke Color button or Fill Color button.

The RGB values for the color you selected are displayed in the R, G, and B windows.

5. Enter the RGB values in each field.

Alternately, you can click the triangle to the right of the field and drag the slider to set the value.

The color you specified is displayed in the appropriate color well and will be applied to the next object you create.

Figure 5-3:
Use the
Color Mixer
menu to
switch to a
different
color model.

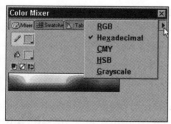

Matching HSB colors

The HSB Color Model also uses three parameters to mix a color, in this case Hue, Saturation, and Brightness. To match a stroke or fill color to a known color designated with the HSB model:

1. **Unless you want to apply the color to the currently selected item, click anywhere in the workspace to deselect the object.**

2. **Choose Window⇨Color Mixer.**

   The Color Mixer panel comes out of hibernation awaiting your next move.

3. **Click the triangle on the top right side of the panel and select HSB from the menu.**

   The R, G, and B fields now become the H, S, B fields.

4. **Click the Stroke Color Well button to replace the current stroke color with the known HSB color; click the Fill Color Well button to replace the current fill color with the HSB color.**

5. **Click the slider to the right of the H window and drag it to set the desired value. Repeat for the S and B fields.**

   The Stroke Color well (or Fill Color well if you if you chose it in Step 4) shows the color you specified; the color will be applied to the next object you create.

Matching CMY colors

Printers use the CMY (cyan, magenta, and yellow) color model to create an ink color that is a perfect match for a known color value. You can match these known colors in Fireworks by doing the following:

1. **Deselect the currently selected item unless you want to apply the color you are creating to it.**

2. **Choose Window⇨Color Mixer.**

   The Color Mixer panel pops in wondering what color you want to mix.

3. **Click the Stroke Color well to match the CMY color to the stroke; Fill Color well to match the CMY color to the fill.**

4. **Click the triangle at the top right side of the panel and select CMY from the drop down menu.**

   The R, G, and B fields become the C, M, and Y fields.

5. **Click the triangle to the right of the C field and when the slider pops up, drag it until the number in the window matches the known value.**

Alternately, you can double-click the current value to select it, and then enter the known value.

6. **Repeat Step 4 for the M and Y fields.**

The color well you chose in Step 2 changes to reflect the values you entered. The color will be applied to the next item you create.

Coloring Objects with the Swatches Panel

You use the Swatches panel to select colors from the loaded palette. (If you haven't been adventurous and opened a different color palette, the loaded palette is the default Fireworks Web-safe palette.) This may seem redundant because you can also select colors from the loaded palette by clicking one of the color wells, but the people who created Fireworks have a reason for the Swatches panel: You can use the panel to create your own custom swatch set or load an existing set.

A swatch is an individual color in the Swatches panel. That's right, each square is a swatch. When you delete swatches or create your own custom colors, you're creating a custom set of swatches.

The default color selection in the Swatches panel is the Web-safe 216 color palette. You can add to, replace, or modify the default color set. But before you can modify the color set in the Swatches panel, you've got to open it.

To open the Swatches panel:

1. **Choose Window⇨Swatches.**

The Swatches panel makes a swashbuckling entrance.

2. **Click the triangle in the upper-right corner of the panel.**

A drop down menu appears showing you the options available for the panel. The Swatches panel and its menu are shown in Figure 5-4.

Modifying a color swatch

When you initially launch Fireworks and open the Swatches panel, your old friend the Web-safe 216 color palette displays its hues. You use this palette in the vast majority of your work. But if the vast majority is deemed half-vast by your client, you'll have to make some changes, and colors may be one of them.

Figure 5-4:
The
Swatches
panel —
looking very
much like a
patchwork
quilt — is
full of pretty
little
swatches.

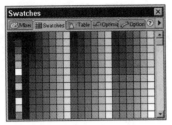

One very immediate option is the replace the Web-safe color swatch with another set. To replace a color swatch set:

1. **Click the triangle at the top right corner of the Swatches panel.**

   The drop-down menu drops down.

2. **From the second section of the menu choose one of the following color sets: Color Cubes (the default set), Continuous Tone colors, Macintosh System colors, Windows System colors, or Grayscale.**

   - The **Color Cubes** set is the Web-safe palette starting with the darkest color (jet black) in the upper left-hand corner and ending with the lightest color; white, which is pure as the driven snow.

   - The **Continuous Tone** color set is also the Web-safe palette, but the colors are arranged differently. In this palette, the colors are arranged according to their tonal value.

   - The **Macintosh System** color set is the default color set that the Mac OS uses to display system software.

   - The **Windows System** color set is the default color set that the Windows OS uses to display system software.

   - The **Grayscale** color set is 256 shades of gray, from white to black.

   The chosen color set replaces the current color set.

You can also add colors to the existing set from within the document. If you created a lovely shade of your favorite color using the Color Mixer panel and want to add it to the currently loaded color set, it's easy. Here's how you do it.

1. **Choose Window⇨Swatches.**

   The Swatches panel opens.

2. **Click the Eyedropper tool in the Toolbox.**

3. **Move the Eyedropper over the color in your document that you want to add to the color palette and click it.**

   The sampled color appears in the Fill Color well.

4. **Move the cursor to an open space in the Swatches panel.**

   The cursor changes from an eyedropper to a paint bucket.

5. **Click to add the sampled color to the color set.**

   A new swatch is born with the color you sampled.

To add a color from anywhere in the workspace, even another document, click the Fill Color Well button that looks like a paint bucket. After the cursor changes to an eyedropper, drag it over the color you want to sample and click. Next drag the cursor over a blank space in the Swatches panel. When the cursor becomes a paint bucket, click to add the sampled color to the current color set.

Sorting swatches

After you've added custom colors to the color set, you may find it beneficial to sort them by hue. To sort the colors in the Swatches panel:

1. **Choose Window⇨Swatches.**

   The Swatches panel opens.

2. **Click the triangle in the upper-right corner of the panel.**

   A drop-down menu appears.

3. **Choose Sort by Color.**

   Fireworks sorts the swatches by color.

Working with color palettes

After going to all the trouble of creating custom colors, adding them to the Swatches panel, and then sorting them, it would be kind of silly to lose them when you open a new Fireworks document. Well, this doesn't have to happen if you exercise another one of your options.

To save the colors currently in the Swatches panel as a custom set:

1. **Click the triangle in the upper-right hand corner of the Swatches panel.**

   The Swatches panel menu appears, waiting to take your order.

2. **Choose Save Swatches.**

   The Save As dialog box appears.

3. **Navigate to the folder you want to save the color set in.**

4. **In the File Name field, enter a name for the color set.**

   Choose a name that has meaning to you, one that you'll be able to identify the color set's contents with.

5. **Click Save.**

   The custom palette is saved for future use.

To receive the Fireworks Seal of Approval, use your computer's operating
system to create a directory for your custom color sets. Okay, you won't win
an award, but you'll be able to locate the color sets easily.

After you've saved a custom palette from extinction, you can load it as needed.

To load a custom palette:

1. **Choose Window➪Swatches.**

   The Swatches panel opens.

2. **Click the triangle in the upper-right corner of the panel.**

   The Swatches panel menu drops down.

3. **Choose Replace Swatches.**

   The Open dialog box appears.

4. **Navigate to the folder your custom color palettes are in, select the
   palette you want to load and click Open.**

   The custom palette replaces the previously loaded color set.

Another neat thing you can do with custom palettes is to add them to the
current color set. This is tremendously useful when you need to use a particularly pungent purple that's part of a palette you saved after creating a little
ol' winemaker's Web site. Rather than trying to recreate it from scratch, load
the color palette and use it.

To add a color palette to the currently loaded palette:

1. **Open the Swatches panel by choosing Window➪Swatches.**

2. **Click the triangle in the panel's upper-right corner; then choose Add
   Swatches from the drop down menu.**

   The Open dialog box opens.

3. **Navigate to the folder you saved the needed color palette in, select the palette, and then click Open.**

   The lovely shade of purple you needed, along with all of the other colors in the custom palette, are added to the currently loaded palette.

Using the Color Table Panel

The Color Table is a panel that you use to keep track of all the colors used in the document you're creating. You use the Color Table panel to manage, edit, delete, and sort the colors in the document. When you initially create a document, you have a background color. Then you start adding objects to the document and assigning strokes and fills to them with colors from either the palette or custom color. These colors all become part of the document's color table. To open the Color Table panel:

1. **Create a document and begin creating items.**

   For a refresher course in creating a new document, refer to Chapter 2. To get the skinny on creating items, take a little trip to Chapter 3.

2. **Choose Window⇨Color Table.**

   The Color Table panel opens, and YIKES, it's empty.

3. **To display the colors used in the document, click the triangle in the upper-right corner of the panel.**

   Hey, lookee here, another drop-down menu.

4. **Choose Rebuild Color Table.**

   All the colors you used in the document are displayed in the panel as shown in Figure 5-5.

As you add more objects to the document with different colors, you can update the table by using the Rebuild Color Table command.

Notice all the icons on the bottom of the panel in Figure 5-5. These icons are used to manipulate and malign the colors into submission. Select a color in the table and then click one of the icons to edit the color. From left to right the icons perform of the following tasks:

✔ **Edit Color:** Opens a color palette that you use to modify the selected color.

✔ **Transparent:** Makes the selected color transparent when the document is exported. Transparent colors allow the background color or background image of a Web page to shine through.

✔ **Snap to Web Safe:** Modifies the color to the nearest hue in the Web-safe palette. Colors that are Web-safe have a small *x* in the center of their swatches.

✔ **Lock Color:** Locks an individual color to prevent removing it or changing it when you change to a different palette or reduce the number of colors in the current palette. Locked colors have a small rectangle in the lower-right corner of their swatches.

✔ **Add Color:** Opens the Color dialog box. Choose the color you want to add to the table.

✔ **Delete Color:** Removes the color from the table.

If you find the colors in a color table useful, you can save them as a custom palette. To save the colors in a document's color table:

1. **Click the triangle at the top right corner of the Color Table panel.**

   The drop-down menu shown in Figure 5-6 appears.

2. **Choose Save Palette from the menu.**

   The Save As dialog box appears.

3. **Navigate to the directory where you save your custom palettes.**

4. **Enter a name for the palette in the File Name field.**

5. **Click Save.**

   The colors in the Color Table panel are saved for future use.

Figure 5-5:
The Color Table helps you keep track of all the colors in a document.

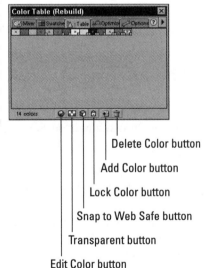

Delete Color button

Add Color button

Lock Color button

Snap to Web Safe button

Transparent button

Edit Color button

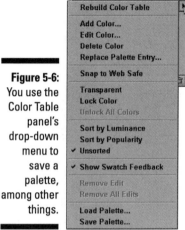

Figure 5-6:
You use the
Color Table
panel's
drop-down
menu to
save a
palette,
among other
things.

Chapter 6

Getting the Word Out with Text

• •

• •

*W*ords — we use them every day. Without words, the world would be a lot quieter because without words we'd have to communicate like cave men, drawing pictures on the wall with burned stubs of wood. Not fun. And without words, there would be no need for text, the subject of this chapter. On a personal note, as a writer, I'm very glad there's text, because without text, I'd have to rely completely on pictures, which doesn't quite get the job done.

In this chapter I show you how to use text in your Fireworks documents. In Fireworks, you use text on banners to let Web surfers know where they are, on buttons to let Web surfers know what will happen when a button is clicked, and sometimes you use whole blocks of text when you've got a lot of things to say.

Using the Text Tool

Text had its rudimentary beginning when a cave man chiseled a symbol on a cave wall that was supposed to be the equivalent of a monosyllabic grunt in the cave man alphabet. Fortunately we've advanced well beyond the monosyllabic grunt — with the notable exception of certain actors who play superheroes.

When it comes time to grace your work with the written word, or perhaps just a letter or two, you use the Text tool. The Text tool is that critter in the Toolbox with the big A icon, which is the same symbol used for the text tool in a lot of programs. I guess it's the same principle involved with the universal icons for the men's and women's restrooms: familiarity.

When you decide to add text to your Fireworks document, you put the Text tool to work. After you select the Text tool, you can specify any font currently in your computer. You can make the text really-really-big for a big message or miniscule so as not to draw attention to itself — you know, like those disclaimers in the car commercials.

To create a block of text:

1. **Select the Text tool.**

2. **Click the spot on the canvas where you want the text to begin.**

   The Text Editor dialog makes an appearance, as shown in Figure 6-1.

3. **Begin typing text in the Text Editor.**

   The letters you type in the Text Editor appear on the canvas. The letters have all the attributes currently assigned to Text tool. The text appears on canvas, giving you a preview of what the finished product will look like.

   To assign attributes such as font style, font color, and other delights to your text, you use the Text Editor. I show you how to use the Text Editor in the next paragraph.

4. **To position the text on the canvas prior to leaving the Text Editor, select the text block and drag it to a new position.**

   Fireworks moves the text block to the desired position.

5. **When you're finished entering text, click OK.**

   Fireworks draws the text block on the canvas.

Figure 6-1:
You write
your text in
this dialog
box.

Making Text Pretty with the Text Editor

The first time you select the Text tool and use it, the Text Editor has the default text characteristics deemed worthy by the creators of Fireworks. But creativity is all about choice, and the Text Editor is all about choice. You can

modify text in with the Text Editor so that it's mundane, ho-hum, or humdrum, or you pull out all the stops and use the Text Editor to create text that
is a thing of beauty.

Fireworks does not have a spell checker. Remember to spell all words correctly so you write right.

Selecting a text font

One of the first things you do with the Text Editor is select a font. Fonts are
fun to work with. You can mix them and match them to give your document
just the touch it needs. To specify a font style:

1. **Select the Text tool and click the spot on the canvas where you want
   the block of text to begin.**

   The Text Editor opens.

2. **Click the triangle to the right of the Font field.**

   A menu full of fonts drops down.

3. **Move your cursor over the fonts.**

   As your move over each font, a window to the right displays the font style.

4. **When you see a font you can't live without, scream "Sold!" and click
   the font to select it.**

   The font will be applied to the text you create.

5. **Begin typing the text.**

   As you type, the text appears on the canvas, giving you a preview of
   what the text will look like when you close the Text Editor.

6. **When you're finished entering text, click OK to close the Text Editor.**

   You've got text on the canvas.

You can also change text attributes using menu commands. Select the text
block with the Pointer tool and then choose an option from the Text drop-
down menu.

Adjusting the text size

You can control the size of the text using the Text Editor. To create really-
really-big text, itty-bitty-infinitesimal text, or anything in between:

1. **Select the Text tool and click the spot on the canvas where want your words of wisdom to appear.**

The Text Editor makes an appearance. As you know, anything that has to do with text requires an editor. Just ask any writer.

2. **Select a font style.**

3. **Click the triangle to the right of the Size field.**

A slider appears.

4. **Drag the slider to select a text size.**

The size you selected appears in the Size window and will be applied to the text you create.

5. **Start typing something.**

As you type, the text appears on the canvas, giving you a real-time preview of what the finished text will look like. At this stage, you can move the text by selecting it and dragging it to a new position on the canvas.

6. **When you're finished typing, click OK.**

Fireworks creates your textual masterpiece on the canvas.

 The maximum text size you can select with the slider is 96 on Windows, 128 on a Mac. If you need bigger text, double-click the currently selected size to select it and then type the size you want. You can enter any value up to 9999. But remember that as you increase the text size, you're increasing the demands on your computer's RAM.

Creating colorful text

Black text on a white background looks good in the newspapers, but you're more creative than that. Why else would you be reading a section about creating colorful text? To add a dash of color to the text you create:

 1. **Select the Text tool and click the spot on the canvas where you want to start creating a block of text.**

The Text Editor pops in for a visit.

2. **Select the font style and font size.**

3. **Click the color swatch to the right of the Size window.**

Your cursor becomes an eyedropper and the color palette pops up.

4. **Drag your cursor across the color swatches in the palette.**

As you move your cursor, the window in the top left corner of the palette changes to the color of the swatch your cursor is over.

5. **Click a color to select it.**

   The color swatch in the text editor changes to the color you selected. The selected color is applied to the text you type.

6. **At this stage of the process, the Text Editor would greatly appreciate it if you'd enter some text.**

   As you type, the text is created on the canvas, giving you an idea of what your colorful text looks like.

7. **After you've entered the text, click OK.**

   Fireworks decorates the canvas with the text object you've created.

After you've created a block of text, you can quickly change the color by selecting the text with the Pointer tool and then changing the fill or stroke color in the Toolbox's Colors section. For more information on working with stroke and fill colors, refer to Chapters 7 and 8.

Styling text

You can use the Text Editor to style your text also. You can't give it a wave or a perm, but you can make it bold, italicized, underline it, or combine the styles. To stylize your text object:

1. **Select the Text tool and click the spot on the canvas where you want to write something.**

   The Text Editor appears.

2. **Select the font style, font size, and font color.**

3. **Click a button to apply a style to the text.**

   - B button to **boldface** the text
   - I button to *italicize* the text
   - U button to <u>underline</u> the text

   You can click more than one button to apply additional styles to the same text.

4. **Type something.**

   The text appears on the canvas as you type.

5. **Click OK to close the Text Editor.**

   Fireworks creates your styled text object on the canvas.

Adjusting kerning

Kerning text has nothing to do with writing corny prose. *Kerning* adjusts the space between two or more letters in a text block. You adjust a text object's kerning in the Text Editor as follows:

1. **Select the Text tool and click the spot on the canvas where you want to get wordy.**

   With a fanfare of techno-wizardry, the Text Editor makes its appearance known.

2. **Select a font style, font size, font color, and add a dash of styling, or not.**

3. **To disable automatic kerning, deselect Auto Kern.**

   Many fonts have built-in kerning information to determine the spacing between letters. Fireworks uses a font's built in kerning by default.

4. **Type some text, any text, as long as it has two or more letters.**

   The text appears in the Text Editor and a carbon copy appears on the canvas, right where you told Fireworks to put it.

5. **To adjust text spacing:**

   - For the entire block of text entered: Click the space before the first letter of text and then drag your cursor over all the letters.

   - For two or more letters in a group of text: Drag your cursor over the letters you want to adjust the kerning for.

   - Between two letters in the block: Click between them.

   The selected letters are highlighted.

6. **Click the triangle to the right of the kerning field and drag the slider to adjust text spacing.**

   As you drag the slider, you'll be able to preview your handiwork by watching the spacing between the selected letters on the canvas.

7. **When the spacing between the letters is to your liking, release the mouse button.**

8. **Click OK to close the Text Editor.**

   Your gapped text is displayed on the canvas.

Adjusting text spacing

You also adjust text spacing (also known as *leading*) in the text editor. When you adjust text spacing, you adjust the distance between two lines of text. You use the multi-talented Text Editor to adjust text spacing. To adjust text spacing:

1. **Select the Text tool and click a spot on the canvas where you want to show off your talents as a wordsmith.**

The Text Editor rushes in.

2. **Select a font style, size, and color, and then apply styling as needed.**

3. **On your mark, get set, go! Start typing.**

As you type text in the Text Editor, it wraps to another line when it reaches the end of the large window in the Text Editor. However, on the canvas, the darned thing keeps running off into oblivion, the next county, or wherever else text disappears to in a computer program.

4. **Press Enter to create a new line of text.**

5. **Continuing typing and creating new lines of text until you run out of things to say or run out of space on the canvas.**

6. **Drag your cursor over all lines of text to select them.**

The selected text is highlighted.

7. **Click the triangle to the right of the text spacing field and drag the slider to adjust the text spacing.**

Drag the slider up to create more space between lines of text; down to scrunch them together. As you drag the slider, the spacing between the lines of text on the canvas changes.

8. **When the spacing is where you want it, release the mouse button.**

9. **Click OK to close the Text Editor.**

Your text block looks marvelous and is spaced to perfection.

 To size a text block prior to entering the Text Editor, select the Text tool and drag it inside the canvas. As you drag, Fireworks creates a bounding box that gives you a preview of the text block's size. When the block is the desired size, release the mouse and Fireworks opens the Text Editor. As you enter text, it wraps to the size of the text block you created.

Aligning text

Aligning text is important. After all, you wouldn't want a document with text that was misaligned, would you? You have several different options when it comes to aligning text. You can have Fireworks display the text vertically, horizontally, or centered, and if you really want to keep your audience guessing, have Fireworks flow the text from right to left. To specify alignment of your block of text:

 1. **Select the Text tool and click the spot on the canvas where you want to display text.**

The Text Editor makes its entrance.

2. **Select a font, font size, font color, and font style.**

3. **Enter the message of your choice.**

   The letters you type in the Text Editor make a simultaneous appearance on the canvas.

4. **Adjust kerning and text spacing.**

5. **Click the alignment buttons, as shown in Figure 6-2, to determine how the text will appear on the canvas. Choose from the following options:**

   - **Horizontal Text** (the default): The text flows horizontally.

   - **Vertical Text:** The text flows vertically, from the top of the canvas down.

   - **Left Alignment:** All text aligns to the left of the text box.

   - **Top Alignment**: All text aligns to the top of the text box. This option becomes available if you select Vertical Text and replaces the Left Alignment option discussed above.

   - **Center Alignment:** All text aligns to the center of the text box.

   - **Right Alignment:** All text aligns to the right of the text box.

   - **Bottom Alignment:** All text aligns to the bottom of the text box. This option becomes available if you select Vertical text and replaces the Right Alignment option discussed above.

   - **Justify Alignment:** The text spread out to fill the text box as evenly as possible, and if possible, creates a block of text with no spaces on the right border.

   The Left, Center, Right, and Justify alignment options are noticeable only when you have more than one line of text in a box.

   - **Stretched Alignment:** Creates a text block where the text you create stretches if you expand the size of the text box with the Pointer tool.

   - **Text Flows Left to Right** (the default): The text flows from left to right.

   - **Text Flows Right to Left:** Creates a block of text that is written backwards.

6. **Click OK to close the Text Editor.**

   Your text marches to the tune of the Fireworks drummer.

Scaling text horizontally

When you scale text, Fireworks stretches (or shrinks if you specify a value less than 100 percent) the letters you create horizontally. To scale text:

1. **Select the Text tool and click the spot on the canvas where you want to say it with text.**

   Fireworks summons its purveyor of things textual, the Text Editor.

2. **Go ahead, make the Text Editor's day, and enter some text.**

   The text you type in the Text Editor also appears on the canvas.

   Some people prefer to set the text attributes first. To see if this method better suits your working preference, first do Step 3 and then Step 2.

3. **Select a font style, size, and color; then adjust other parameters to suit your fancy.**

4. **Select the text by dragging your cursor over it.**

   You can select either the whole block of text or individual letters.

5. **Click the triangle to the right of the Scale field and drag the slider to scale the text.**

   Drag the slider up to increase the width of each selected letter; down to decrease the width. As you drag the slider, the width of each letter you selected changes on the canvas.

6. **When what you see is what you want, release the mouse button.**

7. **Click OK to exit the Text Editor.**

   Fireworks finalizes its creation of the text block, scaling it as you specified.

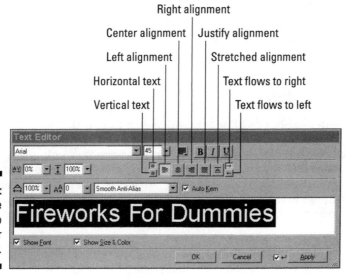

Figure 6-2: Use these buttons to align your text.

Shifting the baseline

When you create a block of text, it has a baseline. The *baseline* is where the bottom is the text is. You can shift text above or below its natural baseline to create special effects, or just because you want to. To shift the baseline of text:

1. **Select the Text tool and click the location on the canvas where you want the text to appear.**

   The Text Editor rushes in from the wings.

2. **Adjust the font style, size, color, and other parameters.**

3. **Enter some text.**

   As you type, a line of text appears on the canvas.

4. **Select the text whose baseline you want to shift.**

   The selected text is highlighted. Normally you'll select one word or a few characters from a block of text when you shift a baseline.

5. **Click the triangle to right of the Baseline Shift field.**

   A slider appears. Drag the slider up to raise selected text above the baseline; down to lower it below the baseline. As you drag the slider, the baseline of the selected letters shifts on canvas, giving you a preview of the transformation.

6. **When the baseline is shifted to your liking, release the mouse button.**

7. **Click OK to exit the Text Editor.**

   The baseline of the selected text is shifted and looks down or up at its fellow letters in the block.

Editing text

The nice thing about creating text with a computer is that nothing is cast in stone. If you're old enough to remember electric typewriters — the author is guilty as charged — then you remember they were very unforgiving beasts. If you had one error in a page of text that you didn't catch as you were typing, you had to resort to white-out to eradicate the error and then try to perfectly align the page in the typewriter so the new text aligned with the old. Not fun. Fortunately, editing text in Fireworks is simple. To edit a block of text:

1. **Double-click the block of text you need to edit.**

   The Text Editor opens.

2. **Drag your cursor over the text in the Text Editor to select it.**

   You can select all the text to globally edit the entire block of text, or select a word or letter to apply a change to just part of the text.

3. **Apply the desired changes to the selected text.**

   When you apply the change, the text updates in the Text Editor and on the canvas. Fireworks applies the changes by default and updates the text on canvas so you can preview the changes as you make them.

   To manually apply the changes, click the box next to the Apply button and Fireworks updates only the text on the canvas when you click the Apply button.

   If the position of the Text Editor prevents you from previewing a block of text as you edit, click on the Text Editor and drag it to the side.

4. **When the text is just the way you want it, quit fiddling with the Text Editor's options. You can't improve upon perfection.**

5. **Click OK to exit the Text Editor.**

   Firework applies your edits to the text.

To create a block of text with different font sizes, colors, or styles applied to individual words or letters, create a block of text, select the text that you want to have a different font, color, or style applied to, and then enter the desired changes. When you exit the Text Editor, Fireworks creates a block of text with mixed styles (you can call it text gumbo).

Attaching Text to a Path

When you attach text to a path, it flows along the path. This is just one of the neat effects you can achieve with text in Fireworks.

A *path* is a series of connected points that defines a line segment or shape. A path can be created with the Pencil tool, Pen tool, or one of the other drawing tools, such as the Ellipse tool.

Attaching text to a path

Text is attached to a path with a menu command. To attach text to a path:

1. **Create a block of text.**

2. **Create a path using any of the drawing tools.**

   I show you how to create paths in Chapter 3.

3. Use the Pointer tool to select both the text and the path.

The text block is surrounded by a blue bounding box, and the path becomes highlighted.

4. Choose Text⇨Attach to Path.

The text block develops a magnetic attraction for the path and clings to it as shown in Figure 6-3. The path loses all of its other attributes such as stroke and fill color. If you want to conform text to a path and still have the path visible, (for example, displaying text around the top a filled oval), you have to duplicate the path first and then attach the text to the original.

I show you how to align text to both sides of an oval in Chapter 20.

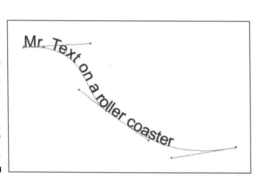

Figure 6-3:
Now listen here, text. I want you to follow this path.

Aligning text along a path

After you attach text to a path, you may need to realign its position along to path. To change the way text aligns along a path:

1. Select a block of text that is attached to a path.

2. Choose Text⇨Align and then choose one of the alignment options from the submenu.

You can align the text to the path's left, center, or right; justify it to the path; or stretch it along the path.

Figure 6-4 shows the text in Figure 6-3 with different alignment options applied.

To edit text attached to a path, double-click it and Fireworks opens the Text Editor.

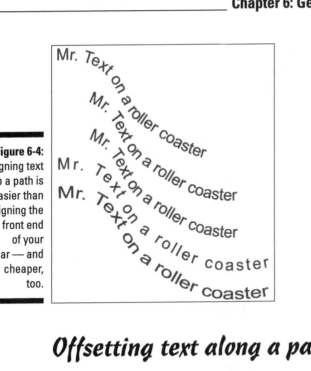

Figure 6-4:
Aligning text
to a path is
easier than
aligning the
front end
of your
car — and
cheaper,
too.

Offsetting text along a path

If the normal alignment options don't get your text to toe the line, you can fix that by offsetting the text a smidge. *Offsetting* the text is like giving it a nudge, nudge, wink, wink, say no more, say no more (I'm a Monty Python fan — can you tell?). How gentle a nudge is up to you, the text's creator. Oh, such power.

To offset text along a path:

1. **Select a block of text that you've attached to a path and then choose Window⇨Object.**

   The Object panel appears.

2. **In the Text Offset field, enter a value.**

   This value determines how far Fireworks nudges the text along the path. Enter a negative value to move the text backwards along the path.

Changing the orientation of text along a path

By default, Fireworks flows the text along the path, orienting each letter perpendicularly (this word was handpicked for your reading pleasure from my thesaurus) to the path you create. If you so desire, you can change the orientation of the text with a menu command. To reorient text along a path:

1. **Select a block of text that is attached to a path.**

2. **Choose Text➪Orientation and choose one of the following options:**

   • **Rotate Around Path** (the default): Orients each letter to the path perpendicularly.

   • **Vertical:** Aligns each letter to the path at a 90-degree angle to its baseline, regardless of the path's curvature.

   • **Skew Vertical:** Maintains each letter's vertical orientation, but adds a vertical skew (slant) to the equation.

   • **Skew Horizontal:** Orients the letters vertically and skews (slants) them horizontally.

Fireworks reorients your text according to the menu command you chose. Figure 6-5 shows the text object in Figure 6-3 with the different orientation options applied.

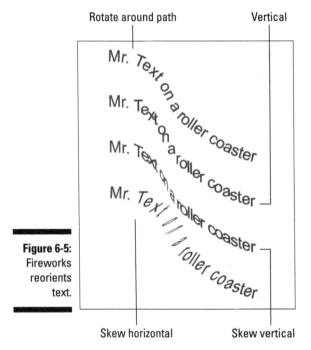

Rotate around path   Vertical

Skew horizontal   Skew vertical

Figure 6-5:
Fireworks
reorients
text.

To reverse the direction Fireworks aligns the letters in a block of text to a path, choose Text➪Reverse Direction.

Tricks with Text

With a little help from your imagination and the proper Fireworks effect, text, like modeler's clay, can be rather malleable. You apply special effects to text when you want to draw your viewer's attention to it; use the Text Editor to create unique looking text and then apply special effects to the unique text to make it really stand out.

Applying special effects to text

Fireworks has a number of effects that work well on text. You can add a drop shadow to make text appear as though it's floating over the page, make text glow, bevel text, or emboss it. You can even mix and match effects to create something really special. To apply effects to text:

1. **Use the Pointer tool to select a block of text you want to apply effects to.**

2. **Choose Window⇨Effect.**

   The Effect Panel appears.

3. **Click the triangle to the right of the current Effect field (the selected option will be None if no effects have been previously applied).**

   A drop-down menu of effects appears.

4. **Choose the effect you want to apply; then adjust the effect's options.**

   Fireworks applies the effect to the text. Figure 6-6 shows text with different options applied.

I show you everything you ever wanted to know but were afraid to ask about using the Effects panel in Chapter 11.

Converting text to editable objects

When you convert text into an editable object, the text becomes a series of points and paths that you can use to distort the text into shapes that would make a contortionist cringe.

When you convert text into editable objects, you can no longer use the Text Editor to modify it.

To convert text into editable objects:

1. **Select the block of text you want to convert.**

2. Choose Text➪Convert to Paths.

Fireworks converts each letter to an editable object comprised of paths and points. You can now use any of the vector editing tools to modify the objects. After you convert the text to an editable object, you can move the position of individual points along the path or adjust the shape of the paths. Figure 6-7 shows an upper case "a" that has been converted to paths and modified.

I show you how to modify editable vector objects with menu commands and tools in Chapter 10.

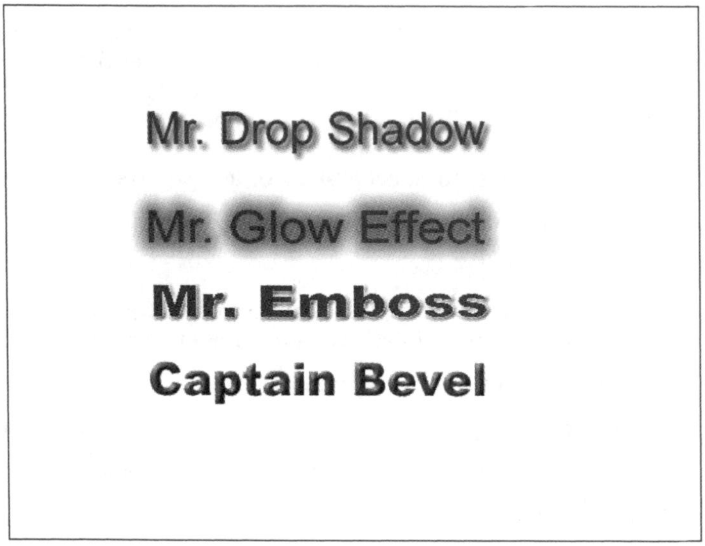

Figure 6-6:
Apply effects to text to make it stand out.

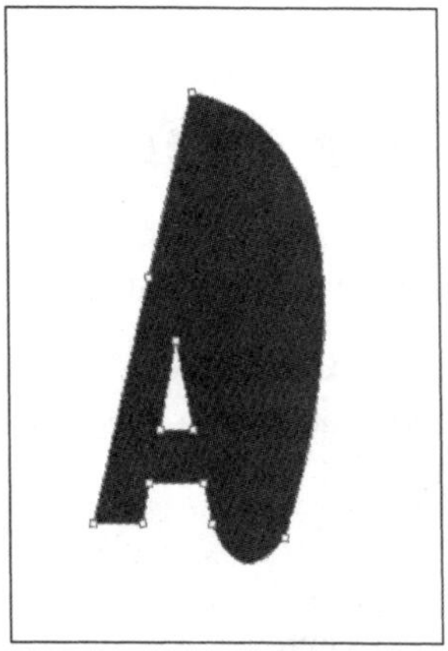

Mr. Drop Shadow

Mr. Glow Effect

Mr. Emboss

Captain Bevel

Figure 6-7:
Convert text to paths and you can create some cool letters.

Part II
Creating Complex Graphics for Fun and Profit

The 5th Wave   By Rich Tennant

"Why don't you try blurring the brimstone and then putting a nice glow effect around the hellfire."

In this part . . .

Whether you use Fireworks to create Web pages for hire or you use the program to create the best home page out there, you need to create artwork with more than just simple ovals or rectangles filled with solid color to pique a visitor's interest. To add visual interest to your Fireworks designs, you need to know how to create visually compelling shapes filled with colorful gradients or patterns. That's what this part of the book is all about, finding out how to create objects for your Fireworks documents that attract attention and keep visitors returning to your Web designs time and time again.

I begin this part by showing you how to create line styles and work with solid fills and gradients. Then I show you how to modify an object's parameters. In other chapters I show you how to create interesting shapes by modifying a basic shape. After reading this section you'll know how to move, rotate, skew, and distort objects to create complex graphics. You also find out how to apply effects to the objects you create and then optimize the artwork for its final destination. And last but not least, I show you how to create reusable graphic elements known as *symbols*.

Chapter 7

Creating Line and Outline Styles

• •

In This Chapter

▶ Using the Stroke panel

▶ Putting on the pressure

▶ Creating a stroke

▶ Saving a stroke

• •

*W*hen you create an object with any of the drawing tools, a *stroke* is involved. Unfortunately for those of you who play the lottery, it's not a stroke of luck; it's a stroke of the lined variety. If you're creating a solid object like an oval or rectangle, the stroke is the outline that surrounds the solid color inside the object. If you're using the Brush, Line, Pencil, or Pen tool, a stroke is all you've got to work with.

A stroke can be solid and skinny, or it can be textured and wide. You can create strokes that look like they were created with a calligrapher's pen or strokes that looked like they were painted with an airbrush. Hmm, I've used stroke three times in the last sentence. Must be that's why Macromedia calls them strokes.

Introducing the Stroke, a Line by Any Other Name

When you create an object with one of the Toolbox's drawing tools, Fireworks assigns the default stroke for that tool. Depending upon the tool you select, this can range anywhere from a wimpy one-pixel slash to the anemic-looking Basic stroke style. In order for a stroke to strut its stuff, it's gotta have some muscle.

To give a stroke muscle, you don't put it on a weight-training regimen. One trip to the Stroke panel is the equivalent of a wimpy stroke working out with free weights for three months.

Creating Line and Outline styles with the Stroke panel

You use the Stroke panel to modify the way a stroke appears. Within the stroke panel are individual fields that you use to select a category, style, or color; modify the tip; or apply texture to a stroke. To modify a stroke with the Stroke panel:

1. **Create a path with one of the drawing tools or select one you've already created, such as a single line or an outline around a shape.**

2. **Choose Window⇨Stroke.**

   The Stroke panel opens (see Figure 7-1).

3. **Select a category, name, and color for the stroke.**

   If you're thinking your friendly author has left you high and dry with no information about how to select a stroke category, name, or color, please read the upcoming sections where I show you how to select all of the above to create a stroke of distinction.

   Fireworks modifies the stroke, and the stroke searches for a mirror to admire its new look.

Figure 7-1:
You use the
Stroke panel
to create a
makeover
for a non-
photogenic
stroke.

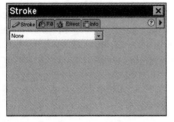

Selecting a stroke category

You select a category in the Stroke panel to modify the overall appearance of a stroke. The default Stroke category depends upon the tool selected. To select a stroke category:

1. **Select a stroke and then choose Window⇨Stroke.**

   The Stroke panel opens.

2. **Click the triangle to the right of the stroke Category field.**

   The drop-down menu shown in Figure 7-2 drops down.

3. Select a category.

Several other parameters you can modify appear in the panel.

4. Adjust the way the stroke looks by modifying each option.

Fireworks transforms the selected stroke.

Figure 7-2:
You select a
different
stroke
category to
give your
stroke
pizzazz.

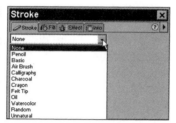

Selecting a stroke color

Web pages are colorful works of art, or at least they should be. The same is true of the strokes you create. To modify a stroke's color with the Stroke panel:

1. Select a stroke and choose Window⇨Stroke.

The Stroke panel opens.

2. Click the stroke color well.

The color palette appears and your cursor becomes an eyedropper.

3. Drag your cursor over the color swatches.

As you drag, the window on the left side of the panel changes to the color your cursor is over.

4. Click a color to select it.

The color appears in the Stroke Color well in both the Stroke panel and the Colors section of the Toolbox.

Selecting a stroke name

Stroke names (or as I prefer to call them, stroke styles) are options that modify the look of a category's default stroke. Each category has several styles to choose from. To modify the appearance of a stroke, you select a different stroke name.

To select a stroke name (style):

1. **Select a stroke and choose Window⇨Stroke.**

   The Stroke panel appears.

2. **Click the triangle to the right of the Stroke name field.**

   A drop-down menu appears, as shown in Figure 7-3.

3. **Click a style to select it.**

   Fireworks modifies the stroke.

Figure 7-3:
Select a
stroke style
to modify
the
appearance
of a stroke.

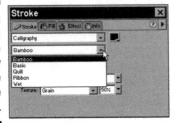

Each stroke category has its own unique set of stroke names/styles. To get a feel of what the different stroke categories and styles look like, create a simple path with the Brush tool. Open the Stroke panel and select strokes from different categories and apply different styles to the path you just created to modify its look. You'll be surprised how many different choices you have.

Modifying a stroke

Every stroke style has parameters that you can modify to change the appearance of the stroke. You can modify the edge of the stroke, change the width of the stroke tip, or apply a texture to the stroke. To modify a stroke style:

1. **Select a stroke.**

2. **Choose Window⇨Stroke.**

   The Stroke panel streaks onto the canvas.

3. **Select a Stroke category and Stroke name.**

   For a refresher course on selecting a Stroke category or name, read the preceding sections.

4. **Drag the slider to the right of the Tip window to control how Fireworks creates the edge of the stroke. Drag up for a stroke with a softer edge; down for a stroke with a harder edge.**

The image in the Tip window updates to give you a preview of the stroke's edge.

5. **Click the triangle to the right of the Tip Size window.**

   A slider appears.

6. **Drag the slider up to create a wider stroke; down to create a narrower stroke.**

   The image in the Tip window changes to reflect the stroke's new width.

7. **Click the triangle to the right of the Texture window.**

   A drop-down menu appears (see Figure 7-4). As you drag your cursor over the choices, an image of the texture appears in a window to the right of the menu.

8. **When you see the texture you want, click the texture's name to select it.**

9. **Click the triangle to the right of the Amount of Texture window.**

   A slider appears.

10. **Drag the slider to vary the texture's intensity.**

    The texture applied to the stroke changes intensity as you drag the slider. When you're finished editing, Fireworks updates the stroke.

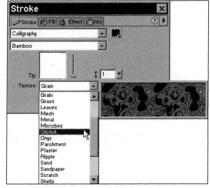

Figure 7-4:
Apply
texture to
create a
stroke of
distinction.

Creating Strokes with Digital Tablets

If you use a pressure sensitive digital tablet to create paths, you can create wonderful effects using the Brush tool with a style from the Air Brush, Calligraphy, or Charcoal stroke categories. Modify the tip size so that it's fairly broad and then vary the pressure as you create the path. Figure 7-5 shows paths drawn with a pressure sensitive digital tablet.

A pressure sensitive tablet is a small drawing pad (made out of high tech plastic or some other space-age material) that you can attach to your computer. The tablet comes with a stylus that you use to draw paths. The stylus looks and feels like a pencil. Using a digital tablet generally gives you much better control when creating paths with the drawing tools, unless of course you're like me and your favorite drawing instrument is a magenta-colored crayon.

For more information on creating paths, refer to Chapter 3.

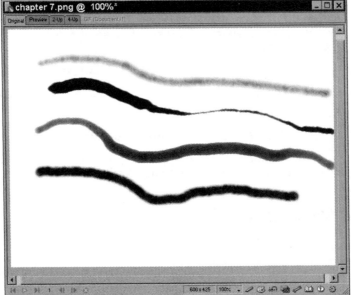

Figure 7-5:
Use a pressure sensitive tablet to create strokes that look like they were painted with an airbrush.

Creating Pressure Effects with a Mouse

If you use a mouse to draw your paths, you can come close to simulating the look of a path drawn with a pressure sensitive digital tablet. To simulate pressure effects:

1. **Select the Brush tool.**

2. **Choose Window⇨Stroke.**

   The Stroke panel opens.

3. **Click the triangle next to the Stroke Category field.**

   A drop-down menu appears.

4. **Choose Air Brush, Calligraphy, or Charcoal.**

5. **Click the triangle to the right of the Stroke Name field.**

   And yet another drop-down menu appears.

6. **Choose a style.**

7. **Drag the Brush tool across the canvas.**

   To simulate pressure effects, vary the speed at which you drag the mouse across the canvas. Begin slowly and then increase speed to create a stroke that is broad at the beginning and tapers off at the end. Hold your mouse over one position to simulate an airbrush spraying a large amount of paint over an area.

Modifying a Stroke with the Scrubber Tool

 You can change the width of a stroke with the Path Scrubber tool. The Path Scrubber tool is actually a group of tools: the Freeform tool, the Path Scrubber tool, the Path Scrubber (additive) tool, and the Path Scrubber (subtractive) tool. In this section I show you how to use the Additive mode to widen a stroke and the Subtractive mode to make a stroke narrower. I show you how to use the other two modes of the Path Scrubber tool in Chapter 10.

To expand the size of a stroke with the Scrubber tool:

 1. **Using the Pointer tool, select the path whose stroke you want to expand.**

   The center of the selected path is highlighted in light blue.

 2. **Click the triangle at the lower-right side of the seventh button down on the right hand side of the Toolbox.**

   The tool group expands.

3. **While holding down the mouse button, click the Path Scrubber (additive) tool to select it.**

   The tool displays on the toolbar.

4. **Drag the tool over the path.**

   As you drag the tool, the stroke expands.

To decrease the size of a stroke with the Path Scrubber tool:

 1. **Use the Pointer tool to select the path whose stroke you want to make smaller.**

   The center of the path is highlighted with a single pixel blue line.

2. **Click the triangle in the lower-right hand corner of the fifth button on the right side of the Toolbox.**

   The tool group expands.

3. **With the mouse button depressed, click the Path Scrubber (subtractive) tool.**

   The tool knocks the last selected tool's icon off the button to make room for itself.

4. **Drag the tool over the path.**

   Wherever you drag the tool, the stroke shrivels into a mere figment of its former self.

Creating Your Own Custom Stroke of Genius

If you're anything like me, you like to be original. It's kind of hard to be really original when you have the same tools that umpteen zillion other Fireworks users have. Well, the designers of Fireworks — bless their pointed techno-geek heads — like to be different, too. That's why they made if possible for you to create your own strokes.

Editing a stroke

To create a custom stroke, you start with one of the preset styles and modify it. I know what you're thinking — you can change the width and apply a texture. Big deal. Well, if that *is* what you're thinking, you're wrong. You have some very powerful editing tools available to create a custom stroke. If I were to cover all the details of editing a stroke, I'd almost need an extra chapter, something that unfortunately is not in the cards. I do get you pointed in the right direction, though.

To create a custom stroke:

1. **Choose Window⇨Stroke.**

   The Stroke panel opens.

2. **Choose a Stroke category and then choose a Stroke name.**

   Choose a stroke you're particularly fond of or use a lot. If you're confused, you obviously didn't read the earlier sections, "Selecting a stroke category" and "Selecting a stroke name."

3. Click the triangle near the top-right corner of the panel.

A drop-down menu appears.

4. Choose Edit Stroke.

The Edit Stroke dialog box appears, as shown in Figure 7-6. The Edit Stroke dialog box has three tabs of options that you use to modify the basic stroke you selected. See, I told you there were a lot of ways to modify a stroke style.

5. Modify any or all of the parameters in the Options section.

At this stage, my suggestion is to click the triangle to the right of each parameter's field. If a slider appears, drag it and watch the window at the bottom of the panel to see how that parameter affects the way the stroke looks. If the parameter has a menu, choose different options to see how it changes to look of the stroke.

Figure 7-6: You create a custom stroke by editing it.

6. Click the Shape tab.

The Shape section of the Edit Stroke dialog box appears. The changes you make in this section determine the shape of stroke's tip. Think of the tip like the end of a calligraphic pen or a paintbrush. You can modify the tip's size, *aspect* (ratio of the tip's width to height), and angle of attack. Figure 7-7 shows a stroke with a square tip being modified. Notice the control for the tip's angle of attack.

7. **After you're through tweaking the stroke's shape, click the Sensitivity tab.**

   Oh look, a section that says Sensitivity. The changes you make in this section affect the sensitivity of several Brush Properties. Figure 7-8 shows the Sensitivity section.

8. **To modify an individual Brush Property, click the triangle to the right of the field.**

   The drop-down menu shown in Figure 7-9 appears.

9. **Select the Brush Property you want to modify.**

   Again, there are no hard-and-fast rules for modifying a stroke. The effects of your changes depend upon the initial stroke you selected before editing and your own artistic vision. Drag the various sliders until you see something you like in the window at the bottom of the panel.

10. **When you're through playing with the sliders and drop-down menus, click Apply to apply your changes to the selected stroke.**

    The stroke you selected is updated to reflect the changes. The edited stroke will be applied to future paths you create with either the Pen, Line, or Brush tool, as well as the Rectangle, Rounded Rectangle, Ellipse, and Polygon tools. If you select the Pencil tool, the stroke reverts to the Pencil default, a skinny single pixel. If you switch to another stroke style, the changes you made to the previous stroke are lost unless you saved the stroke.

Again, my best advice is to let your inner child have a field day playing with the different controls. As you tweak the controls, you can view a preview of the modified stroke in the window at the bottom of the panel.

Saving a stroke

After you go through all the trouble of editing a stroke, you'll be happy to know you can save it for future use. To save a custom stroke:

1. **Choose Window⇨Stroke.**

   The Stroke panel appears.

2. **Create a custom stroke.**

3. **Click the triangle near the upper-right hand corner of the panel.**

   A drop-down menu appears.

4. Choose Save Stroke As.

The Save Stroke dialog box appears.

5. Enter a name for the custom stroke and click OK.

The stroke is saved for future use and is added to the Stroke category's style menu.

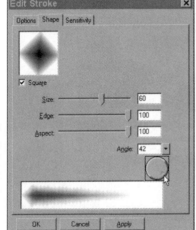

Figure 7-7:
You modify the shape of the stroke in this section.

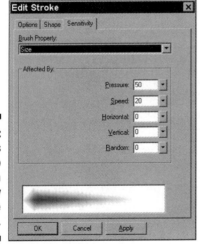

Figure 7-8:
You use this panel to show a stroke how to be more sensitive.

Figure 7-9:
You can
modify any
of these
brush
properties.

Chapter 8

Coloring Solid Objects with Fills

. . . .

. . . .

*L*ike people, some objects have substance, and others don't. To give an object in Fireworks substance, you assign a *fill* to it. You can fill the object with a solid color, a blend of two or more colors, or a pattern. In this chapter I show you how to use the Fill panel to apply a Fireworks ready-made fill and also how to create your own custom fills.

Introducing Fills

When you create a shape with any of the shape tools, the shape has an outline, which is colored with a stroke, and the contents of the outline, which are colored with a fill. A fill can be a single color, a blend of colors, or a tiling pattern.

Creating a fill

You can apply a solid color fill using the fill well in the Colors section of the toolbox, or you can use the Fill panel. When you need to spice things up with a custom fill (such as a blend of many colors) or a pattern, you use the Fill panel.

To create a fill with the Fill panel:

1. **Choose Window⇨Fill.**

   The Fill panel opens (see Figure 8-1).

 2. **Click the triangle to the right of the Fill Category field.**

 A drop-down menu appears.

 3. **Choose a fill category.**

 After choosing the category, the various parameters for that category are displayed. I know, it looks like a lot of stuff. Hang in there, and it will all make sense.

Fill category

Figure 8-1:
The Fill
panel gives
a shape
substance.

Creating solid color fills

The most basic fill you can create is a solid color. Solid color fills, while they may seem mundane or boring, do have their place. Solid colors make excellent fills for shapes you use as background objects in your Fireworks projects. To create a solid fill:

 1. **Using the Pointer tool, select the object you want to apply the fill to.**

 To apply a fill to more than one object, select the first object, and while holding down the Shift key, click additional objects to add them to the selection. When you select a fill, it will be applied to all objects in the selection.

 2. **Choose Window⇨Fill.**

 The Fill panel is at your service, ready to fill 'er up.

 3. **Click the Fill Color well.**

 The color palette appears and your cursor becomes an eyedropper.

 4. **Drag your cursor over the color swatches.**

 As you drag, the window near the top left corner of the panel changes to the color of the swatch your cursor is over.

 5. **Click a color to select it.**

 The selected color appears in the Fill Color well.

6. **Click the triangle to the right of the Edge field.**

   A drop-down menu appears.

7. **Choose one of the following Edge options:**

   • **Hard:** Creates a hard-edged fill.

   • **Anti-Alias:** Creates a smooth transition between the fill and surrounding areas.

   • **Feather:** Blends the fill with the surrounding area. When you choose the Feather option, the window to the right of the field becomes active. Click the triangle to activate the slider and then drag to specify the number of pixels Fireworks uses to blend the fill.

8. **Click the triangle to the right of the Texture field.**

   A drop-down menu appears, as shown in Figure 8-2. You use this menu to apply a texture to the fill.

9. **Drag your cursor over the textures.**

   As you drag, a window opens up, giving you a preview of each texture your cursor passes over, kinda like those coming attractions they add to the start of a rented video to get you to buy more videos.

10. **Click a texture to select it.**

    After you select a texture, the value in the Intensity field increases to 50%.

11. **To tone down the appearance of the texture, click the triangle to the right of the Intensity field and drag it down to select a lower value or up to increase the intensity of the texture.**

    As you drag the slider down, watch the selected object. The texture becomes less apparent at lower settings.

12. **Select the Transparent option, and background objects appear through light areas of the texture.**

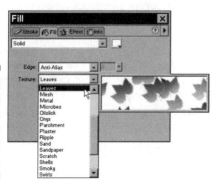

Figure 8-2:
Get your fill
of textures
for your fill
from this
menu.

To create a fill with no texture, use the default Grain texture (or the currently selected texture) with an Intensity setting of 0%.

Creating dithered color fills for the Web

A dithered fill is a different kind of animal. When you create a *dithered fill,* you choose two colors that are blended together to create a reasonable facsimile of a third. Actually, what happens is Fireworks creates a checkerboard pattern of the two colors, but the checkers are so small you don't notice them, and they blend to create a pseudocolor that actually looks quite realistic. What'd he say? In short, you use dithered fills when you want to limit the number of colors in your document.

To create a dithered fill:

1. **Choose Window⇨Fill.**

   The Fill panel fills up part of your workspace.

2. **Click the triangle to the right of the Fill Category field.**

   A drop-down menu appears.

3. **Choose Web Dither.**

   A large Dither Preview window and four mini-windows appear below the Fill field. The small windows with a triangle in their lower-right corner are your color controls.

4. **Click the top color control.**

   A color palette appears and your cursor becomes an eyedropper.

5. **Click a color in the palette to select it.**

   The selected color appears in the color control window and to the left of the bottom color control.

6. **Click the bottom color control.**

   A color palette appears and your cursor becomes an eyedropper.

7. **Click a color to select it.**

   The selected color appears in the bottom color control window and in the window to the left of the top color control. The grid of four colors simulates how the colors will blend together. The dithered color is displayed in the Dither Preview window as shown in Figure 8-3.

8. **Enable the Transparent option to make the selected color from your Web dither transparent.**

9. **Click the triangle to the right of the Edge field.**

   A drop-down menu appears.

10. **Choose one of the following Edge options:**

    • **Hard:** Creates a hard-edged fill with no blending.

- **Anti-Alias:** Blends the edge of the fill with adjacent colors.
- **Feather:** The window to the right of the Edge field becomes active. Click the triangle to activate the slider and drag to choose how many pixels Fireworks uses to blend the fill with neighboring colors.

The Dither Preview window updates to show you the finished fill, Phil.

Create a dithered fill when you want to create a document that you'll export with a limited number of colors. To limit the number of colors to the current color table, choose Window⇨Color Table. If the color table is empty, click the triangle near the top right corner of the panel and choose Rebuild Color. When you create your dithered fill, choose the colors to blend from the color table instead of the pop-up color palette.

Dither preview window

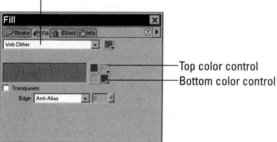

Figure 8-3: You create a dithered fill to get more colors from less.

Top color control
Bottom color control

Filling an object with a pattern

Another option you have for fills are patterns. When you choose a pattern as a fill, Fireworks is actually tiling a photograph within the object you are filling.

To create a pattern fill:

1. **Using the Pointer tool, select the object you want to fill with a pattern.**
2. **Choose Window⇨Fill.**

   The Fill panel appears.
3. **Click the triangle to the right of the Fill Category field.**

   A drop-down menu appears.
4. **Choose Pattern.**
5. **Click the triangle to the right of the Pattern field.**

   Guess what? Another drop-down menu appears, as shown in Figure 8-4.

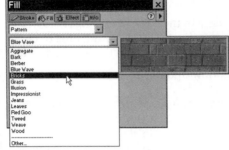

Figure 8-4:
Patterns.
Patterns.
We've got
your
patterns.

6. **Drag your cursor over the selections.**

   As you drag over a pattern name, its image appears in the preview window.

7. **Click a pattern to select it.**

   Fireworks applies the pattern to the selected object, and it looks simply magnificent.

8. **Click the triangle to the right of the Edge field.**

   Another drop-down menu appears.

9. **Select one of the following Edge options:**

   • **Hard:** Gives your pattern fill a hard edge.

   • **Anti-Alias:** Creates a gentle blend between the pattern and adjacent objects.

   • **Feather:** Creates a blend of ten pixels (the default) between the pattern fill and adjacent objects. To change the size of the blend, click the triangle in the small window to the right of the Edge field and drag the slider to specify a different value.

10. **To apply a texture to the pattern, click the triangle to the right of the Texture field.**

    You see the drop-down menu shown in Figure 8-5.

11. **Drag your cursor over the pattern names.**

    A preview window displays an image of the texture.

12. **Click a texture to select it.**

    The value in the Intensity field jumps to 50%. To vary the intensity of the texture, click the triangle to the right of the window and drag to select a different setting. A setting of 0% shows no texture whatsoever.

13. **Select the Transparency option to have any underlying underlings show through the fill.**

    Note: If you select 0% for the Intensity setting, this option is unavailable.

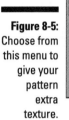

Figure 8-5:
Choose from
this menu to
give your
pattern
extra
texture.

Graduating to Gradients

A blend of two or more colors is known as a *gradient.* You have two gradients
to work with: *linear gradients* that blend colors from left to right, and *radial
gradients* that blend colors in concentric (or circular) fashion.

Applying gradient fills

Use gradient fills to add a bit of pizzazz to your Fireworks masterpiece and to
create visual points of interest. Use linear gradient fills to liven up a static
shape without resorting to shock treatment. Or you can apply radial gradient
fills to round objects to make them appear three-dimensional.

To apply a gradient (blended) fill to an object:

1. **Using the Pointer tool, select the object you want to apply the fill to.**

2. **Choose Window⇨Fill.**

   The Fill panel yawns and ambles in from stage left.

3. **Click the triangle to the right of the Fill field.**

   The drop-down menu shown in Figure 8-6 appears. The fills below the
   dotted line are gradient fills.

4. **Click a fill's name to select it.**

   Fireworks applies the fill to the selected shape.

5. **Click the triangle to the right of the Gradient Preset Color Sets field.**

   A drop-down menu of color presets appears, as shown in Figure 8-7.

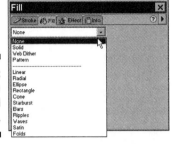

Figure 8-6:
The little
menu's full
of fills.

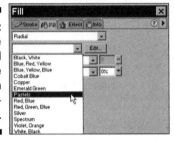

Figure 8-7:
Add a little
color to fill
with the
presets in
this drop-
down menu.

6. **Click a Gradient Preset to select it.**

   Fireworks applies the preset to the gradient, and the object is the center of attention.

7. **Click the triangle to the right of the Edge field.**

   Another drop-down menu appears.

8. **Select one of the following Edge options:**

   - **Hard:** Gives your preset gradient fill a hard edge.

   - **Anti-Alias:** Creates a gentle blend between the preset gradient and adjacent objects.

   - **Feather:** Creates a blend of ten pixels (the default) between the pattern fill and adjacent objects. To change the size of the blend, click the triangle in the small window to the right of the Edge field and drag the slider to specify a different value.

9. **To apply a texture to the gradient fill, click the triangle to the right of the Texture field.**

   A drop-down menu filled with names of textures appears.

10. **Drag your cursor over the texture names.**

    An image of the texture is displayed in the preview window.

11. **When you see a texture you like, click it to select it.**

    The value in the Intensity field jumps to 50%. The texture is readily visible through the gradient. Click the triangle next to the field and drag the slider to select a lower setting. A setting of 0% shows your entire fill without the texture.

12. **Select the Transparency option, and any underlying objects show through the texture.**

To fully realize the power of gradients, I suggest you take a few minutes to explore the effects you can achieve with them. Create a few objects on the canvas and then use the Fill panel to apply different gradients to them.

Editing gradient fills

The Fireworks preset gradients are not cast in stone. You can edit them to create your own effects. You can change the number of colors that appear in a gradient, change where they appear in the gradient, and change the individual colors of the gradient. It's a lot easier than mixing watercolors, and cleaner, too. And if you like what you create, you can save it for future use.

To edit a preset gradient fill:

1. **Choose Window⇨Fill.**

    The Fill panel appears.

2. **Click the triangle to the right of the Fill category field and choose a fill type from the drop-down menu.**

    After the drop-down menu appears, notice that it is divided into two sections. Select a fill type from the lower section of the menu.

3. **Click the triangle to the right of the Preset Gradient Color Sets field and choose a preset.**

4. **Click the Edit button.**

    A window appears below the Gradient Preset Color Sets field as shown in Figure 8-8. The bright color bar in the top window is called the Gradient Definition bar. The individual pointers below it are used to choose individual colors within the gradient and to determine where the colors appear in the gradient. The large window at the bottom shows you what the fill looks like and updates in real time as you edit the gradient.

5. **To edit an individual color on the Gradient Definition bar, click its pointer.**

    The color palette appears and your cursor becomes an eyedropper.

6. **Click a color swatch to select it.**

   Fireworks applies the selected color to the pointer.

7. **To move a pointer, click it to select it.**

   The cursor becomes a rather belligerent looking closed fist.

8. **Drag the fist (and the color pointer) to a new position and then release the mouse button.**

   The color pointer gets accustomed to its new surroundings. Fireworks updates the gradient in the preview window.

9 **To add a new color pointer to the Gradient Definition bar, click just below the point where you want the pointer to appear.**

   A new pointer is added to the Gradient Definition bar. Click the pointer to choose a color from the palette as outlined in Steps 5 and 6.

10. **To remove a color from a gradient, click the color pointer you want to remove and then drag it right off the Gradient Definition bar.**

   The color waves good-bye before it becomes virtual trash.

Color pointers

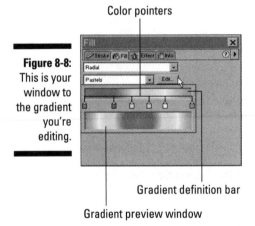

Figure 8-8:
This is your
window to
the gradient
you're
editing.

Gradient definition bar

Gradient preview window

Saving a gradient

After you edit a gradient and bask in the glow of your creativity, you may decide that, hey, this is really neat, and I want to use it again. Fortunately, you can save your handiwork for future use. To save a gradient:

1. **Use the Fill panel to edit a preset gradient.**

2. **When it looks just the way you want it to, click the triangle near the upper right hand corner of the Fill panel.**

A small drop-down menu takes a diminutive step downward.

3. **Choose Save Gradient As.**

The Save Gradient dialog box appears.

4. **Enter a name for the gradient and click Save.**

Fireworks saves the gradient and adds it to the Preset Gradient Color Sets menu.

To create a new gradient fill, select one of the Fireworks presets that looks similar to the gradient you want to create. For example, if you're creating a custom gradient for a round object, you want to start with a radial or ellipse preset. Edit the preset gradient and then save it for future use.

Applying Color with the Paint Bucket Tool

Use the Paint Bucket tool to apply a fill you created in the Fill panel to any object on the canvas. After you've applied the fill to the object, you can use the Paint Bucket tool to modify the way it's aligned within the object.

Applying fills with the Paint Bucket tool

Applying a fill with the Paint Bucket tool is like opening a bucket of paint and throwing it at the side of your house with one important exception: When you use the Paint Bucket tool, Fireworks makes sure the fill stays where you want it, and there's no messy cleanup.

To apply a fill with the Paint Bucket tool:

1. **Choose Window⇨Fill.**

The Fill panel opens.

2. **Create a fill.**

3. **Click the Paint Bucket tool to select it.**

As you drag the tool over the canvas, the cursor becomes a paint bucket.

4. **Click an object on canvas that you want to apply the fill to.**

Fireworks applies the fill.

Editing a fill with the Paint Bucket tool

You also use the Paint Bucket tool to edit a fill you've applied to an object. You can move the center of the fill relative to the center of the object, rotate the fill, and scale the fill. To edit a fill with the Paint Bucket tool:

1. **Using the Pointer tool, select the object whose fill you want to edit.**

   The filled object suddenly sprouts handles. The number of handles depends on the type of object selected and the type of fill applied. The largest number of handles you'll ever have to deal with is three: one to scale the fill horizontally, one to scale it vertically, and one to move its center. The fill in Figure 8-9 is the two-handled variety.

   By default, Fireworks displays fill handles whenever you use the Pointer tool to select an object fill with a gradient. To disable this option, double-click the Pointer tool's icon in the Toolbox and when the tool's option panel appears, deselect Show Fill Handles.

2. **Select the Paint Bucket tool.**

3. **To move the center of the fill, click the center point and drag it.**

   As you drag, the position of the fill changes relative to the position of the object.

Click and drag this handle to move the fill

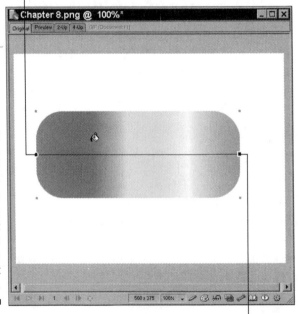

Figure 8-9:
Scaling a fill is easier than climbing Mt. Everest when you use the Paint Bucket tool.

Click and drag this handle to scale the fill

4. **To scale a fill, you use a rope or a good ladder. Kidding. To scale a fill, click the scale handle and drag left or right.**

Dragging away from the fill's center point increases the fill's scale; dragging towards the fill's center point decreases it.

5. **To rotate a fill, move your cursor towards the fill's center.**

As you move towards the center, the cursor becomes a curved arrow. Click and drag clockwise or counterclockwise to rotate the fill.

Using the Object Panel

The Object panel may not become an object of your affections, but you will find it useful when you've created objects with both a fill and a stroke. You use the Object panel to tell Fireworks how you want the stroke drawn in relation to the *path*. (If you missed the section on paths, a path is either a line segment drawn with the Line tool, or a series of connected points that make up a line segment drawn with the Pen tool, Pencil tool, or Brush tool. A path can be closed or open.) To use the Object panel to specify how a stroke is drawn:

1. **Select the object with the Pointer tool.**

2. **Choose Window⇨Object.**

The Object panel appears (see Figure 8-10). The Object panel has three buttons and an option.

3. **Click one of the buttons to determine how Fireworks draws the stroke relative to the path.**

   • Click the first button to have Fireworks draw the stroke inside the path.

   • Click the second button to have Fireworks draw the stroke centered on the path.

   • Click the third button to have Fireworks draw the stroke outside the path.

4. **Enable the Fill over Stroke option to draw the fill on top of the stroke.**

Use this option when you've got a wide stroke centered on the path and you want the fill to eclipse half of the stroke.

Draw stroke inside path

Draw stroke centered on path

Draw stroke outside path

Figure 8-10:
The Object
panel
determines
how a
stroke is
drawn in
relation to
its path.

Object (Rectangle)

Object

Roundness: 0

Stroke:

Fill over Stroke

Controlling an Object's Transparency

When you've got objects filled with patterns, gradients, or solid color, you
can control their transparency. When you change an object's transparency,
objects behind it show through. To change an object's transparency:

1. **Select the Pointer tool and then click the object you want to make
   transparent.**

   The object is selected.

2. **Choose Window⇨Layers.**

   The Layers panel opens up, as shown in Figure 8-11. Just below the
   Layer's panel tab is a little window that says 100. This means that the
   object is 100 percent opaque; in other words, you can't see through it.

3. **Click the triangle to the right of the window.**

   A slider appears.

4. **Drag the slider to determine the transparency of the selected object.
   As you drag the slider, look at the object on canvas.**

5. **When the object is as transparent as you want, stop dragging the
   slider.**

   Notice the bitmap image in Figure 8-11. You'd never see it if transparency
   hadn't been applied to the object above it.

If you drag the slider all the way to 0, the object is invisible, which is something you may find useful if you decide to create animations (something I
show you how to do in Chapter 14).

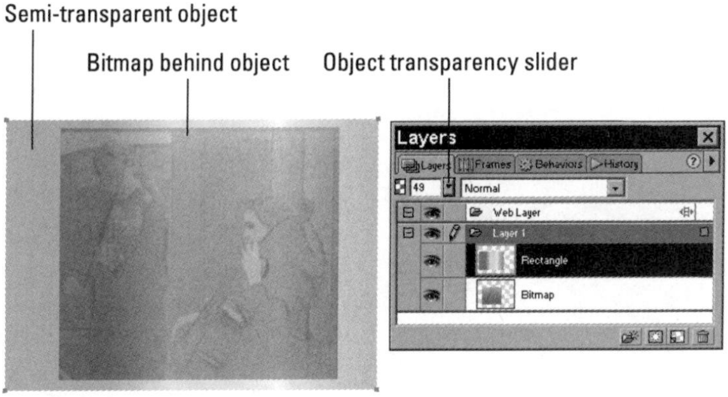

Semi-transparent object

Bitmap behind object   Object transparency slider

Figure 8-11:
Make an
object semi-
transparent
when you
gotta see
what's
underneath.

You may have noticed a whole lot of other doohickeys in the Layers panel. I
show you how to use those in Chapter 10.

Chapter 9

Scaling, Moving, and Rotating Objects

• •

In This Chapter

▶ Manipulating objects with the Pointer tool and Select Behind tool

▶ Using the Info panel

▶ Getting precise with the Numeric Transform command

▶ Flipping, aligning, and arranging objects

• •

*W*hen you create some objects on the canvas, you've got to move them. That is, unless your aim is perfect and you plop them down in the right spot the first time you create them. If you're not that skilled — or that lucky — you're gonna have to do a bit of rearranging to get things just the way you want them. Lucky for you, these objects are virtual objects and therefore light as a pixel. You don't need three men and a young boy to heft them around; a couple of tools and a menu command (or four) work just fine. In this chapter I show you how to use the tools and menu commands to get everything on the canvas just where you want it.

Get a Move On, Little Object

One of the basic editing techniques you'll need to do time and again is move objects. And where you move the objects — whether it's up, down, or sideways — all depends upon you, the creator of the objects on the document. You can even rotate them or make them grow, but that's a gruesome subject best saved for a section or two down the chapter.

Selecting an object

Before you can move anything on the canvas, you've got to select it. The big gun in your selection arsenal is the Pointer tool. The Pointer tool is that arrow-looking critter at the top left-hand side of the Toolbox. To select an object with the Pointer tool:

1. **Select the Pointer tool from the Toolbox.**

2. **Move the tool toward the object you want to select.**

   When the tool passes over an object that can be selected, the points that define the path of the object's outline become highlighted in red.

3. **Click to select the object.**

   The highlighted points become blue, indicating the object has been successfully selected.

The Pointer tool works just great for selecting objects that are in plain view on the canvas. But what do you do when you've got a canvas full of stuff, and some of the stuff is behind other stuff? Well, I'm glad you asked that question. Rather than disturbing the objects in front to get to the objects in back, use the Select Behind tool. (It's a little known fact that the Pointer tool and the Select Behind tool are actually sisters. Er, I guess that would make them the Pointer Sisters.)

You can also select obscured objects by selecting their thumbnails in the Layers panel. I give you the lowdown on the Layers panel in Chapter 10.

To select an object behind an object:

1. **Click the triangle to the right of the first button on the left-hand side of the Toolbox.**

   The tool group expands.

2. **Select the Select Behind tool.**

   The Select Behind tool is selected. Hey, is there an echo in this room?

3. **Move the tool towards the object you want to select.**

   As you move the tool across any object, the points that define the outline path of the object turn red. The difference between this tool and the Pointer tool is that objects hidden or obscured by other objects are also highlighted when the tool is passed over them.

4. **When the outline points of the object you want to select turn red, click it.**

   The Select Behind tool selects a previously unselectable object that was obscured by an always-selectable object. (And that sentence really does make sense.)

Moving an object

After you select an object with the Pointer tool or the Select Behind tool, you can get the object to pull up its stakes and move to another part of the canvas. To move an object:

1. **Select an object with the Pointer tool or the Select Behind tool.**

   The outline points of the object turn blue.

2. **Drag it to another spot on the canvas.**

   Any spot will do as long as that's where you want the object to be.

3. **Release the mouse button.**

   The object stays put until you move it again.

Resizing an object

After you create an object, sometimes you need to cut it down to size; other times you need to just make it grow up. Use the Scale tool to manually resize an object. Here's how:

1. **Select the object you want to resize with the Pointer tool or Select Behind tool.**

   The object is selected and wonders what's up next.

2. **Select the Scale tool.**

   A bounding box surrounds the object with eight tiny square handles on the bounding box's border and, as shown in Figure 9-1, a little dot appears at the object's center for good measure.

3. **To resize the object proportionately, move your cursor towards any of the bounding box's corner handles.**

   As the cursor approaches the handle, it becomes a diagonal line with an arrow at each end.

4. **Click the square and drag towards the center to shrink the object; drag away from the center to increase the object's size.**

5. **To change the width of the object, move your cursor towards one of the middle handles on the side of the bounding box.**

   As your cursor approaches either handle, it becomes a horizontal double-headed arrow.

6. **Click the square and drag away from the center to increase the object's width; drag towards the center to decrease it.**

   The object resizes only from the side you selected.

7. **To change the height of the object, move your cursor towards the handle on the top or bottom of the bounding box.**

   As your cursor approaches the handle, it becomes a vertical double-headed arrow.

8. **Click and drag away from the center of the object to increase its height; drag towards the center to decrease it.**

You can also scale an object by selecting it with the Pointer tool and then clicking and dragging one of the object's corners. To constrain proportions as you resize, hold down the Shift key as you drag.

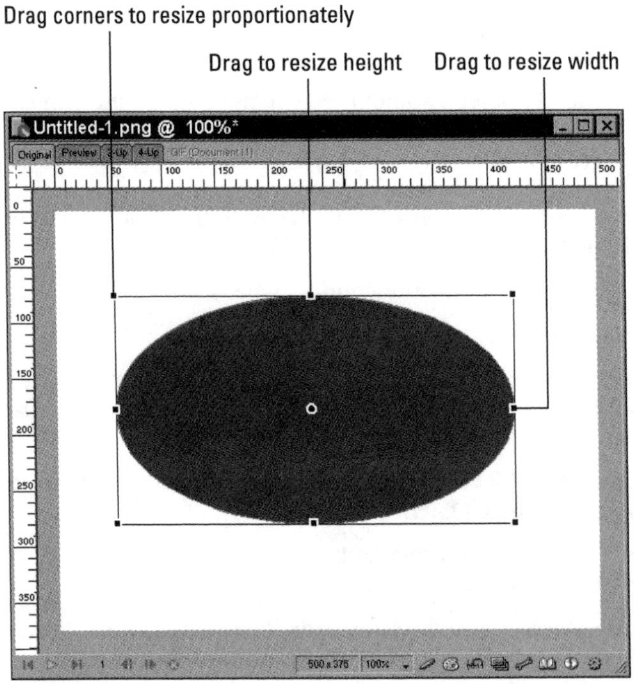

Drag corners to resize proportionately

Drag to resize height   Drag to resize width

Figure 9-1:
You use the Scale tool to resize objects.

Rotating an object

When you need to rotate an object, you use the Scale tool. I know — it makes no sense. To rotate an object you should have a rotate tool. But the Fireworks program designers are multi-taskers at heart, and they believe a tool's gotta carry some weight to earn a position in their program's Toolbox. Therefore, the Scale tool does double duty and also rotates objects. To manually rotate an item:

1. **Use the Pointer tool or Select Behind tool to select the object you want to take out for a spin.**

2. **Select the Scale tool.**

   A bounding box with eight squares surrounds the object.

3. **Move your cursor towards the object.**

   As you near the object, the cursor becomes a curved arrow.

4. **Click and drag clockwise or counterclockwise to rotate the object.**

   The object rotates around the circle in the center of the bounding box, as shown in Figure 9-2. A dotted bounding box appears, giving you an indication of the object's current position.

5. **When you've spun the object to the desired location, release the mouse button.**

You can also use the Resize, Skew, or Distort tools to move an object. When you're using one of these tools to transform an object, move the tool over the object and the cursor becomes a 4-headed arrow, which is a rather becoming transformation for a cursor. When the 4-headed cursor appears, click and drag to move the object.

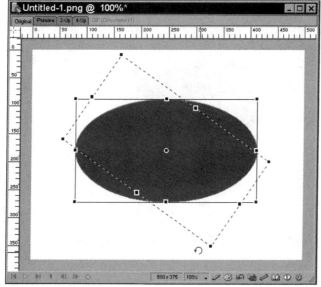

Figure 9-2:
You take an object for a spin with the Scale tool.

Changing an object's center point

Okay, rotating an object around its center doesn't seem all that terribly complicated. But what happens when you don't want to rotate an object around its center? Say, for example, if you're animating a dial for a speedometer? In this case, you'd want the speedometer dial to rotate from the bottom. To change an object's center point:

1. **Select the object with the Pointer tool or Select Behind tool.**

2. **Select the Scale tool.**

   The object is surrounded by a bounding box bordered by eight square handles with a small dot in the center of the object.

3. **Move your cursor towards the small center dot.**

   The cursor changes into a solid black arrow.

4. **Click the center dot and drag it to a new position.**

   When you rotate the object, the center of rotation is from the dot's new position (see Figure 9-3).

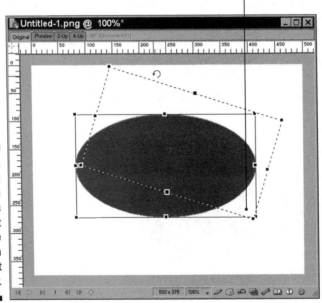

New location of object's center

Figure 9-3:
When you move an object's center, it turns to the tune of a different drummer.

Skewing an object

When you skew an object, you slant it. You can skew an object vertically or horizontally. To skew the object, you use the Skew tool that hangs out with its skewed buddies on the seventh button down on the left side of the Toolbox. To skew an object:

1. **Select the object with the Pointer tool or Select Behind tool.**

2. **Select the Skew tool.**

   A bounding box with eight square handles surrounds the selected object.

3. **To skew the object so that it looks like it's got perspective (meaning that the back end of the object is smaller than the front, just like when you look at objects in the distance), move your cursor towards one of the outer handles.**

   As you move towards either of these handles, your cursor becomes a solid arrow.

4. **Drag outward, inward, or up or down, depending upon the direction you want for your perspective.**

   The object looks different now that it's got perspective. Figure 9-4 shows an object that looks like it's vanishing into the distance, thanks to a subtle skew.

5. **To skew the object horizontally, move your cursor towards the center handle on the top or bottom of the object.**

   As you move towards either handle, the cursor becomes a horizontal double-headed arrow.

6. **Click the handle and drag left or right.**

7. **To skew the object vertically, move your cursor towards the center handle on the right or left side of the object.**

   As you move towards either handle, the cursor becomes a straight vertical double-headed arrow.

8. **Click the handle and drag up or down.**

9. **To rotate the object, move your cursor towards the object.**

   As you move towards the object, the cursor becomes a curved arrow.

10. **Drag clockwise or counterclockwise to rotate the skew.**

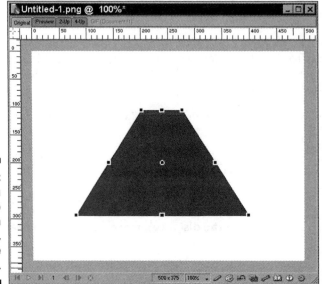

Figure 9-4:
When you
want to
skew up on
purpose,
choose the
Skew tool.

To undo a skew that's gone askew, choose Edit⇨Undo Transform.

Distorting an object

If you have a surrealistic side to you, you can distort an object a la Salvador Dali. To distort an object you use the Distort tool (now that's logic for you). To distort an object:

1. **Choose the subject of your distortion with the Pointer tool or Select Behind tool.**

2. **Click the triangle at the lower-right hand corner of the seventh button on the left side of the Toolbox.**

   The tool group expands.

3. **Select the Distort tool from the group.**

   The tool surrounds the object with eight square handles There is no constraint on any handle's movement; you can move them anywhere within the confines of the canvas.

4. **Click a handle and drag it at will. And if Will's not on the canvas, drag the handle wherever you want to.**

   Click and drag additional handles until the object is distorted to taste.

Transforming Objects with the Info Panel

In Fireworks, there's more than one way to transform an object. For those of you who like to take things into your own hands, you can use the tools. For those of you who prefer the cold hard logic of mathematics — the IRS can always count on you for an accurate return — you can use the Info panel. To transform an object with the Info panel:

1. **Use the Pointer tool or the Select Behind tool to select the object you want to transform.**

2. **Choose Window⇨Info.**

   The Info panel opens. Notice that you have four little fields:

   - The **W field** shows the object's width

   - The **H field** shows the object's height

   - The **X field** shows the object's horizontal location

   - The **Y field** shows the object's vertical location

   The object's location is measured from its upper-left hand corner. For example, if you enter a value of 0 in both the X and Y fields, you place the object at the upper-left hand corner of the canvas.

3. **Enter values in the appropriate fields to change either the object's size or location.**

   To precisely change the object's position, you have to do a little math. For example, if you have an object that measures 100 pixels by 100 pixels centered in a document that measure 500 pixels by 500 pixels, first you have to determine the center of the document, which is X=250 and Y=250. Subtract half of the object's width from the X coordinate and half the object's height from the Y coordinate, and you end up with and X value of 200 and a Y value of 200. Enter these values in the X and Y fields and the object is smack-dab in the center of the document.

To quickly center an object on the canvas, select it with the Pointer tool and then choose Commands⇨Document⇨Center in Document.

The default position for each ruler's crosshair is at the top-left corner of the canvas. If you move either ruler's crosshair, you change the zero coordinates for that ruler.

Transforming Objects with Numerical Precision

Fireworks has a whole lot of menu commands that you use to transform objects. Some of them are exact duplicates of perfectly good tools in the Toolbox. But some people prefer to order from menus, so the Fireworks gurus decided to duplicate some tools on the menu. Your time is valuable so I'm not going to show you anything about tools duplicated on the menu because if you've read the previous sections in this chapter (You have read the previous sections of this chapter, haven't you?), you know how to use them. If you prefer to use menu commands instead of tools, choose Modify⇨Transform and choose the command from the submenu.

But there on the submenu, away from everything else on the submenu, are some perfectly good commands that transform objects with micrometric precision not available from the tools. You use these commands to resize objects, rotate them, and flip them. The following sections describe these commands.

Using the Numeric Transform command

Use the Numeric Transform command to precisely resize objects by scaling objects by percentage or resizing them by choosing the exact size you want the object to be. To resize an object using the Numeric Transform command:

1. **Use the Pointer tool or Select Behind tool to select the object you want to transform.**

2. **Choose Modify⇨Numeric Transform.**

   The Numeric Transform dialog box makes a guest appearance. By default of the designers of Fireworks, the Scale option is selected.

3. **Click the triangle to the right of the transform field and choose one of the following:**

   • Choose **Scale** to scale the object by a percentage. If you choose scale, the value for the width (the horizontal double headed arrow icon) is 100% and the value for height (the vertical double-headed arrow icon) is 100%. To the right of the width and height fields, the actual measurement of the object in pixels appears.

   • Choose **Resize** to resize the object by entering an exact measurement in pixels.

4. **Enable Scale Attributes to transform the stroke, fill, and any applied effect when Fireworks transforms the object.**

5. **Enable Constrain Proportions to keep the width and height proportionate.**

   When this option is enabled, a padlock appears to the right of the width and height fields indicating that Fireworks has locked the proportions of the object. When this option is enabled, you enter one value, and Fireworks computes the other.

   If Constrain Proportions is disabled, the padlock disappears and you can change the proportions of the object by entering width and height values that are not proportionate with the object's original dimensions. For example, you can change a square object to a rectangular object of different dimensions.

6. **Enter one value (if Constrain Proportions is enabled) or both values (if Constrain Proportions is disabled) to resize or rescale the object.**

   Enter a value in the width and/or height field. If you've chosen Scale, enter a percentage less than 100 to shrink the object; enter a percentage greater than 100 to make the object bigger. If you've chosen Resize, enter the desired value in pixels.

7. **Click OK.**

Rotating objects with the Numeric Transform command

You can take an object out for a spin with the Scale tool, but when you need precise rotation by degrees, only a menu command will do. Use the Numeric Transform command to precisely rotate an object by an exact number of degrees. To rotate an object with the Numeric Transform command:

1. **Use the Pointer tool or Select Behind tool to select the object.**

2. **Choose Modify⇨Transform⇨Numeric Transform.**

   The Numeric Transform dialog box appears.

3. **Click the triangle to the right of the Transform field.**

   A drop-down menu appears.

4. **Choose Rotate.**

5. **Click the triangle to the right of the Angle field.**

   The Numeric Transform dialog box appears.

6. **Click the dot in the round wheel and drag until the desired angle value appears.**

   Alternately, you can just type a value in the field.

7. **Click OK.**

   The object rotates.

Flipping Objects

You can teach an old (or new if you just created it) object new tricks. By using the Flip Horizontal or Flip Vertical command, you can put a whole new perspective on an object. These commands are immensely useful. Say, for example, you've imported an image of your client, but it doesn't look quite right. By flipping the image, you can flip his or her good side from right to left. To flip an object:

1. **Use the Pointer tool or Select Behind tool to select the object you want to flip.**

2. **Choose Modify➪Transform and then choose one of these commands:**

   • **Flip Vertical:** The selected object does a 180-degree turn, making its top the bottom and the bottom its top.

   • **Flip Horizontal:** The selected object does a 180-degree flip, making its left become its right and its right become its left.

   The object flips.

Aligning Objects

When you have several objects on the canvas, you may need to align them. For example, if you've created several buttons for a navigation menu, you need to line them up. To align several objects:

1. **Select the first object with the Pointer tool or the Select Behind tool.**

2. **With the Pointer tool or Select Behind tool still selected, hold down the Shift key and click additional objects to add them to the selection.**

   A blue bounding box appears around each object.

3. **Choose Modify➪Align.**

   A submenu appears.

4. **Choose one of the following options:**

- **Align Left:** Aligns the selected objects to the object farthest left on canvas.

- **Center Vertical:** Aligns the selected objects to the vertical center of the two outermost objects.

- **Align Right:** Aligns the selected objects to the object that is farthest right on the canvas.

- **Align Top:** Aligns the objects to the object that is nearest the top of the document.

- **Align Center Horizontal:** Aligns the selected objects to the horizontal center of the two outermost objects.

- **Align Bottom:** Aligns the selected objects to the object nearest the bottom of the document.

- **Distribute Heights:** Equally distributes the vertical space between selected items.

- **Distribute Widths:** Equally distributes the horizontal space between selected items.

5. **After you select the command, Fireworks aligns the objects.**

To align objects vertically, horizontally, and distribute them equally, you'll need to apply more than one alignment command to the selected objects.

Arranging Objects

When you create objects, the last object created appears on top of the others, kind of like when the dealer at a BlackJack table deals card; the last card dealt appears on top of the others. With objects in Fireworks, this is called the *stacking order.* You change the stacking order of objects by using one of the Arrange commands. To keep the order of the stack straight, let me throw another analogy at you: Think of the stacking order like a stack of pancakes at Denny's. The pancake that gets the syrup first is at the top of the stack. The dry pancake is at the bottom of the stack. When you lift a pancake with your fork to slather the next pancake with a slab of butter, you're choosing the next lowest pancake in the stack.

To arrange the way objects appear on the canvas:

1. **Use the Pointer tool to select the object you want to rearrange.**

2. **Choose Modify➪Arrange; then choose one of the following commands from the submenu:**

- **Bring To Front:** Moves the selected object on top of all the other objects.

- **Bring Forward:** Places the object one step higher in the stack.

- **Send Backward:** Places the object one step lower in the stack.

- **Send to Back:** Moves the selected object to the lowest point in the stacking order.

You can also rearrange the stacking order of an object by selecting its thumbnail image in the Layers panel and dragging it to a new position in the stacking hierarchy. I show you how to use the Layers panel in Chapter 10.

Chapter 10

Modifying, Reshaping, and Arranging Objects

. . . .

In This Chapter

▶ Using the Subselection tool

▶ Modifying paths

▶ Using the Reshape Area tool

▶ Using the Freeform tool

▶ Grouping objects

▶ Working with layers

. . . .

The neat thing about vector objects is they're almost like molding clay. You can mold them and stretch them into the shape you want them to be. To modify a vector object, you get right down to the nitty-gritty and edit points along the object's path. If the path you're editing is a closed path, you tweak a couple of points and, voilà, you've got a new shape. In this chapter I show you how to edit paths by modifying their points. I also show you how to organize your documents by grouping objects and putting them on layers. (And if terms like "vector object" and "path" cause you concern, don't worry — just keep reading.)

Putting a New Twist on an Old Path

Whenever you use one of the tools in the Toolbox to create an object, that object is a *vector object.* Vector objects are defined by paths, which are defined by points. Remember, paths are single line segments, a series of line segments, or an outline where the ends meet (a closed path). Points define the start and end of a line segment — you know the shortest distance thing. And whenever you've got one of these little vector beauties gracing your document, you can modify it by changing the points used to create it. Vector paths have two kinds of points: *curve points,* which can be changed to modify the curve, and *corner points,* which connect straight path segments.

Modifying a path with the Subselection tool

Use the Subselection tool to select and modify individual points that make up an object's path. You can use the Subselection tool to select objects, just like you can with the Pointer tool (see Chapter 9 for more on the Pointer tool). When you select an *object* with the Subselection tool, the points that make up the object's path are shown. When you select a *point* with the Subselection tool, Fireworks gets the point and fills it. To modify a path with the Subselection tool:

 1. **Select the Subselection tool from the Toolbox.**

2. **Click the object whose path you want to modify.**

   The selected object's points appear. Corner points appear as squares; curve points as dots.

3. **Click a point to select it.**

   If the selected point is a corner point, Fireworks fills the square to show you that the point has been selected.

   If the selected point is a curve point, Fireworks fills the dot to show you it's selected and creates two tangent handles that you use to modify the curve between the corner points the curve point is connected to.

   If the corner point is the end point of a path, one tangent handle appears.

To modify the appearance of points you create with the Pen tool, double-click the tool in the toolbox to open the Tool Options panel. Select Show Pen Preview and Fireworks creates a preview of the path before you create the next point in the path. Select Show Solid Points and unselected points are filled dots instead of the default hollow dot.

You can create a selection of more than one point by clicking and then dragging the Subselection tool around all the points you want to select. As you drag, a rectangular bounding box appears, showing you the area you're selecting. When you've surrounded all the points that you want to select, release the mouse button. You can also add additional points to a selection by holding down the Shift key while clicking them.

4. **To move a selected corner or curve point, drag it to a new location.**

   Fireworks redraws the path segment connected to the point you moved to reflect the point's new position. If the path is a closed path, the shape's fill changes to reflect the path's new orientation.

5. **To modify a curved path segment, click and drag the dot at the end of a corner point's tangent handle.**

If you've selected a curve point in the middle of a curved path segment, you have two handles to work with. If you've selected a curve point at the beginning of a curved path segment, you have only one tangent handle to work with.

You can nudge selected points to a new position by pressing one of the arrow keys. Each key nudges the point in the direction designated on the keyboard.

Adding and deleting points

Sometimes you have too many points, and sometimes — like a losing football team — you don't have enough. You *add* points to a path when you need to define additional points of reference to create the shape you want. You *delete* points from a path when the additional points serve no purpose and make editing the object more difficult. To add points to a path:

1. **Using the Pointer tool or Subselection tool, select the path you want to modify.**

2. **Select the Pen tool.**

3. **Move the Pen tool towards the path.**

   As you move the tool closer to the path, a plus sign (+) appears in front of the tool.

4. **Click the spot where you want to add the point.**

   Fireworks creates a curve point if you're adding a point to a curved path segment; a corner point the point is added to a straight path segment.

5. **Click additional spots along the path where additional points are needed.**

   Fireworks gives you additional points for being so diligent and persevering.

Converting points

You *convert* a point when you've got a corner point where you need a curve point and vice versa. Politicians wish they could convert constituents as easily as you can convert points. To convert a corner point to a curve point:

1. **Use the Pointer tool or Subselection tool to select the path with the point you need to convert.**

2. **Select the Pen tool.**

3. Click a corner point and then drag.

When your cursor is over the corner point, a minus sign (–) appears next to the Pen tool icon. As you drag the point, two handles appear. You can modify the segment by selecting either handle's dot with the Subselection tool and then dragging it.

To convert a curve point to a corner point:

1. Use the Pointer tool or Subselection tool to select the path where the curve point you want to convert lives.

2. Select the Pen tool.

3. Click the point to convert it.

When your cursor is over the curve point, an angled less than sign (<) appears next to the Pen tool icon. Like a marine snapping to attention, the path segment the point is attached to becomes rigid.

Reshaping a path with the Reshape Area tool

Use the Reshape Area tool to quickly edit a path. The Reshape Area tool does its dirty work by repulsing a path into a new shape. The tool doesn't repulse the path because it's lacking in social manners; it pushes a path away from it as you move the tool towards a path. To reshape a path with the Reshape Area tool:

1. Select a path with the Pointer tool or the Select Behind tool.

2. Click the triangle at the lower-right corner of the seventh tool on the right hand side of the Toolbox.

The tool group expands.

3. Select the Reshape Area tool.

4. Double-click the tool.

The Options panel opens.

5. Click the triangle to the right of the Size field.

A slider pops up, which you drag to determine how large an area the tool affects.

6. Drag the slider to set the tool's effective area.

7. Click the triangle to the right of the Strength field.

Pop goes the slider. The setting determines how much the tool modifies the path you drag it towards.

8. **Drag the slider to set the strength of the tool.**

   Dragging the slider up increases the tool's strength.

9. **If you don't have a digital tablet hooked to your computer, skip to Step 12.**

   A digital tablet is a device you hook to your computer. The tablet is a rectangular drawing surface with a stylus. As you drag the stylus over the tablet, a line appears in your Fireworks document, just like the one you drew on the tablet. A digital tablet enables you to draw naturally. For accomplished artists, using a digital tablet to create artwork is easier than using a mouse.

10 **In the Pressure area, select the options to configure the tool for use with your pressure-sensitive digital tablet. You have the following options to choose from:**

   • Choose **Size,** which is selected by default, and the pressure you exert on the tablet with the stylus determines the effective area of the tool. If you select only this option, the strength of the tool is determined by the setting you chose in Step 8.

   • Choose **Strength,** and the pressure you exert with the stylus on your pressure sensitive tablet determines the tool's strength. If you select this option only, the tool's size is determined by the setting you chose in Step 6.

   • Choose **both** options, and the size and the pressure you exert on the tablet with the stylus affects the strength of the tool. If you switch back to using a mouse to apply the tool, the settings you chose in Steps 6 and 8 will apply.

11. **Select the Preview Option to see a preview of the new shape as you're creating it.**

12. **Drag the tool over the path you want to modify.**

   Fireworks modifies the shape.

13. **Release the mouse button when the path is reshaped the way you want it.**

   This tool is more like virtual morphing. You can use this tool to good effect when you want to create a cartoon character or something unusual. Figure 10-1 shows a shape that was once a circle before the Reshape Area tool got a hold of it.

 When you create a shape with the Rectangle tool or Rounded Rectangle tool, you get a group of points that can't be edited. To edit a shape created with either tool, choose Modify⇨Ungroup to make all the points used to create the rectangle available for editing.

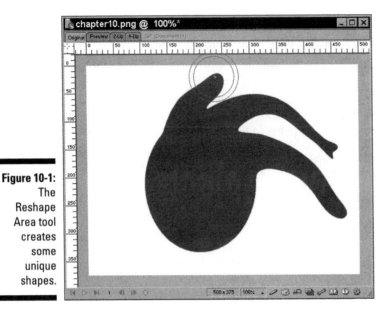

Figure 10-1:
The
Reshape
Area tool
creates
some
unique
shapes.

Reshaping a path with the Freeform tool

The Freeform tool reshapes a path in a freeform manner. If you use the tool with a pressure sensitive digital tablet, applying more pressure to the stylus increases the tool's area of influence. To reshape a path with the Freeform tool:

1. **Select the object that you want to modify with either the Pointer tool or the Select Behind tool.**

2. **Click the triangle in the lower-right corner of the seventh tool on the right side of the Toolbox.**

   The tool group expands.

3. **Select the Freeform tool.**

4. **Double-click the tool.**

   The Options panel appears, which has options you set to determine the effect the tool has.

5. **Click the triangle to the right of the Size field.**

   A slider appears.

6. **Drag the slider to determine how large an area the tool affects.**

7. **Enable the Pressure option if you're using a pressure sensitive digital tablet.**

   With the option enabled, exerting additional pressure on the tablet's stylus causes the tool to modify a larger area.

8. **Enable the Preview option to see a preview of the new shape as you use the tool.**

9. **Drag the tool over the path you want to modify.**

10. **Release the mouse button when the path is contorted to your heart's content. Figure 10-2 shows what was once a star before I modified it with the Freeform tool.**

Figure 10-2:
The Freeform tool is a path contortionist's best friend.

Using the Knife tool

Use the Knife tool when you want to pare a path into pairs. For example, if you create an oval and then drag the Knife tool across the oval, you will have two objects. To split a path using the Knife tool:

1. **Use either the Pointer tool or the Select Behind tool to select the path you want to split.**

2. **Select the Knife tool.**

3. **Drag the tool across the path you want to sever.**

4. **Click anywhere in the workspace to deselect the shape.**

5. **Use either the Pointer tool or the Select Behind tool to select one of the shapes and move it. Figure 10-3 shows an oval that was cut with the Knife tool.**

Hold down the Shift key while dragging the Knife tool to constrain it to 45-degree angles.

Figure 10-3:
The Knife
tool
separates a
path into
separate
pieces.

Reducing points in a path

You reduce the number of points in a path when you want to smooth a shape. Simplifying the number of points in a path reduces the shape's complexity and makes it easier to edit. Oddly enough, the command you use to simplify a complex shape is simply called Simplify. To reduce the number of points in a path:

1. **Use the Pointer tool or Select Behind tool to select the path you want to simplify.**

2. **Choose Modify⇨Alter Path⇨Simplify.**

   The Simplify dialog box appears.

3. **Click the triangle to the right of the Amount field.**

   A slider appears.

4. Drag the slider to determine how much the path is simplified.

Choose a higher setting to remove more points; a lower setting to remove less.

5. Click OK.

Using the Redraw Path tool

You use the Redraw Path tool when you need to modify a path. You can use the tool to extend a path or modify the shape of an existing path. To modify a path with the Redraw Path tool:

1. Select the path you want to modify with either the Pointer tool or the Select Behind tool.

2. Click the triangle to the right of the Brush tool.

The tool group expands.

3. Select the Redraw Path tool.

4. To extend a path, click and drag the tool over the last portion of the path. To modify a path, click the point in the path where you want the modification to begin and start dragging.

As you drag the tool, Fireworks creates a preview of the altered state of the altered path.

5. Release the mouse button when the path is altered to perfection.

If Fireworks creates a lot of additional points when you use the Redraw Path tool, use the Simplify command to reduce the number of points and therefore smooth the path.

Combining Objects with Path Commands

You combine objects when you want to create a shape that would be difficult to create with the drawing tools. When you combine shapes, you can add one shape to another to create a new shape, subtract one shape from another to create a new shape, or create a new shape by intersecting two shapes.

Joining objects for life with the Union command

The Union command creates a new shape out of two or more overlapping shapes. The new shape is identical to the area encompassed by all the objects. To create a new shape using the Union command:

1. **Use the drawing or shape tools to create two or more shapes.**

2. **Use the Pointer tool to overlap the shapes by selecting one shape and then positioning it over the other.**

3. **Select the two shapes with the Pointer tool (see Figure 10-4).**

   Click the first shape to select it and then, while holding down the Shift key, click the second shape to add it to the selection.

   The shape's outlines turn a lovely shade of baby blue.

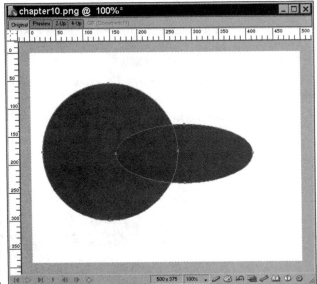

Figure 10-4:
Before you
can join 'em,
you gotta
overlap 'em.

4. **Choose Modify⇨Combine⇨Union.**

   Fireworks joins the two shapes for life unless you decide you don't like the new shape and invoke the Undo command. Figure 10-5 shows two ovals enjoying the bonds of the Union Command.

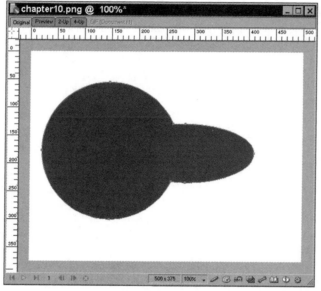

Figure 10-5:
Blessed be
the menu
command
that joins
two shapes
in virtual
union.

Creating cross-town traffic with the Intersect command

You use the Intersect command to join two or more shapes to create a new shape. If you read the previous section and this reads like a rerun, well it is and it isn't. The Intersect command creates a new shape, but this new shape encompasses the area where the two shapes intersect. To create a new shape with the Intersect command:

1. **Create two or more shapes using the drawing tools.**

2. **Select the Pointer tool and arrange the shapes so that they overlap.**

3. **Select all the shapes.**

   Remember, you can select all of the shapes by dragging the Pointer tool around them or by clicking the first shape and the Shift-clicking the second shape.

4. **Choose Modify⊏⊃Combine⊏⊃Intersect.**

   Fireworks creates a new shape that equals the area where the two shapes intersect, as shown in Figure 10-6.

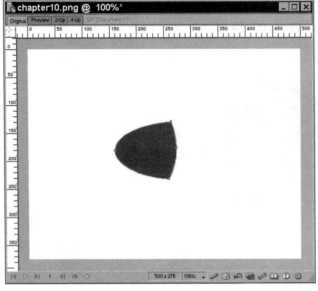

Figure 10-6:
The shapes from Figure 10-4 look decidedly different when you use the Intersect command on them.

Subtracting Object B from Object A with the Punch command

Use the Punch command when you want one shape to cut out the shape it's overlapping. The Punch command is a great tool when you want to punch a hole in something. Ahh, these Fireworks designers. Punch command . . . punch a hole. You can also use the Punch command to cut a chunk out of something. To create a new shape using the punch command:

1. **Create two or more shapes using the drawing tools.**

2. **Use the Pointer tool to arrange the shapes.**

   Remember the last shape created does the cutting because it's the one at the top of the stacking order.

3. **Select the shapes with the Pointer tool.**

   Select the first shape by clicking it and then Shift-click to select additional shapes.

4. **Choose Modify⇨Combine⇨Punch.**

   Fireworks creates a new shape by removing the area where the last shape created overlaps the other shapes from the other shapes. Figure 10-7 shows what the Punch command does to the overlapping shapes in Figure 10-4.

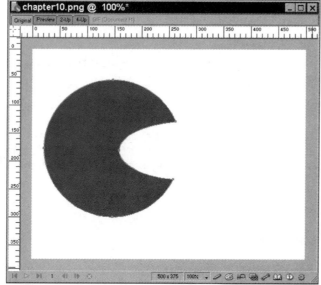

Figure 10-7:
You use the
Punch
command to
cut a shape
out of a
shape.

Select two shapes and then choose Modify⇨Combine⇨Crop to create a new shape by cropping out the area around where the shapes overlap.

Organizing Artwork with Groups

When you start creating full-fledged Web pages with Fireworks, you're going to have a lot of items on the canvas. And when you have a lot of items on the canvas, one slip of the mouse may end up moving the wrong item, and then you have to go back and redo what you've already painstakingly created. Not fun. That's why you *group* items so that they stick together and act as one item when you select them with the Pointer tool. For example, when you have a row of buttons all aligned, group them so that they stay together.

Creating groups

You create a group when you've created objects that you want to behave as a single unit. For example, if you've created text for a banner, created a rounded rectangle for the text backdrop, and then aligned the two objects, you group them. After they're grouped, you can't accidentally move the text or the banner with an errant slip of the mouse. To create a group:

1. Use the Pointer tool to select the objects you want in the group.

After you select the first item you want in the group, hold down the Shift key and then click additional items to add them to the group.

2. **Choose Modify⇨Group.**

Fireworks groups the objects, and dots appear that signify the group's boundary.

You can *nest* a group within a group. For example, you create a button, complete with the text needed to identify the button, and then group the button and text so they behave as one object. Repeat this procedure for each button you need in the document, position each button group on the canvas, and then group all the button groups so they behave as one unit, the navigation menu.

Editing groups

If you ever need to edit an individual item in a group, say to change an oval's color from cherry red to candy-apple green, you can, but first you have to ungroup the item. To edit a group:

1. **Select the group with the Pointer tool.**

Fireworks displays the dots that make up the group's border.

2. **Choose Modify⇨Ungroup.**

Fireworks displays the dots that make up each individual object's boundary.

3. **Click anywhere in the workspace to deselect the objects.**

4. **Select the object you need to change and make your edit.**

5. **Edit any other items in the group and then select them all with the Pointer tool.**

6. **Choose Modify⇨Group.**

Unlike the priceless vase your pet cat smashed into a gazillion pieces last week, Fireworks puts the group back together again.

If you need to make only a minor edit to an object in a group, you can select the object with the Subselection tool. After the object is selected, you can use any of the tools or menu commands to modify the object without destroying the integrity of the group.

Groups are just like any other object you create; the last group created is at the top of the stack. To rearrange the order in which a group appears on the canvas, Choose Modify⇨Arrange and then choose the appropriate command from the submenu to send the group where you want it to go. You can also rearrange the stacking order by clicking an object's thumbnail in the Layers panel.

I show you how to stack the deck in the Arranging Objects section in Chapter 9.

Organizing Objects with Layers (It All Stacks Up)

You use *layers* to organize a complex document. Think of layers as thin sheets of clear plastic that you place over the canvas. Where objects on upper layers overlap objects on lower layers, they partially obscure them. Whenever a document seems to be getting out of hand, consider adding a layer or two to keep things under control.

Using the Layers panel

Use the Layers panel to keep the layers in your document manageable. I know, the layers are supposed to do that, but someone's got to look after the layers. With the Layers panel you can add layers, delete layers, hide layers, lock layers, and rearrange the order of layers. To open the Layers panel:

1. **Choose Window⇨Layers.**

   The Layers panel appears, as shown in Figure 10-8. The Layers panel in this figure has three additional layers created. Notice all the icons next to the layer's name. You can use these icons to control individual layers:

   - The layer with the **pencil icon** is the currently selected layer.

   - The **eye icon** in each layer is used to show or hide the contents of a layer.

   - The **minus sign (–)** at the far left side of each layer's section indicates that the layer has been expanded to show all of its contents. If a layer has a **plus sign (+)** in this column, it indicates that the layer has been collapsed. On the Macintosh version of Fireworks, collapsed groups are signified by a small arrow that points to the right; expanded groups by a downward pointing arrow.

   Also notice there is a thumbnail image of each object in each layer.

2. **To hide the contents of a layer, click the eye icon to the left of the layer's name.**

   The eye icon disappears, and Fireworks hides all the objects on that layer.

3. **To show the contents of a layer, click the blank spot in the layer's Show/Hide column.**

   Fireworks displays the objects and the eye icon is once again visible.

4. **To lock a layer, click the column to the left of the layer's name.**

   A padlock appears in the column, and Fireworks locks the contents of the layer to prevent you from inadvertently mucking up all of your hard work.

5. **To unlock a layer, click the padlock in the layer's Lock/Unlock column.**

   The padlock disappears, and you can once again edit the contents of this layer.

6. **To collapse a layer, click the minus sign (–) in Windows or the arrow with a Mac to the far left of the layer's name.**

   Like a turtle retracting into its shell, the thumbnail object images on that layer disappear, and the group collapses to a single line with only the layer's name displayed in the Layers panel.

7. **To expand a layer, click the plus sign (+) in Windows or the arrow with a Mac in the far left hand column.**

   The layer expands, and the thumbnail images are once again visible.

8. **To move an object from one layer to the next, click the object's thumbnail image in the Layers panel and drag it to another layer.**

When you have more than one object in a layer, you can rearrange the stacking order of an object by clicking its thumbnail image and dragging it up or down within the layer. I show you how to arrange the stacking order of objects in Chapter 9.

Figure 10-8:
Use the
Layers
panel to
keep all
of your
artwork in
order and
prevent you
from going
bonkers
when you
create a
complex
document.

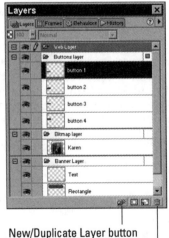

New/Duplicate Layer button

Delete Selection button

Adding layers

You can add a layer whenever a document starts getting to the point that you're having a hard time keeping everything in order. You can also add layers when you feel it's necessary to segregate items in your documents. For example, you may want to keep all of your bitmaps images on one layer and all of your navigation elements on another. To add a layer to the document:

1. **Choose Window⇨Layers.**

   The Layers panel opens.

2. **Click the triangle near the upper right-hand corner of the panel.**

3. **Choose New Layer.**

   The New Layer dialog appears.

4. **Accept the default name for the layer or enter a name.**

   I advise you to get in the habit of naming layers. That way you'll be able to identify what's in a layer by looking at its name in the Layers panel. You'll thank me for this little tidbit when you start creating some complex Fireworks documents.

5. **Enable the Share across Frames option to share all the objects on the created layer across all frames of an animation.**

   I show you how to create animations in Chapter 14.

6. **Click OK to create the new layer.**

   Fireworks creates a blank layer, all ready for your artwork.

To delete a layer, click the triangle near the upper-right-hand corner of the Layers panel and choose Delete Layer.

Arranging the pecking order of layers

When you create layers, the objects on the top layers eclipse the objects on the lower layers where they overlap them. If you decide that an object on a lower layer will look better with more exposure on an upper layer, you can easily rearrange the stacking order of the layers. To move a layer:

1. **Choose Window⇨Layers.**

   The Layers panel opens.

2. **Click a layer in the panel to select it.**

   The pencil icon appears to the left of the layer's name, and the panel's name is highlighted.

If a layer is locked, you must unlock it before selecting it.

3. **With the mouse button still held down, drag the layer to its new position.**

A folder icon appears and a black line gives you a preview of the layer's current position in the stacking order.

4. **When the layer is where you want it, release the mouse button.**

You can add a layer by clicking the New/Duplicate Layer button (it looks like a file folder) at the bottom of the Layers panel. You can delete a selected layer by clicking the Delete Selection button (it looks like a trash can) at the bottom of the Layers panel. You can also delete an item by selecting its thumbnail in the Layers panel and then clicking the Delete Selection button in the Layers panel.

Chapter 11

Creating Special Effects

● ●

In This Chapter

▶ Using the Effects panel

▶ Applying effects to bitmap images

▶ Applying effects to vector objects

▶ Using Photoshop plug-ins

● ●

*W*hen you have the need for something special in a project, there's nothing like a good set of effects. Fireworks has so many effects that they've got their own panel — yup, you guessed it, the Effects panel. You can use effects on vector objects you create in Fireworks or bitmap images you import into Fireworks. Some effects are for vector objects only, other effects are for bitmaps only, while other effects work on both.

You can apply effects in two different ways: using the Effects panel (Fireworks techno-people call these *live effects* because you can always edit them) or by using the Xtras menu. The options on the Xtras menu are more aptly referred to as *filters*. Any change you make using the Xtras menu is permanent.

Transforming Vector Objects with the Effects Panel

You use the Effects panel to apply an effect to an object on the canvas. The Effects panel can be thought of as an eye-candy store. You use the panel to select an effect as well as modify the effect. The following steps show you how to apply an effect with the Effects panel.

The effects as presented in this section refer to vector objects and not bitmap images.

1. **Use the Pointer tool or the Select Behind tool to select the object you want to apply the effect to.**

2. **Choose Window⇨Effect.**

   The Effects panel opens.

3. **Click the triangle to the right of the Effect window (where it says None by default or Untitled if you've applied an effect previously).**

   A drop-down menu of effects drops down.

4. **Choose an effect.**

   The controls for the effect show up in the panel. Figure 11-1 shows the controls for the Inner Bevel effect.

Figure 11-1:
Each effect
has its own
controls.

5. **Adjust the controls.**

   As you adjust the effect's controls, the object you're applying the effect to updates before your eyes.

6. **When what you see is what you like, click anywhere to finish applying the effect.**

   Fireworks applies the effect to the selected object. Figure 11-2 shows an oval that has been duplicated with different effects applied.

Adding additional effects to an object

What's better than one effect? Two! You can add one effect on top of another to double your effective pleasure. For example, you can add an Inner Bevel to an Outer Bevel, which reminds me of the ongoing debate about the perfect bellybutton. To add an effect to another effect:

1. **Use the Pointer tool or Select Behind tool to select an object you've applied an effect to.**

2. **Choose Window⇨Effect.**

   The Effects panel makes an appearance.

3. **Click the triangle in the upper-right corner of the panel.**

   A drop-down menu of effects appears.

Inner Bevel   Outer Bevel

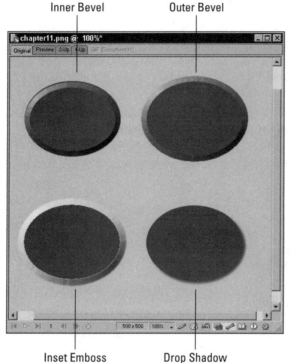

Figure 11-2:
Take your
garden
variety oval,
add a few
effects, and
you've got
something
pretty cool.

Inset Emboss   Drop Shadow

4. **Choose the effect you want to add to the object.**

   The effect's control panel appears.

5. **Adjust the controls until the effect is just the way you want it.**

   The second effect is applied to the object, and the two effects work in harmony to produce a pleasing bit of eye candy for your document.

Deleting effects

What you can add, you can also take away. You can delete any effect you've applied to an object to return the object to its natural state or to replace the effect with another effect. Or if need be, you can delete one effect out of all applied to an object. To delete an effect from an object:

1. **Using the Pointer tool or the Select Behind tool, select the object you've applied the effect to.**

2. **Choose Window⇨Effect.**

   The Effect panel opens and shows all the effects you've applied to the object.

3. **Click the effect you want to delete.**

   The effect's name is highlighted, as shown in Figure 11-3.

4. **If you've applied multiple effects and you're not sure which one to delete, you can momentarily see how the object looks without the selected effect by clicking the box at the left side of the effect's section in the panel.**

   The checkmark is removed from the box and the effect is momentarily deleted from the object. To apply the effect again, click the box; the checkmark appears, and the effect is reapplied.

5. **To delete the effect, click the trash can icon at the bottom of the panel.**

Selected effect

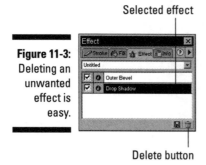

Figure 11-3:
Deleting an
unwanted
effect is
easy.

Delete button

Changing the order of effects

When you apply multiple effects to an object, Fireworks applies the effects in the order you added them in; the last effect applied is applied on top of the other effects. After you've got the object all gussied up with nowhere to go, you may end up deciding that you want the last effect applied before one of the other effects. Fortunately, changing the order in which effects are applied is almost as easy as changing your mind. To change the order in which effects are applied:

1. **Use the Pointer tool or Select Behind tool to select an object to which you've applied multiple effects.**

2. **Choose Window⇨Effects.**

   The Effects panel opens and displays the names of all the effects you've applied to the object.

3. **Click an effect's name to select it.**

   The effect's name is highlighted

4. Drag the effect to the desired position.

Drag an effect towards the top of the list and that effect is applied before other effects. Drag the effect lower in the list to have it applied after the effects that appear above it on the list.

Applying Effects to Bitmap Images

When you get a bitmap image for a Fireworks document, it can come from a multitude of sources. The bitmap image may be an image you downloaded from a public domain Web site, an image a client supplied, an image you scanned, or a scratchy old black-and-white photo of your childhood pet, Zippy the Wonder Pup. After you import the image into Fireworks and start designing your document, you may find that the image is lacking. Fireworks gives you a number of tools to punch up the image and make it look better.

I show you everything you ever wanted to know about importing bitmaps in Chapter 4.

Adjusting a bitmap's color characteristics

You can adjust a bitmap's color characteristics when an image doesn't look quite right. For example, if there's a bit too much orange in a skin tone or the sky is a wonky-looking shade of cyan instead of blue. Or perhaps you have an image that's just a tad dark and you need to brighten it up. To change the brightness and/or contrast of a bitmap image:

1. Select the image you want to modify with the Pointer tool or the Select Behind tool.

2. Choose Xtras⇨Adjust Color⇨Brightness and Contrast.

The Brightness and Contrast dialog box opens.

3. Drag the Brightness slider right to make the image brighter; drag it left to make it darker.

The image gets brighter or dimmer as you drag the slider.

4. Drag the Contrast slider to the right to increase contrast; left to decrease it.

The contrast of the image changes as you drag the slider.

5. Fireworks creates of preview of the changes you make as you make them.

You can click the Preview box to uncheck this option and disable it.

6. Click OK to apply the changes.

The image is modified according to your whims and your tactile dexterity with the sliders. Figure 11-4 shows an image being modified with the Brightness and Contrast command.

When you apply an effect to a bitmap using the Xtras menu, it's permanent and can't be undone. If you want to edit the effect after the fact, choose Window⇨Effect and choose the effect of your choice. If after adding other objects to your Fireworks document you find the effect is lacking, you can edit if by reopening the Effects panel and tweaking the controls to taste.

Figure 11-4:
Make a
bitmap's
day by
brightening
it with the
Brightness
and
Contrast
commands.

Adjusting a bitmap's curves

Contrary to popular belief, this section doesn't show you how to convert a bitmap image of a Jane or Joe Ordinary into one that looks like a supermodel. What this section does show you is how to adjust the color curve of a bitmap to modify individual colors in a bitmap. You can choose to adjust all colors (red, green, and blue) or a single color from the RGB color format. You can put Fireworks on autopilot to do this or you can adjust the controls manually.

For more information on using color in Fireworks, refer to Chapter 5.

To have Fireworks automatically adjust a bitmap's tonal range:

1. **Select the bitmap image whose tonal range you want to modify with either the Pointer tool or the Select Behind tool.**

2. **Choose Xtras⇨Adjust Colors⇨Curves.**

   The Curves dialog box appears.

3. **Click the Auto button.**

4. **Click OK to apply the change.**

   Fireworks automatically adjusts the image's tonal range. If Fireworks automation doesn't give you the results you want, you can adjust individual parts of the image's tonal curve.

To manually adjust an image's tonal range:

1. **Use the Pointer tool or Select Behind tool to select the bitmap image you want to adjust.**

2. **Choose Xtras⇨Adjust Color⇨Curves.**

   The Curves dialog box swoops in, as shown in Figure 11-5. By default the Preview box is checked. Leave this option enabled to see a preview of your changes as you make them.

   Below the Auto button are three eyedroppers:

   - Use the eyedropper on the left to select a shadow color.

   - Use the middle eyedropper to select a midtone color. Midtone colors are the brighter colors in your document, not the darks or lights.

   - Use the right eyedropper to select a highlight color.

3. **Click the left eyedropper and then click a color in the image to select it as the shadow color.**

   Fireworks updates the image.

4. **Repeat Step 3 with the middle and right eyedroppers.**

   Fireworks applies the selected colors and adjust the image's tonal range.

5. **Click OK to apply the changes.**

If you're into absolute control, you can modify the image's tonal range by manually adjusting its curve. To modify a bitmap's color range by adjusting its tonal curve:

 1. **Use the Pointer tool or Select Behind tool to select the bitmap image you want to adjust.**

2. **Choose Xtras⇨Adjust Color⇨Curves.**

   The Curves dialog box twists into view.

Figure 11-5:
Use the
eyedroppers
to modify
individual
parts of an
image's
tonal range.

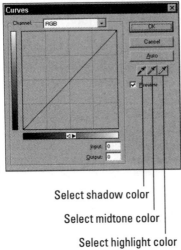

Select shadow color
Select midtone color
Select highlight color

3. **In the Channel field, accept the RGB default to modify the image across the entire color range, or click the triangle to the right of the field.**

   A drop-down menu appears. Choose R to modify the red tones, G to modify the green tones, or B to modify the Blue tones.

4. **To begin modifying the image's tonal range, click a point on the diagonal line and drag it to a new position.**

   The lowest part of the diagonal line represents the darkest or shadow colors in the image. Click a point on the lower point and drag right to darken shadow colors; left to lighten them.

   The middle part of the line represents the midtones of the image. Click a point in the middle of the graph and drag right to darken midtones; left to lighten them.

   The top part of the line represents the highlight tones in the image. Click a point near the top of the line and drag left to lighten highlights; right to darken them.

5. **As you drag the points you add to the line, it becomes a curve. Continue adding points and dragging them until the tonal image is to your liking.**

6. **Click OK to apply the changes.**

   Fireworks modifies the tonal range of the bitmap image. In Figure 11-6 you see the original bitmap on the left and a copy of it on the right being modified with the curves command. Notice the curve in the dialog box.

Figure 11-6:
The Curves command modifies a bitmap's tonal range.

Inverting a bitmap's colors

Inverting a bitmap's color makes the image look like a photographic negative. Or if the image already looks like a photographic negative, this command makes it look a photographic positive. To invert a bitmap's colors:

1. **Select the bitmap whose colors you want to invert with either the Pointer tool or Select Behind tool.**

2. **Choose Xtras⇨Adjust Color⇨Invert.**

   Fireworks inverts the image's colors. Figure 11-7 shows an image before and after the Invert command has done its handiwork.

If you like working with graphs that look like Rorschach ink blots to edit the color range in your images, choose Xtras⇨Adjust Color⇨Levels. I'll warn you that this method of editing colors in your bitmaps can get tricky.

Sharpening a bitmap's image

If you've got an image you want to use in a Fireworks document that's a little blurred, you can snap it back into focus with the Sharpen command. When you use the Sharpen command, Fireworks makes the change from one color's edge to the next more pronounced, thus producing the sharpening effect. To create a razor-sharp image:

1. **Select the image you want to sharpen.**

2. **Choose Xtras⇨Sharpen⇨Sharpen.**

   Fireworks sharpens the image. To produce a more pronounced sharpening effect, choose Xtras⇨Sharpen⇨Sharpen More.

Figure 11-7:
Invert a bitmap's colors when you want an image to look like a photographic negative.

Using Effects for Both Bitmap and Vector Images

Some Fireworks effects are primarily used to correct deficiencies in a bitmap image while other effects are used to create special effects with both bitmap and vector images. Use the Effects panel to apply effects that work on both types of images. (These effects are beveling, embossing, and creating a glow or drop shadow.)

Beveling an object

You *bevel* an object when you want it to stand out from the background. You can use a bevel to create a frame-like effect for a bitmap image or to create a navigation button. You have two bevels to choose from, an inner bevel and an outer bevel.

For the Outer Bevel effect, follow this same set of steps to select the Outer Bevel effect. The controls are the same with the exception of the color swatch that you use to select a color for the outer bevel.

To bevel an object inward:

1. **Use either the Pointer tool or Select Behind tool to select the object or bitmap you want to bevel.**

2. **Choose Window➪Effects.**

   The Effects panel opens.

3. **Click the triangle to the right of the Effect window (where it says None by default or Untitled if you've applied an effect previously).**

   A drop-down menu appears.

4. **Choose Bevel and Emboss➪Inner Bevel.**

   The Inner Bevel controls are shown in Figure 11-8.

5. **Click the triangle to the right of the Bevel Edge Shape field.**

   A drop-down menu appears.

6. **Choose a shape from the menu.**

7. **Click the triangle to the right of the Width field and then drag the slider to adjust the width of the bevel's edge.**

8. **Click the triangle to the right of the Contrast field and then drag the slider to determine the amount of contrast in the bevel's edge.**

9. **Click the triangle to the right of the Softness field and then drag the slider to determine how the bevel blends with the top of the object.**

   A lower value creates an abrupt blend between the bevel and the object; a higher value creates a smoother blend.

10. **Click the triangle to the right of the Angle field.**

    A rotary dial appears.

11. **Drag the dial to determine which direction the light source shines on the bevel from.**

12. **Click the triangle to the right of the Button Preset field and select an option from the drop-down menu.**

13. **Click anywhere outside of the Effects panel to apply the bevel.**

Bevel edge shape   Softness

Width   Contrast   Angle

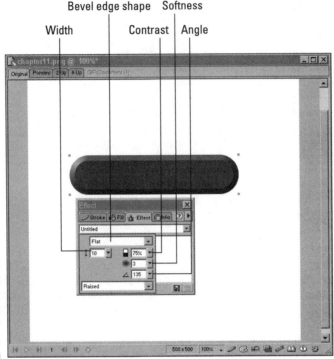

Figure 11-8:
Inner bevels
make great
borders for
buttons.

Embossing an object

Use one of the emboss effects when you want to make an object look like it's indented (Inset Emboss) or raised (Raised Emboss). This effect works best when shown on a canvas with a color other than white.

The Raised Emboss effect has the same controls as the Inset Emboss effect. When you apply the Raised Emboss to an object, it appears to be raised above the canvas. This effect works best when shown on a canvas with a color other than white.

To apply the Inset Emboss effect to an object:

1. **Use the Pointer tool or Select Behind tool to select the object you want to emboss.**

2. **Choose Window➪Effects.**

   The Effects panel appears.

3. **Click the triangle to the right of the effect field (where it says None by default or Untitled if you've applied an effect previously).**

   A drop-down menu appears.

4. **Choose Bevel and Emboss⇨Inset Emboss.**

   The Inset Emboss controls appear, as shown in Figure 11-9.

5. **Click the triangle alongside the Width field and then drag the slider to set the width of the bevel's edge.**

6. **Click the triangle alongside the Contrast field and then drag the slider to adjust the amount of contrast in the bevel's edge.**

7. **Click the triangle to the right of the Softness field and then drag the slider to determine how the bevel blends with the top of the object.**

   A lower value creates an abrupt transition between the emboss and the object; a higher value creates a smoother transition.

8. **Click the triangle to the right of the Angle field.**

   A rotary dial appears.

9. **Drag the dial to determine from which direction the light source shines on the emboss.**

10. **The Show Object option is enabled by default. Deselect the option and only the emboss is visible.**

11. **Click anywhere outside the Effects panel to apply the settings.**

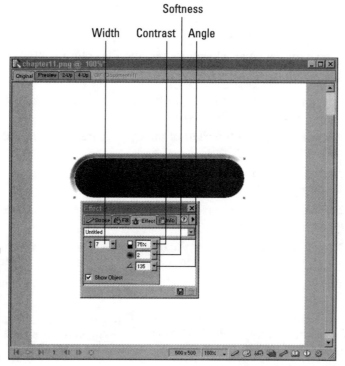

Softness

Width   Contrast   Angle

Figure 11-9:
I'll show you who the emboss is around here.

Creating a glow

You use one of the glow effects to draw attention to an object. When you choose the Inner Glow effect, an aura appears inside the object; the Glow effect creates an aura outside the object. This effect is perfect for putting halos on angels or for applying a different effect to one of a rollover button's states. The Inner Glow and Glow have identical controls. To save some of your valuable time, I'll present my favorite, the Glow effect. To create a glowing object:

1. **Select the object you want to glow with either the Pointer tool or the Select Behind tool.**

2. **Choose Window⇨Effects.**

   The Effects panel pops in.

3. **Click the triangle to the right of the Effect field (where it says None by default or Untitled if you've applied an effect previously).**

   Just when you thought it was safe to venture in the workspace, another drop-down menu appears.

4. **Choose Shadow and Glow⇨Glow.**

   The Glow effect controls appear, as shown in Figure 11-10.

5. **Click the triangle to the right of the Halo Offset window and then drag the slider to determine how wide the aura around the object is.**

6. **Click the Halo Color swatch.**

   Your cursor becomes an eyedropper and the color palette appears.

7. **Click a color to select it.**

   The selected color surrounds the object you're applying the glow to and appears in the halo color swatch.

8. **Click the triangle to the right of the Opacity field and drag the slider to adjust the setting.**

   Drag the slider up to create a more opaque glow; down to create a more transparent glow.

9. **Click the triangle to the right of the Softness field and drag the slider to adjust the setting.**

   This setting determines how the halo blends in with the surrounding objects. High values create gentle blends; low values create harsh blends.

10. **Click the triangle to the right of the Offset field and drag the slider to offset the halo.**

    You use this control if you want some distance between the halo and the object you're applying it to. The default setting of 0 butts the halo up against the perimeter of the object.

11. **Click anywhere outside of the Effects panel to apply the glow.**

Halo color   Softness

Halo offset   Opacity   Offset

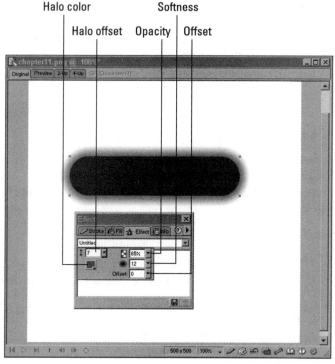

Figure 11-10:
Make
objects
appear
angelic with
the Glow
effect.

Creating a drop shadow

Apply the Drop Shadow effect to an image or object when you want to make it appear as though the object is floating off the canvas and casting an actual shadow. The drop shadow is probably used more than any other effect on Web pages. But they look great, so drop shadows have not worn out their welcome. To apply a drop shadow to an object or image:

1. **Using either the Pointer tool or the Select Behind tool, select the object or image you want to apply the effect to.**

2. **Choose Window⇨Effect.**

    The Effect panel drops in with no shadow, but a Fireworks PI has it under investigation.

3. **Click the triangle to the right of the Effect field (where it says None by default or Untitled if you've applied an effect previously).**

    A drop-down menu appears.

4. **Choose Shadow and Glow⇨Drop Shadow.**

    The Drop Shadow effect controls appear, as shown in Figure 11-11.

5. **Click the triangle to the right of the Distance field and then drag the slider to determine how far from the object the shadow extends.**

   Choose a high setting to make the object appear as though it's floating quite a distance from the canvas.

6. **To change the shadow's default black color, click the Shadow Color swatch.**

   The cursor becomes an eyedropper and the color palette appears.

7. **Click a color to select it.**

   The object's shadow color and the shadow color swatch changes to the one you selected.

8. **Click the triangle to the right of the Opacity window and then drag the slider.**

   This setting determines how dense the shadow is. Choose a high setting, and the shadow is very dark; choose a low setting, and objects underneath the shadow are visible.

9. **Click the triangle to the right of the Softness field and drag the slider.**

   This setting determines how abruptly the shadow ends. Choose a low setting and the shadow ends abruptly; high setting and the shadow blends in gently with its surroundings.

10. **Click the triangle to the right of the Angle field.**

    A rotary dial appears.

11. **Drag the dial to determine where the light source responsible for the shadow is coming from.**

    The object's shadow moves.

12. **Enable the Knock Out option if you want only the shadow to be visible.**

    Enabling this option makes the object disappear, leaving only the shadow of the object.

13. **Click anywhere outside of the Effects panel to apply the drop shadow.**

Blurring an object

Another neat effect you can apply is blurring an object. Use the effect to good effect on an optometrist's Web page and you'll increase his or her business by leaps and bounds. But seriously, use the effect any time you want an object to appear slightly out of focus.

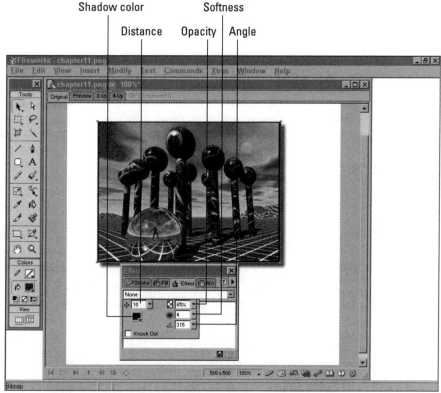

Figure 11-11:
Levitate objects off the canvas with ease when you use the Drop Shadow effect.

You have three different blur options:

- **Blur,** which blurs an object.
- **Blur More,** which intensifies the blur.
- **Gaussian Blur,** which applies a dreamlike blur, almost like you were looking at an object through a piece of gauze.

To apply a blur to a bitmap image:

1. **Using the Pointer tool or Select Behind tool, select the bitmap image you want to blur.**

2. **Choose Xtras➪Blur and then choose the type of blur you want to apply to the object.**

   The Blur and Blur More commands have no controls. The Gaussian Blur control has a slider that you use to apply more or less blur to the selected bitmap.

To simulate an object in motion, use the Lasso tool to select a car or plane from a bitmap image, Choose Xtras and then choose one of the effects from the Blur menu.

Editing effects

After you apply a live effect to an object, you can easily edit it. (A *live effect* is any effect that you apply through the Effects panel. Live effects can be edited at any time.) Say for example that you've applied a drop shadow to an image. It looked just great when you created it, but now that you've got other objects on the canvas, you need to modify it. To edit an effect:

1. **Use the Pointer tool or Select Behind tool to select the object the live effect is applied to.**

2. **Choose Window⇨Effects.**

   The Effects panel opens.

3. **Click the edit icon (it looks like the universal lowercase *i* used to designate information) to the left of the effect's name.**

   The effect's controls appear.

4. **Modify the effect as needed.**

   As you tweak the effect's controls, the object is updated.

5. **When you're through playing with the effect's controls, click anywhere outside the Effect panel to apply the effect.**

Using Photoshop Plug-ins in Fireworks

If you have other image editing software programs and you're using Photoshop type plug-ins with them, you can also use these plug-in filters to modify bitmaps directly in Fireworks. All you've got to do is tell Fireworks where to find the plug-ins. Here's how.

1. **Choose Window⇨Effects.**

   The Effects panel opens.

2. **Click the triangle near the top right corner of the panel.**

   A drop-down menu appears.

3. **Choose Locate Plugins.**

   The Select the Photoshop Plugins Folder dialog box opens.

4. **Navigate to the folder where your Photoshop plug-ins are filed and double-click the folder's name.**

   The folder's name appears on the Select button on the bottom of the dialog box.

5. **Click the Select button.**

   A warning dialog appears telling you the Fireworks must be restarted.

6. **Close Fireworks and then re-launch it.**

   The plug-ins appear as part of the Xtras menu and depending upon the plug-ins you selected, some may appear on the Effects menu. When you select a plug-in, its controls appear in Fireworks, just like they do in your other image editing programs.

Chapter 12

Optimizing Artwork for Export

● ●

● ●

*W*hen you visit a Web page created by people who know what they're doing — present company included, of course — the images are crisp and clear and download quickly into your browser. Unfortunately, some Web sites aren't created by people in the know. And you know which Web sites these are. They're the ones you never wait around for because the pages take so long to download.

Understanding Image Formats

Bitmap images come in many flavors, and Fireworks can import all the common ones, such as TIFF, Targa, BMP, and Photoshop. When you're creating an image for a Web page, you only need to concern yourself with the JPEG, GIF, and PNG formats, the major formats used by Web developers. These formats yield the best results with the smallest possible file sizes.

The JPEG (*Joint Photographic Experts Group* for those in the audience who are into acronyms) format supports millions of colors, which in my book is a lot. This format is also a lossy format, which means the image can be compressed. When an image is compressed certain information is lost, hence the term *lossy*. For example, if two neighboring pixels are close in color, they will be converted to a single color, which results in a smaller file size than the original. The JPEG format is well-suited for images.

The GIF *(Graphics Interchange Format)* format is an 8-bit format, which means you've got 256 colors to work with — no more, no less. The default Fireworks palette is the Web-safe 216 palette. These 216 colors will look the same in most browsers with both Macintosh and Windows operating systems. The GIF format supports transparency, which means you can specify colors that render as transparent when the document is exported. For example, use a transparent color when you want a tiling background image to show through certain areas of a Web page. The GIF format works best when you have images with blocks of large color.

The PNG *(Portable Network Graphics)* format can support up to 32 bits of colors (which is more than just a little bit of color) and can contain transparency. Unfortunately, not all Web browsers are equipped to handle PNG's versatility without plug-ins.

Understanding Resolution

Bitmap images are resolution-dependent. An image's *resolution* is the number of pixels used per inch to create it. The size of a bitmap image is also measured in pixels. (Think of pixels as dots.) And here's where the resolution part comes in: If you create a bitmap image that's 400 pixels x 300 pixels at a resolution of 72 pixels per inch, you get 72 pixels x 72 pixels for every square inch of picture on your computer monitor. If you try to blow this image up to, say, 800 pixels x 600 pixels, you're doubling the size of the image, yet you still only have 72 pixels per inch to work with. So when you ask an image-editing program to modify the size of an image, pixels must be redrawn. In the example above, you're doubling the size of a pixel and the results aren't necessarily pretty. Figure 12-1 is a tale of two bitmaps. The image on the left is the original; the image on the right has been doubled in size. Notice the distortion in the resized image.

So what, you ask, is an acceptable resolution? For a high quality photograph that will be output on a printer, acceptable resolution is generally 300 pixels per inch or better. For an image on the Internet, that's a different story. If you're thinking that more is better and that you need a lot of pixels to have a pretty picture, in most cases, you're right, especially if you're going to print the picture you create. So how many pixels do you need for the Internet? The standard resolution for a computer monitor is 72 pixels x 72 pixels. Therefore, you don't need an image resolution greater than 72 pixels per inch for images you post to the Web.

Figure 12-1:
Bitmap
images are
resolution
dependent:
you resize
them, and
they get
distorted.

Using the Document Window (WYSIWYG)

When you *optimize* (choose a format and settings for exporting) an image, you use the document window to view your document in different formats. The document window has four tabs: Original, Preview, 2-Up, and 4-Up (see Figure 12-2). As you create the document, all of your editing is done under the auspices of the Original section. (If you're in either 2-Up or 4-Up mode, the results of your edits in the Original part of the split-view are apparent in the preview window.) The Original section is the document with no optimization applied. You click the other tabs to preview the document with different optimization settings applied.

Use one of the other three tabs to preview the optimized document. I know, I haven't shown you how to optimize yet — I explain optimization settings in detail in the section "Optimizing Your Images for the Internet" later in this chapter. But you've got to know how to use the document window properly to properly optimize an image.

Click the Preview tab to see how the document looks with the current optimization settings. Figure 12-3 shows a document being previewed. Notice the information to the right of the last tab in the window. Fireworks shows you the file size of the document, how long it will take the document to download at an Internet connection speed of 28.8 kbps, plus the currently selected export format.

Use the 2-Up and 4-Up tabs to preview multiple versions of the object at different optimization settings. In the 2-Up window, you get one window with the original document and one Export Preview window. In the 4-Up tab version, you get one window with the original version and three Export Preview windows. It all adds up, you see. Figure 12-4 shows the Document window with the 4-Up tab selected. Notice that Fireworks shows you the file size, download size, plus the chosen settings for that particular window.

Figure 12-2:
The document window is your multi-tabbed passport to export.

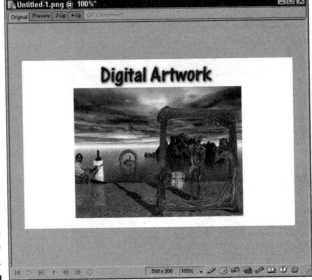

Optimizing Your Images for the Internet

You sit back and beam with pride while you look at your Fireworks masterpiece. You've created the perfect beast with wonderful images, great buttons, and really cool text. You've got enough sweat equity involved to fill a shot glass. But your task isn't done yet. You need to optimize the image for the Internet. Fortunately, you won't need a shot glass for the sweat equity you'll expend when optimizing the image. A thimble will do just fine.

File size

Download time

Current optimization format

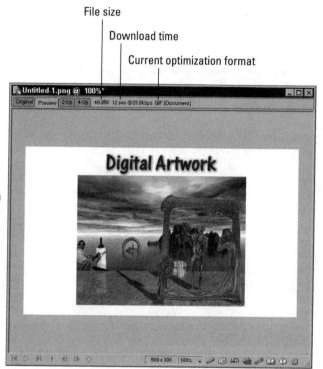

When you *optimize* an image, your goal is to create the best-looking image with the smallest possible file size. Small file sizes download quickly and have a low bandwidth. Remember bandwidth? The Internet is all about bandwidth. *Bandwidth* is the amount of information a modem can receive per second. The larger the file size, the longer it takes to load. To optimize an image, you use your old friends the document window and the Optimize panel.

In the following sections, I show you how to work with and optimize in the GIF and JPEG format. Fireworks is capable of working with other image formats; however, GIF and JPEG are the most popular formats in use for Web pages. Feel free to experiment with the other formats if you have a need for them in your work.

Download time

File size

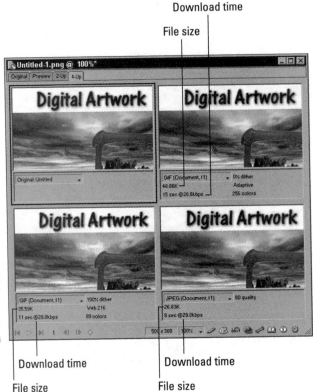

Figure 12-4:
Use the
4-Up tab to
preview four
different
versions of
the
document.

Download time

File size

Download time

File size

Working with GIF images

When you optimize a GIF image, you're choosing the number of colors that are used when the image is exported as well as the dithering and compressions settings. By comparing the original with the optimized image, you're able to determine the proper settings for export. To optimize a GIF image:

1. **Click the 2-Up tab in the document window.**

2. **Choose Window⇨Optimize.**

   The Optimize panel appears at the optimal moment.

3. **Click the triangle to the right of the Export File Format field; then choose GIF.**

4. **Click the triangle to the right of the Indexed Palette field.**

   A drop-down menu appears. There are many choices for color palettes. In Step 5, I show you the four most commonly used palettes. Feel free to experiment with the others if you have some spare time, something I rarely have these days.

5. Choose one of the following palette options:

- **Adaptive:** Creates a custom palette derived from actual colors used in the document.

- **Web Adaptive:** Creates a custom palette in which colors in your document are transformed to the closest Web-safe color.

- **Web 216:** Applies the Web-safe 216 palette to your document. These are colors deemed "safe" because they look consistent in most Web browsers in both the Macintosh and Windows platforms.

- **Exact:** Creates a plate with the exact colors used in the document. If the number of colors exceeds 256, the palette is switched to Adaptive.

To create a document with colors that are Web-safe at any speed, Choose Window➪Color Table. Click the triangle to the right of the last tab and choose Rebuild Color Table. If you see any color swatches that don't have a small dot in the center, select them and then convert them to Web-safe colors by clicking the Snap To Web Safe button (third button from the left on the bottom of the panel).

6. Click the triangle to the right of the Loss field and drag the slider.

This setting compresses the GIF image to create a smaller file size. If you decide to use this option choose a setting less than 15 percent for the best results.

7. Click the triangle to the right of the Dithering field and drag the slider to set the value.

Dithering is used to create colors not in the current palette. For example, if you have a bitmap image in your document, dithering mixes two colors from the selected palette to create a color that is not present in the current palette.

8. To assign transparency to a color, click the third eyedropper at the bottom of the panel and then, in either the Original window or one of the windows that displays the optimized image, click the color you want to be transparent.

When the document is exported, the background color or image on a Web page shows through the transparent color. A checkerboard pattern shows through transparent colors in any Document window that displays the image with optimized settings.

9. To create additional transparent colors, click the first eyedropper; then click a color in either the Original window or a window where the image is displayed in optimized format.

A checkerboard pattern shows through additional transparent colors.

To remove transparency from a color, click the middle eyedropper and then in the Original window (or in any other window), click the color you no longer want to be transparent.

As you make changes in the Optimize panel, pay careful attention to the document window. As you make each change, compare the image in the Original window to the image in the Preview window. If the image in the Preview window degrades below a value you deem acceptable, go back to the last setting you applied and change it until the optimized image is acceptable. Remember, your goal is to create an image that downloads quickly, not one that looks ugly. Figure 12-5 shows the Optimize panel with settings for a GIF export. Notice the two figures in the document window look almost identical. Also notice the file size, settings, and download time in the lower left corner of the Preview window.

To quickly begin the GIF optimization process, open the Optimize panel and then click the triangle to the right of the Saved Settings field. Choose an optimization setting from the drop-down menu and then tweak the individual settings until you've got a good looking, skinny GIF that downloads in a jiff.

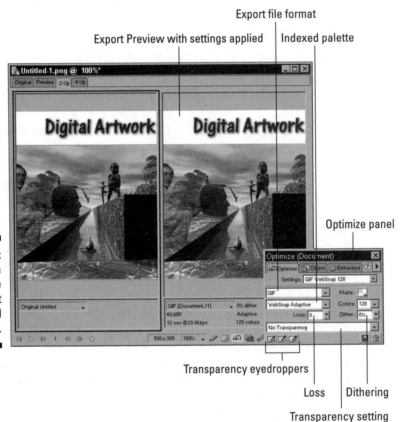

Figure 12-5: Optimizing a GIF image makes it download quickly.

Optimal download time

When it comes to the subject of download times, I use my own Internet impatience factor as a benchmark. If I see a download time greater than 15 seconds in the Preview window, I drop back ten, punt, and then tweak the settings to get an acceptable image that downloads in fifteen seconds or less. Fifteen seconds may not seem like much when you're flying along the interstate with the stereo playing classic rock (is there any other kind?) at 60 miles-per-hour, but when you're sitting in your computer chair waiting for a Web page to download, 15 seconds can seem like an eternity.

Interlacing a GIF image

If you end up creating a large document that takes longer than fifteen seconds to download, there is a remedy. You can *interlace* a GIF image. When you interlace a GIF image, it downloads into a Web browser in segments, which gives viewers something to look at while they're waiting. I'm not a big fan of interlacing because my patience factor is rather low, and I'd rather see the finished product on the first pass. But if you've exhausted all other options and you must export a hefty GIF, here's how to interlace the rascal.

1. **Choose Window⇨Optimize.**

   The Optimize panel opens for business.

2. **Adjust the export settings for the GIF image.**

   If you don't know how to tweak the settings, you probably didn't read the preceding "Working with GIF images" section. Sigh. It's some of my best work. Now go back and read the section before proceeding to Step 3.

3. **Click the triangle near the upper right-hand corner of the panel.**

   A drop-down menu appears.

4. **Choose Interlaced.**

   When the exported document is used in a Web page, the image downloads into a Web browser in segments.

You can also use the Optimize menu to remove unused colors from a palette, save the current settings as a preset for future use, delete a saved setting, or optimize a document to a particular file size.

Working with JPEG images

When you export JPEG images, colors are no longer an issue because you've got millions of them. When you optimize a JPEG image for the Internet, you're concerned about loss. Before you go thinking that this is a treatise on how to minimize your losses on the stock market, JPEG *loss* refers to lowering the quality of the exported image. When you lower the quality of the image, you lose information (which is why JPEG is referred to as a *lossy* format). The trick is to lose enough information to create a file that downloads quickly, but not so much information that you create an ugly graphic. To optimize a JPEG image for export:

1. **Click the 2-Up tab in the document window.**

2. **Choose Window⇨Optimize.**

   The Optimize panel appears at the optimal moment.

3. **Click the triangle to the right of the Export File Format field and choose JPEG from the drop-down menu.**

   The JPEG settings appear.

4. **Click the triangle to the right of the Quality field.**

   A slider appears.

5. **Drag the slider to adjust the setting.**

   Higher values produce better quality images but larger file sizes. As you drag the slider, pay attention to the image in the Preview window. To create the smallest file size, drag the slider until the image degradation is no longer acceptable, and then select a slightly higher setting.

6. **Click the triangle to the right of the Smoothing field.**

   A drop-down menu appears.

7. **Select a setting to determine the amount of smoothing Fireworks applies to the JPEG image.**

   When you apply smoothing to an image, Fireworks blurs hard edges which otherwise would not compress well. The more smoothing you apply, the smaller the file size. Depending upon the beginning quality of the image you're exporting, you can apply a setting of 3 to 4 and still achieve acceptable results. After you select a smoothing value, look at the image in the Preview window. If the image quality is still acceptable, apply additional smoothing to further decrease the file size.

And that's all there is to optimizing a JPEG image. Remember to compare the original to the image in the Preview window so you know exactly what's going on. When you export the document, Fireworks applies the settings you chose.

Using Selective JPEG quality

Fireworks now makes it possible for you to use different JPEG quality settings on different parts of an image, which is great news if you want to export an image with text using the JPEG format. JPEG is notorious for doing a lousy job of compressing text, but by using selective JPEG quality, you can apply low compression to the text area of your document and the maximum compression to the rest of the image to still yield a good, quality image. Talk about having your cake and eating it, too. To apply selective JPEG quality to an image:

1. **Click the 2-Up tab in the document window.**

2. **Choose Window⇨Optimize.**

   The Optimize panel opens.

3. **Click the triangle to the right of the Export File Format field and choose JPEG from the drop-down menu.**

4. **Click the triangle to the right of the Quality window.**

   A slider appears.

5. **Drag the slider to determine the amount of compression Fireworks applies to the image.**

   Drag the slider up to apply less compression; down to apply more. As you drag the slider, pay attention to the image in the Export Preview window. When the image quality is now longer acceptable, drag the slider to a slightly higher setting.

6. **Select one of the Marquee tools.**

   What you're going to do now is create the selection that you will apply the selective setting to. Choose either the Rectangular Marquee tool or the Oval Marquee tool. To create an irregular selection, say around a face, select the Polygon Lasso tool.

7. **In the original window (the one on the left), create a selection with the chosen Marquee tool.**

   An army of marching ants surrounds the selection.

8. **Choose Modify⇨Selective JPEG⇨Save Selection as JPEG Mask.**

   The mask is highlighted in a lovely shade of lavender.

9. **Enter a value in the Selective Quality field.**

   The default value is 90, which is very little compression. Enter a higher value for a higher quality selection; lower value for a lower quality selection. Figure 12-6 shows a JPEG image with selective quality applied. The army of marching ants around the violinist's face signifies the JPEG mask. The area around the JPEG mask has high compression applied for demonstration purposes.

Never export an image with this much compression applied unless you like blocky pixels.

You can edit Selective JPEG Settings by clicking the button to the right of the Selective Quality field.

You can use Fireworks to optimize artwork for other formats; for example, if you're going to have a document you're creating printed professionally. Choose Modify➪Image Size, match the resolution to the printer's output device, and then enter the desired print size. Fireworks does the math and resizes the pixels to match. Use the Optimize panel and select TIFF 32 for the Export File Format. The TIFF format doesn't compress your image. Remember that if you have bitmap images in your document, you cannot resample the bitmap without introducing some distortion.

Figure 12-6:
Apply selective JPEG quality when you want part of your image to shine.

Using Progressive JPEG

There will be a point in your career as a Web designer that a client's going to give you an absolutely gorgeous JPEG image that he or she wants displayed in all its glory on his or her Web page. Try as you may, you just can't create a small file size and still keep the image quality to the specs. And you know that if you post the image as is, people who visit the Web site will leave in flocks because the image takes a while to download. Choose Progressive JPEG to solve this problem. *Progressive JPEGs* download in segments like interlaced GIFs. The viewer first sees a low-resolution version of the image that increases in quality as it downloads. To create a progressive JPEG:

1. **Choose Window⇨Optimize.**

   The Optimize panel opens for business.

2. **Click the triangle near the upper right-hand corner of the panel.**

   A drop-down menu appears.

3. **Choose Progressive JPEG.**

   When the exported image is downloaded into a Web browser, it downloads in stages, each stage presenting a higher quality image than the last.

Selecting the optimal optimization setting

After you've selected an optimization setting, you determine the optimal optimization setting by comparing optimization variations side by side in the document window's 4-Up mode. To optimize an image with the 4-Up mode:

1. **Click the 4-Up tab in the document window.**

   One original and three Export Preview windows appear.

2. **Choose Window⇨Optimize.**

   The Optimize panel appears.

3. **Click the first Preview window.**

4. **Use the Optimize panel to select optimization settings for this Preview window.**

   The image in the window is changed based on the settings you apply. The optimization settings, file size, and download time are listed in the lower corner of the window.

5. **Click the next Preview window.**

6. **Use the Optimize panel to select optimization settings for this Preview window.**

   The image in this window is updated based on the settings you applied.

7. **Click the last Preview window and apply optimization settings in the Optimize panel.**

   You know the drill. The image in this window changes.

8. **Compare the images in the four windows.**

   As you compare the image, note the file size and download times in the bottom of each Preview window. Compare the image quality in each window with the original uncompressed version of the document.

You're able to view only a portion of the image in the 4-Up mode. To view a different part of the image, select the Hand tool and then drag in any window to pan to a different part of the image. Or if the image is only slightly smaller than the document window, click the bottom-right corner and drag to increase the size of the document window. The images in the other windows will change to the same view.

9. **Click the Export Preview window that is the best compromise between image quality and download time.**

    The settings applied to that window appear in the Optimize panel.

10. **Click the Original tab.**

    The optimal optimization settings will be applied when you export the image. Figure 12-7 shows an image being optimized in the 4-Up mode. Notice the difference in image quality, optimization settings, file size, and download time in each of the Preview windows. The image in the lower right corner is the best looking one of the lot and coincidentally has the smallest file size and quickest download time. Talk about your win-win-win situation.

You can apply different optimization settings to different areas of the document by creating a slice with the Slice tool. For example, if you have a JPEG image in the middle of your document, use the Slice tool to make a slice with just the JPEG image and then apply JPEG optimization to it. Apply GIF optimization to the other parts of the document. (Check out Chapter 16 for more on the Slice tool.)

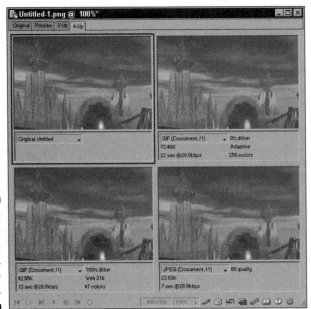

Figure 12-7:
For the optimum in optimization, click the 4-Up tab.

Chapter 13

Creating Reusable Artwork

● ●

In This Chapter

▶ Going over symbols and instances

▶ Understanding symbol types

▶ Creating symbols

▶ Modifying symbols

▶ Using the document Library

● ●

Symbols are reusable artwork that you can use over and over again. Symbols can be blocks of text, graphic objects, multi-state rollover buttons, or animations. The original symbol is stored in the document's Library, which I discuss in this chapter. To use a symbol in your Fireworks document, you simply drag it out of the document Library and onto the canvas to create a copy of it, which is called an *instance*. And if after diligently creating your Fireworks document you feel the symbol doesn't quite match your high artistic standards, you can edit it. When you edit the original symbol, all copies (instances) of the symbol are updated in one fell swoop. So keep reading to find out how to create and modify symbols, as well as how to get the most bang for your buck by using symbols out of the Library.

Understanding Symbols and Instances

Whenever you create a symbol, you're creating a blueprint for a reusable graphic. Every time you open the Library and drag the symbol onto the canvas, Fireworks creates a carbon copy of the symbol, which is known as an *instance*. The beauty of symbols is that they save you time. For example, if you're creating a document that uses a lot of buttons for navigation, create one button symbol and then create instances of the symbol as needed. Then all you need to do is create a text object to identify what the button does, align it to the button symbol's instance, group it, and you're done, ready for a nice cup of your favorite beverage. It's just that easy.

Getting to Know Symbol Types

Trying to get a symbol to behave the way you want is much easier than getting a child, or say your hair, to behave on a bad day. To get a symbol to behave the way you want it to, you assign a *type* to it. You have three types to choose from:

- ✔ You use the **Graphic** type for a symbol that is a *static* (read: stationary, meaning that it doesn't move) piece or artwork. The symbol can be a single object or a group of objects.

- ✔ You use the **Animation** type for a symbol that moves or is *animated.*

- ✔ You use the **Button** type to create a symbol that is used as a navigation device. The button symbol can have multiple rollover states. A button with multiple rollover states reacts differently depending upon where the user's mouse is.

I show you how to create rollover buttons in Chapter 17.

Creating Reusable Graphic Symbols

To create a graphic symbol, you use the same tools that you use to create other Fireworks graphics. The big difference is that you tell Fireworks to make the objects you create into symbols. You can do this in two different ways: create a symbol from scratch or convert an existing graphic to a symbol.

Creating symbols from scratch

You create a symbol from scratch when you decide that you will need an object more than once in the document you're creating. Navigation buttons are a perfect example of this. To create a symbol from scratch:

1. **Choose Insert⇨New Symbol.**

   The Symbol Properties dialog appears. The Name field is selected by default. The default Fireworks name for a symbol is Symbol, which is highly original. Not. I advise you to enter your own name for a symbol, one that you'll recognize when you have a lot of symbols in your document.

2. **In the Name field, enter a name.**

3. **Choose a Type for the symbol.**

   The Type you choose determines how the symbol behaves when you use it in the document. (If you don't understand what the different types do, you must have inadvertently skipped reading the preceding section.)

4. Click OK.

A new window opens up. The actual window that appears depends upon the type you assign to the symbol.

I show you how to create animation symbols in Chapter 14 and button symbols in Chapter 17.

5. Use any of the drawing tools to create the artwork for the symbol.

Figure 13-1 shows a graphic symbol under construction.

You can use more than one object to create a symbol. For example, you can use two concentric ovals to create a symbol that looks like a cartoon character's eyes.

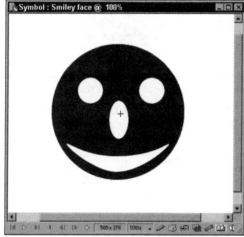

Figure 13-1:
You create
reusable
symbols in
their own
window.

6. When you're done creating the symbol, close the window.

The new symbol appears on the canvas and is added to the document Library. All symbols are designated with a dotted rectangular border and a curved arrow in their lower left hand corner (see Figure 13-2).

Converting objects to symbols

You convert an object to a symbol when you've created an object or some artwork that you absolutely fall in love with and decide to use more than once in a document. You can start with a graphic object and convert it to a symbol using any of the three symbol types. To convert an object to a symbol:

Figure 13-2:
When you create a symbol, it's branded with a curved arrow to its lower left.

1. **Select the object or objects you want to convert to a symbol with either the Pointer tool or the Select Behind tool.**

   If you're converting more than one object to create the symbol, click to select the first object and then Shift-click additional objects to add them to the selection.

2. **Choose Insert➪Convert to Symbol.**

   Alternately, you can press F8.

   The Symbol Properties dialog box appears.

3. **Enter a name for the symbol in the Name field.**

   I advise you to name all symbols. Editing is much easier when you can identify your symbols by name.

4. **Choose a Type for the symbol.**

   For more on symbol types, see the section "Getting to Know Symbol Types" earlier in this chapter.

5. **Click OK.**

   A window opens up. The window differs depending upon the symbol type you've chosen.

6. **Use the Toolbox tools to modify the object or accept it as is.**

   If you're creating a button or animation symbol, you'll need to use the tools to modify the object. Buttons and animations have more than one frame, and you need to edit the objects so that they appear different in each frame. I show you how to create animations in Chapter 14 and buttons in Chapter 17.

7. **Close the window.**

   Fireworks adds the converted symbol to the Library.

Using the Library to Store Your Symbols

Every symbol you create ends up in the Library. But the neat thing about this Library is that you don't need a card to get in, you'll never get fined for an overdue symbol, and you don't have to be quiet. But before you can do anything in the Library, you've got to open it. To open the Library, choose Window⇨Library (or you can click the Library button on the Launcher bar). The Library opens, as shown in Figure 13-3.

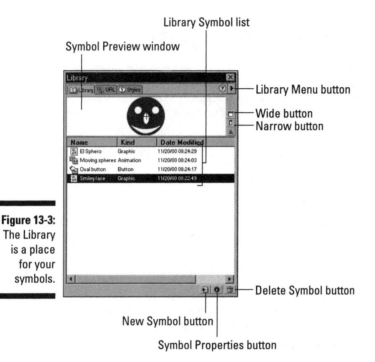

Library Symbol list

Symbol Preview window

Library Menu button
Wide button
Narrow button

Delete Symbol button

New Symbol button

Symbol Properties button

Figure 13-3:
The Library
is a place
for your
symbols.

Figure 13-3 shows the Library in Wide mode (as opposed to Narrow mode). The Library is divided into two windows: The top window is for previewing a symbol, and the bottom window is a list of all the symbols in the Library. Notice the icon to the left of each symbol's name. You use the icon to identify the symbol's type. The second column also identifies the type of symbol by name. The third column tells the date the symbol was last modified. The third column comes in handy if more than one person is working on a project or if you simply have to know the last time the symbol was fiddled with. After you have the Library open, there's a multitude of things you can do.

✔ To preview an animation (of more than one frame) or button symbol, click the **Play** button.

✔ Click the **Wide** button to show all columns.

✔ Click the **Narrow** button to minimize the size of the Library.

✔ To get information about a symbol, click the **Symbol Properties** button to open the Symbol Properties dialog box.

✔ To delete a symbol from the Library, click the **Delete Symbol** button (it looks like a trash can) at the bottom corner of the Library window.

✔ To change the width of a Library column (Windows only), move your cursor over a column's divider, click and then drag right or left. Release the mouse button when the column is the desired width.

Creating instances of symbols

You create an instance of a symbol when you need another copy of the symbol in your document. For example, if you've created a rectangular symbol and you need a rectangular background for a text object, you create an instance of the symbol rather than creating a rectangle from scratch. Here's how.

1. **Choose Window⇨Library.**

   The document Library opens.

2. **Click the symbol's name to select it.**

   The selected symbol appears in the preview area. If the symbol is a button or an animation consisting of more than one frame, you can click the Play button to preview it.

3. **With the symbol still selected, drag it onto the canvas.**

   Fireworks copies the symbol to the canvas. The instance of the symbol has a curved arrow at its lower left corner that tells you and the rest of the objects on the block that this is a clone (or *instance*) of the symbol.

4. **Use the Pointer tool to move the instance into the desired position.**

5. **Use any of the other tools or menu commands to modify the instance.**

You can modify an instance by scaling, skewing, rotating, or distorting it, but you cannot change the instance's shape. Therefore, you can select the instance with the Subselection tool, but you can't edit the instance's points. You can, however, edit the original symbol, in which case all instances of the symbol change as well.

Adding symbols to the Library

You can add a symbol to the Library when you need artwork that you'll use more than once in a document. Whenever you create a symbol, it is automatically added to the Library.

Each document has its own Library. All the symbols you create or objects you import are automatically added to the Library. You can also create a new symbol and add it to the Library from within the Library. This comes in handy when you're perusing the Library for artwork and you don't find what you're looking for.

To add a symbol to the Library from within the Library:

1. **Click the New Symbol button (the plus sign at the bottom of the Library).**

   The Symbol Properties dialog box appears.

2. **Enter a name for the symbol and choose a symbol type.**

   Fireworks opens the Symbol Editing window.

3. **Use the drawing tools to create the symbol and then close the window.**

   Fireworks adds the new symbol to the Library.

Managing the Library

If you do a lot of experimentation when creating a Fireworks document, you may end up with unused items in the Library. While this glut of symbols doesn't affect the exported document, it does increase the file size of the Fireworks document on your hard drive. If you don't foresee needing unused Library symbols in the document, delete them. To delete unused symbols from the Library:

1. **Choose Window⇨Library.**

   The Library is open for business.

2. **Click the triangle near the upper right-hand corner of the Library window.**

   A drop-down menu appears.

3. **Choose Select Unused Items.**

   Fireworks highlights all unused symbols.

4. **Click the Delete Symbol button (it looks like a trash can).**

   Fireworks banishes the selected symbols to be seen nevermore in the Library.

Editing symbols

The beauty of working with symbols is that you can change the original symbol and all instances of it within the document are also changed. Say, for example, you don't like the shape you've created for a button, and you just happen to have six buttons in the document. If the buttons were separate graphics, you'd have to edit each one. The fact that you took the time to read this chapter probably means that you chose to make the button into a symbol, which means that you have to edit only the original symbol. After editing, any instances of the button automatically change to match the original. To edit a symbol from within the document:

1. **Select the Pointer tool and then double-click the symbol you want to edit.**

   Fireworks opens up the symbol in the Symbol Editing window.

2. **Use the tools and/or menu commands to apply the edits to the symbol.**

3. **Close the window.**

   All instances of the symbol are updated.

There may be times when you're browsing through the Library and you decide to tweak a symbol to make it look better. To edit a symbol from within the Library:

1. **Double-click the symbol's name.**

   The Symbol Properties dialog box appears.

2. **Click the Edit button.**

   The symbol appears in the Symbol Editing window.

   You can quickly open a symbol in the Symbol Editing window by selecting it in the Library and then double-clicking its preview in the Library preview window.

3. **Use the drawing tools or menu commands to edit the symbol.**

4. **Close the window.**

   All instances of the symbol are updated to reflect your editing handiwork.

Importing symbols

You can import artwork you've already created and add it to the Library as a symbol. Importing artwork you've already created is a real timesaver. To import a graphic into the document Library:

1. **Choose Window⇨Library.**

   The Library opens.

2. **Click the triangle near the upper right-hand corner of the window.**

   The Library menu opens.

3. **Choose Import Symbol.**

   The Import Symbol dialog appears.

4. **Navigate to the location of the item you want to import as a symbol and then click Open.**

   The symbol you select can be any image such as a GIF or JPEG. The selected file is added to the Library and linked with the original graphic you imported. If you move the original graphic to another folder, Fireworks will still have the exact duplicate in the Library ready for when you need it.

After you create a few Fireworks documents, you can use symbols from other documents (saved in Fireworks native .png format) in a new document rather than create a new symbol. To import a symbol from another Fireworks document Library:

1. **Choose Window⇨Library.**

   The document Library opens.

2. **Click the triangle near the upper right-hand corner of the window.**

   The Library menu awaits your choice.

3. **Choose Import Symbol.**

   The Import Symbol dialog box appears.

4. **Choose the native Fireworks document (it's a .png file type) that the symbol is stored in and then click Open.**

   A new Import Symbols dialog box opens, showing the contents of the other document's Library (see Figure 13-4).

5. **Click a symbol to see it previewed in the Preview window.**

Figure 13-4:
You can import symbols directly from other Fireworks document Libraries.

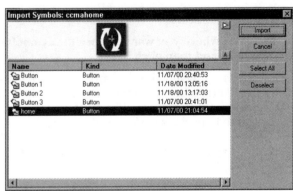

6. **Click a symbol to select it.**

   The symbol is highlighted. To add to the selection, hold down the Shift key and click additional symbols in the Library. To select all symbols, click the Select All button.

7. **To import the selected symbol(s), click the Import button.**

   The Import Symbols dialog box closes, and the imported symbols are added to the Library.

Exporting symbols

Did you ever have one of those days when you created something that was so perfect, you just knew you were going to use it again? When you create the perfect symbol in a Fireworks document, you can indeed save it for a rainy day or for another document by exporting the symbol. To export a symbol:

1. **Choose Window⇨Library.**

   The document Library opens.

2. **Click the triangle near the window's upper right-hand corner.**

   The Library menu opens.

3. **Choose Export Symbols.**

   The Export Symbols dialog box appears.

4. **Click a symbol's name to select it.**

   The symbol's name is highlighted. To add to the selection, hold down the Shift key and click other symbol's names. To select all the symbols in the Library, click Select All.

5. **Click Export.**

   The Save As dialog box appears.

6. **Navigate to the folder where you want to store the symbols, enter a name for the symbols, and then click Save.**

   The exported symbols are saved as a Fireworks .png file. To use an exported symbol in a future Fireworks production, use the Library's Import Symbols command, import the document, and then choose the symbol(s) you want to import for the current document.

If you find yourself exporting a lot of symbols, create a separate folder to store your Fireworks symbols.

Using the Styles Library

The Styles Library is a collection of preset effects that you use to change the appearance of objects in your documents. For example, one of the styles quickly bevels a selected shape and turns it a lovely shade of blue. You use the Fireworks Styles Library, as shown in Figure 13-5, to quickly modify an object. You can use the different styles to create buttons, backdrops for text, and even modify text objects. When you're under a tight deadline and need to get a project out quickly, the Styles Library saves you the time you'd spend tinkering with the Effects panel to create an effect.

To apply a style to an object:

1. **Select the object with the Pointer tool or Select Behind tool.**

2. **Choose Window⇨Styles.**

   The Styles Library opens (see Figure 13-5).

3. **Click a style to select it.**

   The style is applied to the object. If the object doesn't look quite right with the style you selected, click a different style.

After a style has been applied to an object, you can modify the style as it is applied to the object by choosing Window⇨Effect. All the effects used to create the style are listed in the Effects panel and can be edited. You can also modify the object's stroke or fill by opening the appropriate panel. For a refresher course on editing effects, refer to Chapter 9.

I show you how to create your own styles and add them to the Styles Library in Chapter 19.

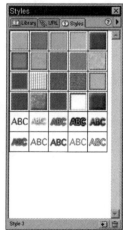

Part III
Making Fireworks Even Hotter: Creating Animations and Dynamic Web Elements

The 5th Wave   By Rich Tennant

"Well, it's not quite done. I've animated the gurgling spit-sink and the rotating Novocaine syringe, but I still have to add the high speed whining drill audio track."

In this part . . .

With Fireworks 4 you can create dynamic elements for your Web pages like rollover buttons, pop-up menus, and hotspots without breaking so much as a sweat. Without Fireworks, you'd need a Ph.D. in HTML and JavaScript to create interactive elements like these.

In this part I show you how to use the most popular Fireworks features to add interactive elements to your Fireworks designs. I show you how to quickly create animations and animated banners. In Chapters 16 and 17, I show you how to create cool hotspots, how to link the objects in your design to other Web pages, and how to apply behaviors to the artwork in your design, as well as other amazing feats of Web interactivity. You say you want an image map in your Web page, but your road atlas doesn't have directions? I map out image maps for you in Chapter 17 and also show you everything you wanted to know about Fireworks pop-up menus but were afraid to ask. And last but not least, I show you how to export the image for use on the Internet.

Chapter 14

Creating Animations

● ●

In This Chapter

▶ Creating animation symbols

▶ Working with frames

▶ Tweening instances

▶ Bringing images to life

▶ Previewing your animations

● ●

*A*nimation is eye-catching. It's eye-catching because it moves, and anything that moves catches the eye. In this chapter, I show you how to animate objects in your Fireworks productions. The animations can be stand-alone files or part of an entire Web page.

Animation in Fireworks is no different than what you did when you were a kid when you scribbled a stick figure on the first sheet of a small pad and then drew the figure in slightly different poses on each consecutive page. When you ran your thumb across to turn the pages, you got motion. In Fireworks, the *frame* takes the place of the individual page. You create an object on the first frame, and then do something different to the object on the second page — maybe move it, make it more transparent, or perhaps rotate it. Perhaps the animation is just a series of images that change in each frame. No matter what you chose to put in each frame, when you export the document as an Animated GIF file and incorporate it into an HTML document, it plays back frame-by-frame in a Web browser, and the viewer sees motion.

Creating Animated Symbols

Animations are fun to create. If you're going to use a single animation more than once in a document, create an animation symbol. Animation symbols are added to the document's Library. When you use an animation symbol from the Library, Fireworks creates a copy, or *instance,* of the symbol.

Creating a reusable animation: The animation symbol

The most basic type of animation you can create in Fireworks is the animation symbol. An *animation symbol* is a reusable piece of animated artwork that you can use — like that pink bunny with the sunglasses and the drum — over and over and over again. To create an animation symbol:

1. **Use the drawing tools to create the object(s) that you want to animate.**

   You can also import objects created in other programs or saved Fireworks documents.

2. **Using the Pointer tool, select the objects you want to animate.**

3. **Choose Modify⇨Animate⇨Animate Selection.**

   The Animate dialog box appears.

4. **Accept the default number of frames (5), or if you want a different number of frames, click the triangle to the right of the Frames field.**

   A slider appears.

5. **Drag the slider to specify the number of frames in the animation.**

   More frames create smoother motion, but also increase the file size of the animation.

6. **Accept the default Move value of 72, or if you want a different Move value, click the triangle to the right of the field.**

   This value determines the distance in pixels that the selected object moves. If you click the triangle, a slider appears which lets you adjust how far the object moves. You can enter a value between 0 and 250.

7. **Click the triangle to the right of the Direction field.**

   A rotary dial appears. Accept the default value of 0 if you want the object to move in a parallel direction; otherwise, drag the slider to enter the direction in degrees that you want the object to move.

8. **Click the triangle to the right of the Scale field.**

   A slider appears. Accept the default value of 100 if you don't want to scale the object as you animate it; otherwise, drag the slider to select a value. Larger values cause the object to get larger during the animation; smaller values shrink it.

9. **In the Opacity section, you have two fields: The first field determines the opacity of the object at the beginning of the animation; the second field determines the opacity of the object at the end of the animation. Click the triangle to the right of each field to adjust the setting.**

When the triangle is clicked, a slider appears. Drag the slider to determine the opacity. To have the object appear as though it were materializing from thin air, drag the first slider to zero to make the object invisible in the first frame of the animation and drag the second slider to 100 to have the object fully visible in the last frame. When the animation is played back, the object appears as though it is materializing.

10. **To have the object rotate during the animation, click the triangle to the right of the Rotate field.**

    A slider appears that you drag to set the number of degrees the object rotates. Select a value from 0 to 360. Accept the default CW (clockwise) option, and the object rotates clockwise; select CCW (counter-clockwise), and the object rotates counter-clockwise during the animation.

11. **Click OK.**

    A warning dialog box may appear, telling you that animation for the symbol will require more frames. To have Fireworks add the frames, click OK.

    Additional frames add to the file size of the animation. If Fireworks adds enough frames to create a large file that takes a long time to download, the only way to pare the file down to size is to delete frames.

12. **To preview the animation in the document window, click the Preview tab and then click the Play button (see Figure 14-1).**

    The animation plays from beginning to end, loops back to the first frame and repeats. Click the Stop button before you get mesmerized or hypnotized or something.

    You can preview the animation in the Original window, but it will play faster than it will when you export the document. To preview the animation as it will appear in a Web browser, refer to the Previewing and editing animations section towards the end of this chapter.

After you create the animation symbol, Fireworks adds it the document Library and gives it the default name of Symbol. To rename the symbol:

1. **Choose Window⇨Library.**

   The document Library opens.

2. **Double-click the new symbol's name.**

   The Symbol Properties dialog box opens.

3. **In the Name field, enter a new name for the symbol.**

   Choose a name that reflects what the animation does.

4. **Click OK.**

   Fireworks renames the animation symbol.

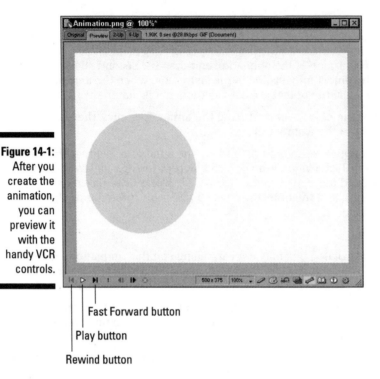

Figure 14-1:
After you
create the
animation,
you can
preview it
with the
handy VCR
controls.

Fast Forward button

Play button

Rewind button

 For more information on creating symbols and the document Library, stuff a
bookmark here and jump back to Chapter 13. Do not, I repeat, do not bend
back the page. Books have feelings too, you know.

Editing an animation symbol

After you create the animation symbol, you may need to edit it in order to get
it to play just the way you want it to. You may need to change the number of
frames to make the animation play smoother, or you may need to change one
of the other parameters, for example, the rotation if your pet gets sick all
over your keyboard while previewing the animation. To edit an animation
symbol:

 1. Using the Pointer tool, select the animation on the canvas.

2. Choose Modify➪Animate➪Settings.

The Animate dialog box appears.

3. Adjust the settings to fine-tune the animation and then click OK.

Fireworks applies the new settings to the animation.

4. **Click the Play button to preview the animation with the new settings.**

   Fireworks rolls your animation. Steven Spielberg watches in awe.

5. **If the animation plays to your satisfaction, you're done. If not, revert to Step 2 and tweak the settings again, Sam.**

You can remove all animation from a symbol by choosing Modify➪Animate➪ Remove Animation.

Creating Action with Frames

If you're creating a document with the sole purpose of animating it, you need to create *frames*. On each frame, you create some change that generates action when the document is exported as an Animated GIF and played back in a Web browser.

Adding frames

After you decide to animate, the first thing you need to do is add frames. After all, it's impossible to get something to move with just one frame. It also helps — but isn't essential — if you know how many frames it will take to do the animation before you begin. But if you change your mind, you can always add or delete frames at any time.

If you have a visual picture of the animation, sketch each major action change to get an idea of how many frames it will take to pull off your master-piece. (When you create a sketch of each phase of your animation, you are creating a *storyboard.*)

To add one or more frames to the document:

1. **Choose Window➪Frames.**

   The Frames panel opens up.

2. **Click the triangle near the upper right-hand corner of the panel.**

   The Frames menu appears.

3. **Choose Add Frames.**

   The Add Frames dialog box appears (see Figure 14-2).

4. **Click the triangle to the right of the Number field.**

   A slider appears. Drag the slider to select the number of frames you want to add.

5. **Choose an option to determine where the added frames will be placed.**

   - Choose **At the beginning** to place the frames at the beginning of the animation.

   - Choose **Before current frame** to place the new frames before the current frame.

   - Choose **After current frame** to add the new frames after the frame you selected when you called up the Add Frames command.

   - Choose **At the end** to add the new frames at the end of the animation.

6. **Click OK.**

   Fireworks adds the frames to the document, and they appear in the Frames panel.

Figure 14-2:
Adding
frames to
your
animation.

Duplicating frames

You can duplicate a frame to quickly copy the contents of one frame to a new frame. After you've duplicated the frame, you use tools and menu commands to create a desired change to the objects within the frame. To duplicate a frame:

1. **Choose Window⇨Frames.**

   The Frames panel opens.

2. **Select the frame you want to duplicate and drag it to the New/Duplicate Frame button.**

   Fireworks creates a new frame with a carbon copy of the original frame's contents, placing it directly below the original frame, and gives the duplicated frame the next available frame number. If the frame is named, Fireworks duplicates but does not append the frame's name; you'll have to rename it. I show you how to name frames in the "Naming frames" section of this chapter.

Moving selected objects from one frame to another

You can also use the Frames panel to move selected objects from one frame to another. This technique comes in handy when you decide that one object in a frame should actually appear in another frame in the animation. To move an object from one frame to another using the Frames panel:

1. **Choose Window⇨Frames.**

   The Frames panel opens.

2. **Select the frame that the object you want to move appears in.**

   The frame is highlighted.

3. **Using the Pointer tool, select the object on the canvas that you want to move.**

   To add to the selection, hold down the Shift key and click the objects you want to add. A blue rectangle appears in the far right corner of the frame's section in the panel.

4. **In the Frames panel, click the blue rectangle and drag it to the frame you want to move the object(s) to.**

   As you drag over a frame, Fireworks creates a flashing black square so you'll know where you are.

5. **When the flashing black square is over the frame you want the object to appear in, release the mouse button.**

   Fireworks moves the selected object(s) to the frame you specified. Figure 14-3 shows an object on its way to a new home.

Figure 14-3:
The object
in limbo is
part of a
Fireworks
frame
relocation
project.

To quickly copy an object to another frame, select the object you want to copy; then click the blue rectangle to the right of the frame's section in the Frames panel and drag the blue rectangle to another frame while holding down the Alt key (Windows) or Option key (Macintosh). Release the mouse button when the flashing black square is over the frame you want to copy the object to.

Naming frames

When you add frames to an animation, Fireworks automatically creates their names — Frame 1, Frame 2, and so on. In addition to being boring names, these names are also nondescript; the frame name tells you nothing about what's in the frame or what it does. In order to create a more perfect animation, one that makes sense to you when you go to edit the animation, I advise you to get in the habit of playing the Frame Name Game and naming your frames. To name a frame:

1. **Choose Window➪Frames.**

   The Frames panel opens.

2. **Double-click the frame you want to name.**

   A blank window appears on top of the frame's current name.

   Make sure you double-click the frame's name. If you click the panel to the right of the name, you open the Frame Delay dialog box.

3. **Type a name for the frame and then press Enter or Return.**

   Fireworks renames the frame. Figure 14-4 shows a frame in the process of being renamed.

Figure 14-4: Name your frames so you can easily identify their contents.

Deleting frames

You can delete a frame from your animation. This action becomes necessary if the animation has too many frames to download quickly, or you simply no longer need a particular frame's contents in your animation. To delete a frame do one of the following:

✔ Click the frame to select it and then press the Delete Frame button (looks like a trash can).

✔ Click the frame and then drag it to the Delete Frame button.

Arranging frames

When you export a document with frames as an Animated GIF, the frames play one after the other in the order they were created. You can rearrange the order of frames to change the sequence of events in your animation. To rearrange the sequence of frames in an animation:

1. **Choose Window⇨Frames.**

   The Frame panel opens.

2. **Click the frame you want to move and then drag it a new position in the Frames panel.**

   As you drag the frame, a small document icon appears above the cursor. A bold black line flashes when the frame can be positioned between two other frames in the animation.

3. **When the frame is in the desired location, release the mouse button.**

   Fireworks relocates the frame to the desired position. If the frame has the default Fireworks naming convention, the frame is renamed, and the number to the left of the frame's name changes as well to reflect its new position. If you christened the frame with a name, the name remains the same.

Animating Objects

There are many ways to animate objects. All you need to do for action to occur is create a couple of frames, create an object (or objects) in the first frame, and then change them in subsequent frames. You can move the object, rotate it, resize it, skew it, or change its opacity, just to name a few possibilities. Changing an object in consecutive frames is how cartoon animators go about their work — to have the Road Runner outfox Wile E. Coyote for a few seconds requires hundreds of frames of hand-drawn artwork.

In Fireworks you can go the route of the cartoon animator and create a change in every frame, or you can let Fireworks automate the process for you by tweening symbols. Tweening is quick and efficient and works especially well when you're pressed for time. Read on . . . .

Tweening Symbol Instances

In animation, *tweening* is when you create two instances (copies) of a symbol and then change one instance to make it appear different. When you apply the Tween Instances command to the instances, Fireworks fills in the blanks and creates action that you can distribute over a number of frames.

You can use tweening only on symbol instances. Tweening does not work on your garden-variety objects that you create with drawing tools and don't convert to symbols.

To create a tweened animation using an existing symbol:

1. **Choose Window⇨Library.**

   The document Library opens.

2. **Click the name of the symbol you want to animate and drag it onto the canvas and position it.**

   If you haven't created a symbol, the Library (like old Mother Hubbard's cupboard) will be bare. Create an object using any of the drawing tools and then convert it to a symbol by pressing F8.

3. **Select the symbol instance with the Pointer tool, press down the Alt key (Windows) or Option key (Macintosh), and then drag anywhere on the canvas.**

   Fireworks creates another instance of the symbol.

   Holding down the Alt/Option key while dragging a symbol instance is the quickest way to create another instance. If you like, you can also reposition the new instance as you create it by dropping it at the desired point on the canvas.

4. **Use tools or menu commands to make one of the symbol instances appear differently than the other.**

   You can move an instance to a different position, scale it, skew it, rotate it, change its opacity, or even apply an effect to it with the Effects panel. You can apply multiple changes to animate the instance, for example, rotating it and resizing it.

5. **Using the Pointer tool drag a rectangular marquee around both symbol instances.**

   Both objects are selected.

6. **Choose Modify⇨Symbol⇨Tween Instances.**

   The Tween Instance dialog box appears.

7. **Enter the number of steps you want Fireworks to create when tweening the symbol instances.**

   The number of steps you choose determines the number of objects Fireworks creates to tween from one instance to another. If you choose the Distribute to Frames option, discussed in Step 8, each step of the tween is distributed to a frame. Choosing more steps creates more frames, which creates smoother motion in an animation. However, a tween animation with more steps creates a larger file size.

8. **Enable the Distribute to Frames option.**

   When you choose Distribute to Frames, Fireworks creates a separate frame for each step. If you do not choose this option, Fireworks tweens the instances on a single frame and no animation takes place, but you do have multiple objects on the canvas, blending from the first instance to the second instance in the number of steps you specified.

9. **Click OK.**

   Firework adds an equal number of frames as the steps you chose in Step 7. On each frame, Fireworks creates an intermediate shape that looks different than the beginning instance of the shape. These intermediate shapes create a blend from the first instance to the second instance.

10. **To preview the animation, click the Preview tab; then click the Play button.**

    Fireworks plays the animation. Figure 14-5 shows a few examples of instances being tweened.

To preview the animation as it will appear in a Web browser, refer to the "Previewing and Editing Animations" section that appears towards the end of this chapter.

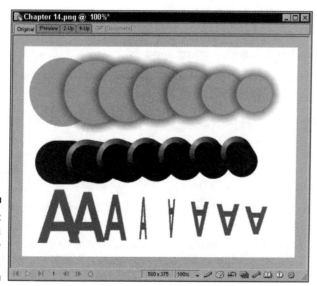

Figure 14-5: Tweening is a great way to animate.

Animating Images

In addition to animating objects and tweening symbol instances, you can create animations using JPEG or GIF images. If you've ever been to a Web site and seen a series of pictures playing like a slide show, you've seen an image animation. In this section I show you how to animate images for fun, and hopefully for profit.

Animating still images

There are several ways to animate still bitmap images in Fireworks. You can modify the way a bitmap appears over time by changing one or more of its characteristics. You can animate a series of still images by changing them from frame to frame. You can also import a series of images, for example, pictures of a person speaking. When you compile the images in an animation, it appears as though it's an actual movie and not just a series of still images.

To animate a single bitmap image:

1. **Choose Window⇨Library.**

   The document Library opens.

2. **Click the triangle near the upper right-hand corner of the window.**

   The Library menu opens.

3. **Choose Import Symbols.**

   The Import Symbols dialog box appears.

4. **Navigate to the image you want to animate and then click Open.**

   Fireworks adds the image to the Library.

5. **Drag an instance of the symbol from the Library to the canvas.**

   Your next move depends on how you want to animate the image. For example, if you want the image to appear gradually over the course of the animation, use the Scale tool to shrink the image and adjust the image's opacity to almost 0.

6. **Create a second instance of the symbol by dragging it from the Library to the canvas.**

   To quickly create another instance of an instance on canvas, select the instance, and then while holding down the Alt (Windows) or Option (Macintosh) key, drag the instance to any location on the canvas.

   Modify the second instance of the object. If you want the object to appear gradually as described in Step 5, don't modify opacity of the second instance at all.

7. **Select both instances and choose Modify⇨Symbol⇨Tween Instances.**

   The Tween Instance dialog box appears.

8. **Enter the number of steps you want Fireworks to use when animating the image; then choose Distribute to Frames.**

9. **Click OK.**

   Fireworks creates additional frames to animate the image.

10. **Click the Preview tab and then click the Play button to preview the animation.**

    Fireworks plays the animation.

To preview the animation as it will appear in a Web browser, refer to the "Previewing and Editing Animations" section that appears towards the end of this chapter.

Animating a series of images or an image sequence

You can also animate a series of images or an image sequence. A *series of images* is a collection of images that are the same size, but of different subjects. An *image sequence* is a collection of images that are the same size, but show different poses of the same subject; for example, a sequence of images of a ballerina dancing. When the sequence of images is compiled, animated, and exported as an Animated GIF, it almost looks like a movie. You use the same technique to animate both types of images. To animate a series of images or an image sequence:

1. **Choose File⇨Open.**

2. **Select the series of images or the image sequence.**

   Select the first image by clicking it. Add additional images to the selection by holding down the Shift key and clicking adjacent image files, or by holding down the Ctrl key and clicking non-contiguous files.

3. **Select the Open as Animation option and then click Open.**

   Fireworks creates a single frame for each image.

When you import a series of images, make sure they are all the same size. If you import images of different sizes, Fireworks creates a document that is large enough for the biggest imported image.

Determining Frame Delay

When a motion picture is created for the silver screen, the number of frames displayed per second determines how the action looks as it occurs. With Animated GIFs however, you can't display a whole lot of images in a second — it would take forever to download. Instead, *frame delay* is what determines how the animation will play. The default frame delay is 7/100 of a second. In other words, the next frame is delayed from displaying for 7/100 of a second. And in even more other words, the frame displays for 7/100 of a second before the next frame is displayed. You can vary the frame delay during the course of the animation. If one frame is more important than others, you can assign a longer frame delay, and Fireworks displays the frame longer when the animation is exported. To set the frame delay for your animations:

1. **After creating an animation, choose Window⇨Frames.**

   The Frames panel opens. The number to the right of each frame's name is the frame's time delay.

2. **Double-click the frame's delay rate.**

   The Frame Delay dialog box opens, as shown in Figure 14-6.

3. **Double-click the current frame delay rate to select it.**

   The frame delay is highlighted.

4. **Enter a new value.**

   Higher values cause a frame to display longer; lower values cause a frame to display for a shorter duration.

5. **Press Enter or Return.**

   Fireworks assigns the new frame delay to the frame.

6. **Repeat Steps 2 through 6 for the remaining frames of the animation.**

To quickly adjust the frame delay for all frames in an animation to the same rate, select the first frame of the animation, and then, while holding down the Shift key, click the last frame in the animation to add them all to the selection. Double-click any frame's delay rate to open the Frame Delay dialog. Type in the desired frame rate; then press Enter or Return, and Fireworks applies the rate to the selected frames.

Figure 14-6:
You change a frame's delay rate in this itty-bitty dialog box.

Using Onion Skins to Preview Animation Frames

When you create an animation of any complexity at all, say for example animating a character's head, you have to make edits on individual frames to pull the whole animation off. When you need to edit across multiple frames, use onion skins, which lets you see more than one frame at a time. *Note:* When you choose the Onion Skins option, images on frames not selected are dimmed.

To use Onion Skins:

1. **Choose Window➪Frames.**

   I know. If you've been reading all along, you know that the Frames panel opens. First off, I thank you for reading the entire chapter. The redundancy is for those folks who aren't reading this book word for word. And you know who you are.

2. **Click the Onion Skins button as shown in Figure 14-7.**

   A drop-down menu appears.

3. **Choose from the following options:**

   - **No Onion Skinning** (default): You see only the selected frame.

   - **Show Next Frame:** Displays only the next frame as an onion skin.

   - **Before and After:** Displays the frames sandwiching the selected frame as onion skins.

   - **Show All Frames:** Displays all frames in the animation as onion skins, except of course for the selected frame, which is displayed normally.

If you're the adventurous sort, choose the Custom option and specify how many frames you want displayed as onion skins and then choose the opacity of the onion skins. I warn you, though, that this involves opening another dialog box and making additional choices.

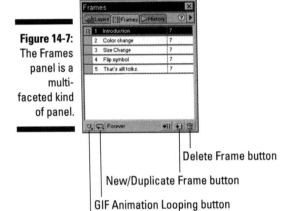

Figure 14-7:
The Frames
panel is a
multi-
faceted kind
of panel.

Delete Frame button

New/Duplicate Frame button

GIF Animation Looping button

Onion Skins button

4. **Choose Multi-Frame Editing (the default) to be able to edit all visible onion-skinned frames, regardless of the selected frame.**

   The Multi-Frame Editing option lets you modify objects in frames other than the current frame. If your animation has a lot of frames and you're using layers to segregate your artwork, you may want to turn this option off to prevent inadvertently editing the wrong object.

   After choosing Onion Skins options, Fireworks displays onion skins as you specified in the drop-down menu. Figure 14-8 shows a document with onion skins enabled. Notice how the images in the onion-skinned frames are dimmed.

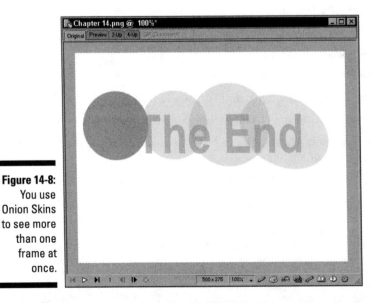

Figure 14-8:
You use
Onion Skins
to see more
than one
frame at
once.

Previewing and Editing Animations

After you've created your animation, you can preview it to determine if everything is playing as you'd envisioned. You can click the Play button in the Original section of the document window and you'll see motion; however, the frame delay rate isn't taken into account in this window. To preview the animation as it will play in a viewer's Web browser:

1. **Choose Window⇨Frames.**

   It's a good idea to have the Frames panel open while previewing your animation. If the animation doesn't play to your liking, you can easily pinpoint which frame is awry.

2. **Choose Window⇨Optimize.**

   The Optimize panel makes a guest appearance.

3. **Click the triangle to the right of the Export File Format field and choose Animated GIF from the drop-down menu.**

   For a refresher course on optimizing artwork for export, refer to Chapter 12.

4. **Click the Preview tab in the document window.**

   The Preview window becomes active.

5. **Click the Play button.**

   Fireworks plays the animation as it will appear in a Web browser after you export it as an Animated GIF. Figure 14-9 shows the Preview window as it appears when previewing an animation.

6. **If the animation is good to go, export it as an Animated GIF.**

   I show you how to export Animated GIFs in Chapter 18.

As you preview the animation, pay attention to how the action flows from frame to frame. If you see a flaw in the animation, you can use the controls in the Preview window to play the animation one frame at a time. When you come to the flawed frame in the animation, click the Original tab to do your editing. Here are a couple of things you can do to fine-tune an animation:

✔ If the animation plays too quickly, increase the frame delay.

✔ If a motion sequence seems too jerky, add additional frames and decrease the distance that objects move between frames.

✔ If an object moves too quickly, either increase the frame delay between frames or add additional frames and decrease the distance that the object moves between frames.

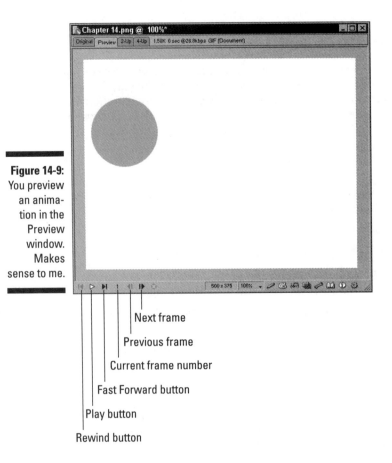

Figure 14-9:
You preview an animation in the Preview window. Makes sense to me.

Chapter 15

Creating Animated Banners and Graphics

Static Web pages have no motion and are, quite frankly, boring. Adding a little motion to a Web page can spice up an otherwise dull site. The motion can take the form of an animated banner that advertises a product or service, or it can be a small animation at the corner of a page's header. Animations are also great introductions to a Web site. In this chapter I show you how to create animations and animated banners for the Web.

Before you plunge headlong into the chapter, I'd like to clarify a few terms for you. A *graphic* is an image that is generally created with vector-based drawing tools. Graphics can, however, incorporate bitmap images. *Image* generally refers to a bitmap, which is an image created in a photo-paint program or a scanned photograph. An *object* is an individual shape or line you create with one of the drawing tools. When you combine shapes and export them, you have a graphic image.

In the last chapter (you did read the last chapter, didn't you?), I introduce you to animation and show you how to incorporate animation symbols (reusable animations) into your Fireworks documents. This chapter deals specifically with creating animations that will be incorporated as artwork within HTML documents as opposed to creating a full-fledged Web page with a Fireworks document.

Getting a Handle on File Size

When you create an animation for a Web page, there are many things you must consider. First and foremost is the size of the file. Most Web surfers are an impatient lot. I know I am. If I visit a Web page and something doesn't download quickly, I'm outta there. You can create the neatest animation in the world, but if no one's around to see it fully downloaded, it's not doing anybody much good.

File size goes hand in hand with many other factors, and it seems that almost everything adds to the size of the file: frames, colors, the number of objects you're animating, and the actual dimensions of the animation itself. Before you blindly rush in and create an animation for the Web, a little thought is in order.

Getting the skinny on bandwidth

Bandwidth is the amount of data that can be downloaded in kilobytes per second at a given connection speed. The faster the connection viewers have, the more data they can download per second, in this case your animation. I could get all technical here and quote you the actual amount of data that can be downloaded per second at a given connection speed, but that's pretty boring stuff, and I'd hate to think you might nod off and collapse face first into the book. So I'll skip that super-techie stuff, which isn't necessary to know, and just tell you to remember this: When you create an animation for the Internet, *less is more.* Every time you add something to an animation or a Web page, it takes longer for the file to appear in the user's Web browser. If the people who will be viewing your animations on the Internet have slow connection speeds, keep your animations as small as possible. When you exceed the bandwidth of a user's connection, the data backs up and the user has to wait for the frames of the animation to fully download before being able to view it in its entirety, all of which can take a very long time.

Connection speeds vary depending upon what part of the country (or world) your audience is in. If your Web pages are geared towards major metropolitan markets, you are fairly safe in assuming most viewers access the Internet with connection speeds close to 56K. If your target audience is wide-ranging, tailor your documents for 28.8K connection speed, which incidentally is the speed that Fireworks uses to display download times in the Preview section of the document window.

Fireworks' document Preview windows give you your best clue as to what a viewer can expect when downloading your animation from the Internet. Both the download time and file size in kilobytes are listed in the window. Whenever you change an optimization setting, add a frame to the animation, change the number of colors in the animation, or add more objects to the

Planning the action

After you've decided what type of banner you're going to create, it's time to think about lights, camera, and action (I've always wanted to say that). Before you begin to create frames and objects, you need to *script* the action. Remember that you're dealing with a limited amount of frames to keep the file size small, so a little bit of preplanning helps you achieve that goal.

To begin scripting your action, create a storyboard. A *storyboard* is a rough sketch of the action that you'll be creating with the banner, which gives you an idea of how many frames you need for the banner.

Less is more.

The storyboard doesn't need to be anything artistic. You can scribble the storyboard on the back of a cocktail napkin, grocery bag, or my all-time favorite, the legal pad. Simply draw a couple of rectangles the approximate dimensions of the banner and start filling in the blanks. When you start filling in the blanks, you can decide whether to use text for the introduction, images, or a combination of both. If you're using images, decide whether you will create them in Fireworks or import a ready-made image, such as a client's picture or logo. The ideal introductory sequence is a single frame; however, if you're going to animate some text, you'll need two or three frames. This won't bloat the file size too badly if you create the banner with a limited color palette and refrain from using bitmap images.

I show you how to animate text in the "Animating text" section of this chapter.

After you've got an idea of what the introduction will be, create the storyboard for the middle of the banner, or the action sequence. This is where you'll animate a character, put objects in motion, or display some images. The amount of action you create determines the number of frames you'll need. If you're contemplating creating a complex character animation, you can skip a lot of the detail and let your viewer's imagination fill in the blanks.

The famous final scene, or *dénouement,* of your animation banner generally calls upon the viewer to take some action. If you've done your job properly and created a small file that downloads quickly and has a clever action sequence, you may just achieve that goal. You can display a button with a text overlay or use the ever present "Click Here" for the banner's final frame. Figures 15-2 through 15-6 show a 5-frame animation that weighs in at a dainty 4.3 kilobytes.

Figure 15-2:
You use the first frame of the animation to get the viewer's attention.

Figure 15-3:
You use the second frame of the animation to begin the action sequence.

Figure 15-4:
As the animation continues, you combine action with a message.

Figure 15-5:
The message builds viewer interest.

Figure 15-6:
The banner
ends with a
call to
action.

Determining the time delay between frames

Certain frames of your animated banners are more important than others. As the director of your production, you determine how long each frame is displayed. The longer a frame is displayed, the more importance a viewer attaches to it.

Use the Frames panel to determine how long each frame is displayed. Fireworks lets you choose different frame delays for each frame. You can choose to display each and every frame for the same amount of time or display the most important frames in your animated banner for a longer period of time. Figure 15-7 shows the Frames panel for an animated banner with different frame delay rates.

If you need a refresher course on the Frames panel or frame delay, refer to Chapter 14.

Figure 15-7:
Use the
Frames
panel to
vary the
amount of
time each
frame in
your banner
is displayed.

Animating text

Text plays an important part in your animated banners because it gets a message (literally) across to the people who are viewing the banner. You can create plain-Jane, ho-hum, here-I-am, yawn-look-at-me text or jump-out, wow, I've-really-got-your-attention-now, snazzy animated text. When you've got a short banner at the top of a tall Web page, animated text can be just the thing to distract viewers' attention to the banner rather than them jumping right into the site.

There are several ways to animate text:

✔ Choose Text➪Convert to Paths to convert the text to editable objects and then use the Freeform tool, Reshape Area tool, or Subselection tool to modify each letter of the text object in subsequent frames. This effectively morphs the text into objects.

✔ Create a block of text in the first frame and then use the Text tool to change to color of the text in subsequent frames, change the text spacing in subsequent frames, or change the baseline of the text in subsequent frames. Remember you can also use the Text tool to modify only part of a text block by selecting certain letters. (If you need a review on working with the Text tool and how to convert text to paths, take a side trip to Chapter 6.)

✔ Create a block of text and flip it, resize it, skew it, or rotate it in subsequent frames.

✔ Create a block of text and then align it to different paths in subsequent frames.

✔ Convert a block of text into a symbol and then use the Tween Instances command to animate different instances of the text block. (To hone up your skills on modifying paths, refer to Chapter 10, which I'm sure held your rapt attention when you read it.)

✔ Create a block of text and then choose Modify➪Animate➪Animate Selection to create an animated text symbol. (I show you how to animate a selection in Chapter 14.)

Linking the banner

After you create the banner, you many want link it to another Web site. You use an HTML editor such as Macromedia's Dreamweaver to link an entire banner to another Web page. However, you can link a specific part of a banner to another Web page by creating a hot spot or button and then assigning a URL to the hot spot or button.

I show you how to create hot spots and URLs in Chapter 16 and rollover buttons in Chapter 17.

Creating Animated GIFs for Web pages

You add Animated GIFs to a Web page to spice things up with a bit of motion. The type of motion is entirely up to you. You can have animated arrows guiding viewers to points of interest or buttons on a Web page. You can have animated characters welcoming viewers to a Web site. Animations also make great introductions to Web sites. Create a small animation with five or six frames that loops one time. Create a hotspot or button in the animation that admits viewers to the site when clicked. Put on your thinking cap and let your inner child run amuck to come up with new and innovative ways to use animations on your Web pages.

If your Animated GIF will be used as an element in a Web page, your first job is to decide how large to create the document that you use to make the Animated GIF. When you incorporate an Animated GIF in a Web page, it is generally fairly small but positioned to attract viewer interest. To incorporate an Animated GIF in a Web page created in Fireworks:

1. **Create the document that will be the Animated GIF within the actual Web page.**

   When you choose the canvas size for the document, consider where the animation will be placed within the main Web page. For example, if you're placing it alongside a static text banner, size the document so it's the same height as the banner.

2. **Create the animation using any of the methods outlined in this chapter or in Chapter 14.**

   Experiment with the different animation methods presented in each chapter. You can animate objects you've created with the drawing tools, animate text, or animate still images to play like a slide show. Remember that you can also create symbols and use the Tween Instance command to quickly animate them. You can also create or import an object and use the Animate Selection command. The animation in the figure that accompanies this section is a series of images that were animated.

3. **Choose Window➪Optimize.**

   The Optimize panel opens. Optimize the document as an Animated GIF.

4. **Export the document.**

   I show you how to export documents in Chapter 18.

5. **Create the document that will serve as the main Web page.**

   Add the necessary elements to flesh out the page such as bitmaps, navigation menus, buttons, pop-up menus, and the like.

6. **After the document is set up just the way you want it, choose File➪Import.**

   The Import dialog box opens.

7. **Navigate to the Animated GIF you just created and click Open.**

   A warning dialog appears, telling you the animation in the symbol extends beyond the last frame in the document. The dialog asks if you want Fireworks to add the necessary frames.

8. **Click OK.**

   Fireworks imports the Animated GIF into the document.

9. **Select the Animated GIF with the Pointer tool and drag it to the desired position in the document.**

10. **With the animation still selected, choose Insert⇨Slice.**

    Fireworks creates a slice the same size as the animation (see Figure 15-8).

11. **With the slice still selected, choose Window⇨Optimize.**

    The Optimize panel opens.

12. **Optimize the slice as an Animated GIF.**

13. **Click anywhere to deselect the slice.**

    The settings in the Optimize panel change back to the default settings for the document. Modify the settings to suit the artwork other than the animation in the document.

14. **Export the entire document.**

    When you export the document as images and HTML, Fireworks exports the animation as an Animated GIF and exports the rest of the document in the format you specified.

Figure 15-8:
Import an Animated GIF into a document, slice it, and you've got motion, baby.

Imported Animated GIF

You can also use an HTML editor to create tables and insert the Animated GIF in one of the cells.

Creating the background

You can use just about anything for the background of an Animated GIF. You can use a pattern, a photograph, or a solid color, or you can create an object the same size as the document with a stroke and a fill. Images created in vector drawing programs such as Macromedia's Freehand (which you can't get for free, but it does give you a free hand to design whatever your heart pleases) are particularly well suited for backgrounds.

You can also use the Fireworks vector-based drawing tools such as the Line tool, Oval tool, or Rectangle tool to create backgrounds. You can create impressive backgrounds, even if you stick with solid colors and a limited palette. Your goal is to create a good background for the animation without creating a file the size of New York City.

Creating the animation

Decide which method you're going to use to create the animation. If you're working with a symbol, use the Tween Instances command to animate different instances of the symbol. Try to create the animation by using a blend of six steps or less and choose the Distribute to Frames option. If the animation isn't to your liking when you preview it and the file size is still fairly small, Undo the command and then redo it using more steps to blend the two instances. (See Chapter 14 for more details.) You can also create an animation by creating an object and then changing it in subsequent frames. Again, remember to work with a limited color palette and a limited number of frames to keep the file size down.

Or you can create a frame-by-frame animation as follows:

1. **Create a new Fireworks document.**

2. **Use the any of the drawing tools to create the object you want to animate.**

   Remember you can use as many objects as you'd like. You can also use layers to segregate the pieces used to create your masterpiece.

   If you create an animation with multiple layers, make sure to enable the Share Across Frames option whenever you create a new layer. By doing this, the layer is available for use when you create new frames. (I show you how to create and manipulate layers in Chapter 10.)

3. **Choose Window⇨Frames.**

   The Frames panel opens.

4. **Select the first frame (at this stage it's all you've got) and drag it to the New/Duplicate Frame button.**

   Fireworks creates a carbon copy of the first frame. Remember to name the new frame, which helps you identify its contents when editing the animation.

5. **Use the Toolbox tools or menu commands to change the object in the new frame.**

6. **After you're done modifying the object in the second frame, create another duplicate frame as outlined in Step 4.**

   Fireworks creates another frame, duplicating the contents of frame 2.

7. **Modify the object in this frame to create action.**

8. **Continue adding frames and modifying the object as needed, but please end the animation before you've got so many frames that the download time is measured in hours instead of seconds.**

9. **Export the document as an Animated GIF.**

   When the file is played back in a Web browser, it will move your viewer.

Looping an Animation

When you create an animation for a Web page, in most cases you want it to play more than once. When you create an animation that plays more than once, you are *looping* the animation. A looped animation will play over and over and over and over . . . well, you get the picture. When a looped animation reaches its last frame, it loops back to the first frame and starts again. When you see an animation in a Web page, it's generally a looped animation. To get you in the loop on looping, do the following:

1. **Create an animation.**

2. **Choose Window⇨Frames.**

   The Frames panel opens.

3. **Click the Gif Animation Looping button (it looks like an oval race-track) at the bottom of the panel.**

   A drop-down menu appears.

4. **Choose one of the following loopy options:**

- Choose **No Looping,** and the animation plays once.

- Choose one of the **number options** (1, 2, 3, 4, 5, 10, or 20), and the animation loops that many times.

- Choose **Forever,** and the animation loops forever or until the person viewing it lapses into a state of severe hypnosis, catatonia, or simply switches to another Web site.

When the Animated GIF is viewed in a Web browser, it loops the specified number of times.

Working with Transparent Color

When you create Animated GIFs, you can assign transparency to colors within the document. Assign transparency to a color when you want the Web page's background color to show in parts of your animation or you want a tiling background image to appear behind your animation.

Matching the canvas and background colors

You can create a transparent canvas color when you create a new document, but you may experience a halo around the objects, especially on a Web page with a dark colored background. In this case, you match the canvas color to the background color of the Web page and then use the canvas color as the transparent color. To match the canvas color with a Web page's background color:

1. **Choose File⇨New.**

   The New Document dialog box appears.

2. **Enter the Width and Height you want the animation to be.**

3. **In the Canvas Color section, select Custom; then click the Custom Color swatch.**

   Your cursor becomes an eyedropper and the color palette appears.

4. **In the Hexadecimal field, enter the value for the background color of the Web page in which the animation will appear.**

   The selected color appears in the color swatch.

5. **Click OK to create the new document.**

6. **Create an animation.**

See all previous sections if you have any questions on creating an animation.

7. **After you create the animation, choose Window⇨Optimize.**

The Optimize panel opens, as shown in Figure 15-9.

8. **Click the triangle to the right of the Export File Format field and choose Animated GIF from the drop-down menu.**

9. **Click the Index Transparency button and then click the canvas color in the document window.**

Be sure to pick an area on the canvas where there are no objects so you don't accidentally select the wrong color.

10. **Export the file.**

When the animation is played back in a Web browser, the selected color is transparent and the Web page's background color shines through.

Figure 15-9:
Choose a
transparent
background
color when
you optimize
the
document.

Set Transparent Index
Color button

Matching the canvas color to a background image's color

If your animation is going to play over a Web page's tiled background image, the best results are achieved if you use the most prominent color in the background image as the canvas color for your Fireworks document and then make the canvas color transparent. The easiest way to match the canvas color to a color from a background image is as follows:

1. **Choose File⇨Open.**

The Open dialog box appears.

2. **Navigate to the Web page's background image and then click Open.**

The image appears in the workspace.

3. **Choose File⇨New.**

   The New Document dialog box appears.

4. **Enter the Width and Height you want the animation to be.**

5. **In the Canvas Color section, select Custom and then click the Custom Color swatch.**

   Your cursor becomes an eyedropper and the color palette appears.

6. **Drag your cursor over the Web page's background image you previously opened.**

   As you drag over the image, the color displayed in the swatch changes.

7. **When your cursor is over the color you want to match, click it.**

   The sampled color appears in the color swatch. After you've sampled the custom canvas color, you can close the background image file.

8. **Click OK to create the new document.**

9. **Create the animation and choose Window⇨Optimize.**

   The Optimize panel appears.

10. **Click the triangle to the right of the Export File Format field, choose Animated GIF from the drop-down menu, and then adjust the other optimization settings.**

11. **Click the Index Color Transparency button and then click the canvas color in the document window.**

12. **Export the file.**

    When the animation is played back in a Web browser, the selected color is transparent and the tiling background image shows through.

Chapter 16

Creating Image Hotspots and Internet Links

- -

- -

*W*hen you create a Fireworks document, it generally ends up on a Web page. Unless you're creating a single page Web site (boring), you'll need to create some kind of navigation for the document that links to other pages within the site or to other sites that have information relevant to the site you're creating the Fireworks document for. You can create buttons or pop-up menus to navigate (I show you how to do this in Chapter 17), or you can create hotspots within the document.

In this chapter, I show you how to create hotspots in your Fireworks document and how to assign URLs to them. I also show you how to use the Slice tool to slice your document into separate pieces, which Fireworks conveniently reassembles for you when you export the document. (You slice an image to create an area that will be interactive or to create an area of the document that will be exported with different optimization settings.)

Creating an Image Map with Hotspots

You create an image map with hotspots to create a navigation system within a Web site. This navigation system doesn't rely on directions or a compass to direct someone who surfs onto the Web page; it uses areas of the image that you designate as hotspots. When users pass a mouse over the hotspot, the cursor changes into a hand signifying that they've discovered a clickable link. So a hotspot isn't an actual image; it's a bit of HTML code that gets exported with the document.

You can assign a hotspot to an existing item in your document or create a hotspot with one of Fireworks handy hotspot tools (fire extinguisher not included). When you create a hotspot in a Fireworks document, the area is tinted an aqua blue. Figure 16-1 shows a document with a few hotspots.

Hotspots

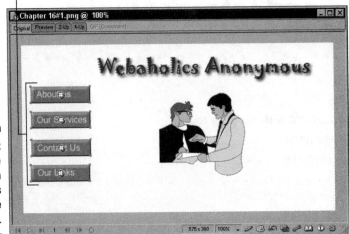

Figure 16-1:
An image map with hotspots is cool to the touch.

Assigning a hotspot to an object

You assign a hotspot to an object to create an interactive link within a document. For example, you can assign a hotspot to a rectangle grouped with a text object. To assign a hotspot to an existing object:

1. **Use the Pointer tool to select the object you want to assign a hotspot to.**

    A blue bounding box appears around the object.

2. **Choose Insert⇨Hotspot.**

    A light blue overlay with a circle in the center appears on top of the object (like you see in Figure 16-1). You use the circle to assign behaviors to the hotspot, something I show you how to do in Chapter 17.

Creating multiple hotspots

You can also create more than one hotspot at a time. This technique is handy if you're pushed for time, and who isn't these days? To create more than one hotspot simultaneously:

1. **Select the first object you want to assign a hotspot to.**

   A bounding box appears around the object.

2. **Hold down the Shift key and click additional objects you want to assign hotspots to.**

   Bounding boxes surround each additional object you add to the selection.

3. **Choose Insert⇨Hotspot.**

   A warning dialog box appears.

4. **Choose an option from the dialog.**

   Click Single to create one hotspot that encompasses the area of the selected objects. Click Multiple to create a hotspot for each of the selected objects. The hotspot(s) are colored aqua blue.

Creating rectangular hotspots

You create a rectangular hotspot when you want to create a rectangular area of the document that is interactive. You can also create a rectangular hotspot when you want to create a larger target area for an object that you want to function as a link, for example, a block of text. To create a rectangular hotspot:

1. **Click the Rectangle Hotspot tool icon in the Toolbox.**

2. **Click the area on the canvas where you want the hotspot to start and then drag down (or up if you're a positive thinker) and to the left or right.**

   As you drag, a blue bounding box gives you a preview of the hotspot's shape and position.

3. **When the hotspot is the size you want, release the mouse button.**

   Fireworks creates a light blue rectangle, signifying the position of the hotspot, with a white circle in its center (see Figure 16-2).

4. **If need be, you can reposition, resize, or otherwise modify the hotspot using tools or menu commands.**

To create a perfectly square hotspot, hold down the Shift key while dragging the tool. Release the mouse button when the square hotspot is the desired size. Remember to release the mouse button before releasing the Shift key.

Figure 16-2:
What's
rectangular
and light
blue? A
rectangular
hotspot.

Creating circular hotspots

You create a circular hotspot to define a circular area of the image that is interactive. You can also use circular hotspots to create a larger target area for a circular section in your image that you want to be interactive, for example, a person's face. To create a circular hotspot:

1. **Click the triangle to the lower right of the tenth icon on the left side of the Toolbox.**

   The tool group expands.

2. **Select the Circle Hotspot tool.**

3. **Click the area on the canvas where you want the hotspot to begin and drag.**

   A light blue circular outline appears, giving you a preview of the circular hotspot's size and location.

4. **When the hotspot is the desired size, release the mouse button.**

   An aqua blue oval with a small white circle in the center graces your canvas, as shown in Figure 16-3. You use the white circle to assign behaviors to the hotspot, something I show you how to do in Chapter 17.

5. **You can now use any of the tools or menu commands to modify the circular hotspot's size or position.**

A hotspot created with the Circle Hotspot tool is perfectly round. You can make it an oval by using the Scale tool.

Figure 16-3:
A circular
hotspot is
the essence
of rotundity.

Creating polygonal hotspots

You create a polygonal hotspot when you have an odd shaped area that you
want to become interactive, say for example a client's logo or a stop sign. To
create an odd shaped hotspot:

1. **Click the triangle in the lower right hand corner of the tenth icon on
   the left side of the Toolbox.**

   The tool group expands.

2. **Click the Polygon Hotspot tool to select it.**

3. **Click the spot on the canvas to define the first point of the hotspot.**

   A blue dot appears on the canvas.

4. **Click to define the second point of the hotspot.**

   The shortest distance between two points appears; yup, a line. A white
   circle appears in the middle of the line.

5. **Continue adding points to define the oddly shaped hotspot.**

   As you add points, the outline of the hotspot takes shape. The hotspot
   shape becomes the lovely aqua blue the program designers seem to
   favor for hotspots.

6. **To close the hotspot shape, click the first point you created.**

   A blue border connects all of the points, and the white circle resides in
   the center of the hotspot. You use the white circle to assign behaviors to
   the hotspot, something I show you how to do in Chapter 17. Figure 16-4
   shows a polygonal hotspot that was created by clicking points along the
   outline of an image.

Figure 16-4:
You use the
Polygon
Hotspot tool
when a
regular
shape just
won't do.

Linking a URL to a hotspot

After you've created a hotspot, you generally link it to something, such as another page within the site or a page at a different Web site. A URL (which stands for *Uniform Resource Locator* and is pronounced *you-are-el)* is like a phone number in the yellow pages, but in this case, your fingers don't do the walking; instead, a click of the mouse on a hotspot with a linked URL transports the clicker to another Web page. To assign a URL to a hotspot:

1. **Use the Pointer tool to select the hotspot.**

   A bounding box surrounds the selected hotspot.

2. **Choose Window⇨Object.**

   The Object panel makes an objective appearance, as shown in Figure 16-5.

3. **To assign a URL to the hotspot, in the Current URL window, drag your cursor over the default No URL, No HREF to select it.**

   The text is highlighted.

4. **Enter the URL you want to assign to the hotspot.**

   Type the full URL of the Web page you want to link to the hotspot using the correct syntax. For example: `http://www.tightwad.com/ scrooge.htm` creates a link to a page called scrooge at a site called tightwad.com.

5. **To keep your Web visitors entertained while the page is downloading, enter some text in the (alt) field. (This is optional.)**

   For example, if you entered "Scrooge's page" in this field for the imaginary Web site in Step 4, "Scrooge's page" displays in the user's Web browser when you pass the mouse over the hotspot.

6. **To open the link in a different target, in the panel's Target section (the red bull's eye) type the name of the HTML frame in which you want the document to open.**

7. **To open the link in a different Web browser window, click the triangle to the right of the Link Target section that is signified by a red bulls-eye icon.**

   A drop-down menu appears.

8. **Select one of the following target options:**

   • **_blank** opens the linked document in a new and unnamed browser window.

   • **_parent** loads the linked document in the window of the frame that contains the link. If the frame isn't nested (meaning it's a frame within a frame Web page), the linked document loads in the full browser window.

   • **_self** loads the linked document in the same frame or window as the link.

   • **_top** loads the document in the full browser window, removing all frames.

9. **To change the color of the hotspot's overlay, click the color swatch and then select a color from the palette that appears.**

   Selecting a different overlay color for a hotspot may come in handy when organizing multiple hotspots in a document.

10. **To change the shape of the hotspot, click the triangle to the right of the Shape field and choose a hotspot shape from the drop-down menu.**

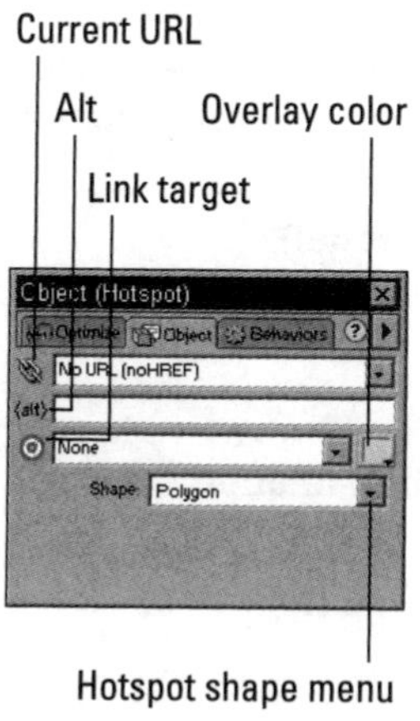

Current URL

Alt   Overlay color

Link target

Figure 16-5: Use the Object panel to assign a URL to a hotspot.

Hotspot shape menu

Assigning a hotspot to an image

Fireworks gives you almost every imaginable tool known to Web designers to create interesting objects to spice up a Web page. Yet sometimes you or your client feel the need to display a photograph on a Web page. And then you want the image to link to something, like another Web page or some tasty bit of scandalous Internet news associated with the smiling face on the image. Lucky for you, Fireworks gives you the capability of creating a hotspot the same size as the image with a mouse click here and a mouse click there. Here's how you do it:

1. **Use the Pointer tool to select the image you want to assign the hotspot to.**

   The image is surrounded with a blue bounding box.

2. **Choose Insert⇨Hotspot.**

   A blue overlay appears over the image with a single white circle in its center.

3. **With the hotspot still selected, choose Window⇨Object.**

   The Object panel appears, and No URL(No HREF) appears in the Current URL field.

4. **If you've already assigned URLs to the document, click the triangle to the right of the Current URL field. If this is the first URL you're using in the document, you may skip to Step 6.**

   A drop-down menu of URLs appears.

5. **Click a URL to select it.**

6. **If you have no URLs assigned to the site, type the URL you want to link to the image.**

   Enter the full URL for the page you want to link to the image. Be sure to use the correct syntax including the proper extension, for example, http://www.mysite.com/mybio.htm.

7. **Enter a message in the (alt) section (optional).**

   The text you enter here will be displayed in the Web browser when you run your mouse over the hotspot.

8. **In the panel's Link Target section (the red bull's eye icon), type the name of the HTML frame to open the link in another target.**

9. **To display the linked page in a different Web browser window, click the triangle to the right of the Link Target field.**

   A drop-down menu appears.

10. **Select one of the following target options:**

    - **_blank** opens the linked document in a brand spanking new browser window.

    - **_parent** loads the linked document in the window of the frame that contains the link. If the frame is not nested, the linked document loads in the full browser window.

    - **_self** loads the linked document in the same frame or window as the link, which happens by default, anyway.

    - **_top** loads the document in the full browser window and gets rid of any frames.

11. **If you don't like the aqua blue color of the hotspot's overlay, click the color swatch and then select a color from the palette that appears.**

    If you've got a lot of hotspots, assigning different colors to the overlays will prevent you from getting hot under the collar when trying to figure out which hotspot goes to which URL and why.

Slicing Images

You create a *slice* in your Fireworks document when you want a part of the image to be exported with different optimization settings. You can also create a slice to add interactivity to your document, such as image swapping or a pop-up menu. Web designers have been slicing and dicing images for their Web pages for years. With other programs, you have to do the math and make sure things line up perfectly and then go through the drudgery of creating a table in an HTML document and hope everything lines up as you planned. Lots of work. With Fireworks, you do the slicing and dicing and then export the document. When you open the document in a Web browser, Fireworks neatly assembles the whole thing in a table, and it all magically fits.

Creating slices

When you decide to get surgical with your Fireworks document and create a slice or four, you have a couple of different options available to you. You can have Fireworks automatically create a slice using an existing object or you can put the document under the knife with the Slice tool.

After you create a slice, you can modify it using tools or menu commands.

Creating a slice using an existing object

Use the automated method of creating a slice when you want to apply different optimization settings to a bitmap image within your document. You can also use an existing object as a slice when you want to assign a behavior to an object, something I show you how to do in Chapter 17. To create a slice using an existing object:

1. **Use the Pointer tool or Select Behind tool to select the item you want to slice.**

   A bounding box appears around the selected object.

2. **Choose Insert⇔Slice.**

   Fireworks wields its mighty scalpel and creates a slice the same size as the object. The only evidence of the slice is the light green overlay with a white circle in its center. At the upper-left-hand corner of the slice the word Slice appears followed by the optimization setting used for the slice (see Figure 16-6).

You can assign a URL to a selected slice by using the Object panel.

Figure 16-6: Fireworks surgeons create slices painlessly.

Using the Slice tools to create a slice

You use the Slice tool to create a slice in a specific area of a document that's a specific size and for a specific purpose. You have two slice tools to work with: the Slice tool, which creates rectangular slices, and the Polygon Slice tool, which creates irregularly shaped slices. To create a slice with the Slice tool:

1. **Select the Slice tool.**

   It's part of the tenth tool group on the right-hand side of the Toolbox.

2. **Click the spot on the canvas that defines the upper-left corner of the slice and then drag down and across.**

   As you drag the tool, a blue bounding box gives you a preview of the slice's size and position.

3. **When the slice is the size you want it, release the mouse button.**

   A light green overlay with a white circle appears where you used the tool. The word Slice appears in the upper-left-hand corner of the slice followed by the optimization method currently applied to the slice.

4. **You can resize the slice or move it using menu commands or tools.**

To delete a slice, select it with the Pointer tool and press the Delete key or choose Edit➪Cut.

You use the Polygon Slice tool to create an irregularly shaped slice. The Polygon Slice tool gives you point-to-point control over the slicing process, much like carving your Thanksgiving turkey. After you create the slice, you can modify the position of individual points in the slice to create the perfect slice. To create a slice with the Polygon Slice tool:

1. **Select the Polygon Slice tool.**

   The Polygon Slice tool hangs out with his buddy the Slice tool. They're the tenth tool group on the right-hand side of the Toolbox. If the Slice tool is displaying its smiling edifice, click the triangle to the lower right of its icon and then click the Polygon Slice tool to select it.

2. **Click a spot on the canvas where you want the irregularly shaped slice to begin.**

   A blue dot signifies the beginning of the slice.

3. **Click the spot on the canvas that defines the next point of your slice.**

   A line connects the two points, and the slice begins to take shape.

4. **Continue clicking to add additional points to the slice.**

   Line segments connect the points.

5. **To close the slice, click the first point you created.**

   Fireworks creates a bounding box that connects all the points, and a green overlay with a white dot appears in its center. Fireworks brands the slice by printing the word Slice in the slice's upper left hand corner, followed by the optimization method used on the slice. You can now move the slice or otherwise modify it using tools or menu commands. Figure 16-7 shows an irregularly shaped slice created with the Polygon Slice tool.

If the slice isn't perfect, you can modify the slice by using the Subselection tool to move individual points.

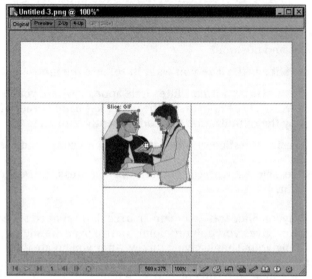

Figure 16-7:
For a slice
of the
irregular,
the Polygon
Slice tool is
the tool
to use.

You can create guides for your slices. The Slice tool will snap to guides, a useful feature when you need to create several slices of exact measurements in a document. To get the skinny on how to create guides, refer to Chapter 2.

Optimizing slices

One of the big advantages of slicing a document is that it gives you the ability to use different optimizations on different parts of your document. Bitmap images look better when exported in the .jpg format and, as a rule, have smaller file sizes than if they had been exported in .gif format. Text objects and other objects with solid color look better and are more bandwidth friendly when exported in the .gif format. When you have a potpourri of different objects in a document, create slices for those you want to export with different settings and then optimize each slice. To optimize a slice:

1. **Use the Pointer tool or Select Behind tool to select the slice you want to optimize.**

   A bounding box surrounds the slice, and the word Slice, along with the current optimization format method, are displayed.

2. **Choose Window➪Optimize.**

   The Optimize panel appears at the optimal moment.

3. Select the desired settings for the slice.

After you select the settings for the slice, the new format (if indeed you chose a new format rather than modify the settings for the existing format) is displayed next to the word `Slice`. When you export the document, Fireworks applies the optimization settings you specified to the slice.

To learn how to optimize in the optimal amount of time, check out Chapter 12.

Using the URL Panel

The Internet is always in a state of flux. New domains appear, old domains disappear, pages that once were aren't anymore, and so forth and so on. All of these Internet sites that are fluxing about have URLs, which is how you find them when you're surfing the net. When you create a Fireworks document that uses a lot of links, you end up having a lot of URLs to bother about. If you've had more than just a passing fancy with the Internet, you know that some of these URLs can be quite long and quite a bother to type. Isn't it nice to know that instead of having to type `http://www.my_supercreative_artful_imaginative_website.com` 20 times, you can rely on Fireworks to take care of the grunt work?

Use the URL panel to manage all the URLs used in the current document. You can also use the URL panel to import URLs, export URLs, add URLs to the Library, and delete URLs from the Library. But before you can do anything with the URL panel, you have to open the URL panel, shown in Figure 16-8. Do so by choosing Window⇨URL.

Current URL

Currently loaded URL Library

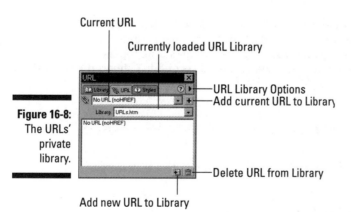

Figure 16-8: The URLs' private library.

URL Library Options

Add current URL to Library

Delete URL from Library

Add new URL to Library

As you can see from the figure above, URLs aren't pretty — although their creators think they are. URLs are Web addresses that you use to create links to parts of your documents such as buttons, hotspots, and slices. When a URL is assigned to an interactive area of the document, the area becomes a hyperlink that when clicked, transports the viewer to another Web site.

Adding URLs

You can save yourself a lot of work if you learn how to use the URL Library. If you're going to use the same URLs repeatedly in a project, you can add them to the URL Library. Every URL in the URL Library can be assigned to a button, hotspot, or slice by using the Object panel. Adding URLs to the URL Library takes the drudgery out of typing in a Web address for each and every button, hotspot, or slice you create. Of course if you're into drudgery, feel free to skip to the next chapter.

To add a URL to the URL Library:

1. **Choose Window➪URL.**

   The URL panel opens.

2. **Click the Add New URL to Library button at the bottom of the panel.**

   The Add New URL window opens.

3. **Type the URL into the dialog box being careful to use correct syntax and then click OK.**

   Fireworks adds the address to the URL Library, and it becomes available in the Object panel whenever you create a button, hotspot, or slice object.

When you add a URL to the URL Library, it is added to the currently loaded URL Library (URLs.htm by default). When you select a hotspot or slice and then open the Object panel, you may see two lists. The top list shows the URLs used in the current document, and the second list shows the URLs that are in the currently loaded URL Library.

Deleting URLs

Just as you can add, you can also delete. To delete a URL from the URL Library:

1. **Choose Window➪URL.**

   The URL panel opens.

2. **Click the URL that you want to delete.**

   The URL becomes highlighted.

3. **Click the Delete URL button (looks like a trash can).**

   The URL is deleted from the Library.

Creating URLs for an entire site

If you're creating a Web site from scratch using Fireworks, you can save yourself an immense amount of time by using the URL panel. As soon as you know the domain name for the site, determine how many individual links you'll need within the site. A simple site may consist of the home page, an About Us page, an Our Services page, and an Our Links page. To quickly create URLs for the entire site:

1. **Choose File⇨New.**

   The New Document dialog box appears. Fill in the fields to create the document that will become the home page for the site. On most Web servers, the home page is referred to as index.htm.

2. **After creating the new document, choose Window⇨URL.**

   The URL panel opens.

3. **Click the Add New URL to Library button at the bottom of the URL panel.**

   The new URL dialog box appears.

4. **Enter the URL for the domain, for example,** `http://www.mysite.com`**, and then click OK.**

   The URL is added to the URL Library and is displayed in the Current URL window.

Now it's time to add the URLs for the pages in the site. For the hypothetical Web site in this example, you have four pages:

- ✔ The home page, which will be index.htm
- ✔ The About Us page, which will be called about.htm
- ✔ The Our Services pages, which will be called services.htm
- ✔ The Our Links page, which will be called links.htm

You can enter any name you want for a page, but keep in mind that somewhere along the line, someone may actually have to type the address in a Web browser. So it's best to follow the KISS theorem when creating names for your pages: Keep It Small, Simple.

If you're creating a name for a Web page and you must use more than one word, do not leave a space between words. Web browsers do weird things when they see space. To differentiate the two words, use an underscore between them. For example, `http://www.mysite.com/two_words.htm`.

After you've named the pages and assigned a URL to each, it's time to add the URLs to the Library. To finish adding your site's URLs to the URL Library:

1. **To enter the address for the home page, click inside the Current URL field and position the cursor to the right of the address already in the window.**

   If you've been following this example, you'll see a flashing vertical bar to the right of `http://www.mysite.com`.

2. **Type a forward slash (/) and then type** index.htm.

3. **Click the Add Current URL to Library button (it looks like a plus sign) to the right of the Current URL field.**

   Fireworks adds the current URL to the URL Library.

4. **Click the base URL for the domain, which for this example is** `http://www.mysite.com`.

   Fireworks displays the selected URL in the Current URL field.

5. **To add the URL for the About Us page, position the cursor to the right of the URL, type a forward slash followed by about.htm (/about.htm), and then click the Add Current URL to Library button.**

   Fireworks adds the URL to the URL Library.

6. **Repeat Steps 3 through 5 for the remaining pages in the site (services.htm and links.htm).**

   Fireworks adds the URLs to the URL Library. The completed URL Library for `http://www.mysite.com` is shown in Figure 16-9.

Figure 16-9:
You can use the URL Library to quickly create URLs for a Web site.

URL
Library URL Styles
No URL (noHREF)
Library: URLs.htm
No URL (noHREF)
http://www.mysite.com
http://www.mysite.com/about.htm
http://www.mysite.com/index.htm
http://www.mysite.com/links.htm
http://www.mysite.com/services.htm

Saving a URL Library

When you use Fireworks to create several different pages for a site, you can save a lot of time by saving the URL Library from the home page. When you save a URL Library, Fireworks creates an HTML document with all the URLs in the Library. To save a URL Library:

1. **Create a home page and add all of the site's URLs to the URL Library.**

   If you don't know how to do this and just randomly jumped to this point in the chapter because it sounded cool, please read the previous section.

2. **Open the URL panel by choosing Window⇨URL.**

   The URL panel opens.

3. **Click the triangle near the upper right-hand corner of the URL panel.**

   A drop-down menu appears.

4. **Choose Export URLs.**

   The Save As dialog box appears.

5. **Navigate to the folder where you want to store the URL Library.**

   I suggest you save the URL Library in the same folder where you're storing the rest of the documents for the Web site.

6. **Enter a name for the URL Library and then click OK.**

   Fireworks saves the file as an HTML document for future use.

When you create additional documents for a Web site, you can use a saved URL Library instead of typing URLs for the new document. Simply open the URL Library for the new document by choosing Window⇨URL. After the URL panel opens, click the triangle near the top-right corner of the panel, choose Import URLs and import the HTML document the URL Library was saved in.

Managing URLs

You can also use the URL panel to add, edit, or delete URLs within the document and import URLs from other documents. To manage URLs within a document, you use the URL panel Options menu. To open the URL panel Options menu:

1. **Choose Window⇨URL.**

   The URL panel opens.

2. **Click the triangle near the upper right corner of the panel.**

   The URL panel Options menu opens.

3. **Select the desired command to manage the URLs in your document.**

Chapter 17

Creating Interactive Web Pages

● ●

In This Chapter

▶ Creating buttons

▶ Linking up with the Link Wizard

▶ Making a navigation bar

▶ Creating pop-up menus

▶ Assigning behaviors

▶ Swapping images

● ●

*W*eb sites should be exciting and give the user something to do when he or she gets there. Just about every Web site has links to other pages in the site; many of them are your garden-variety text links that are quite predictable and quite boring. Just about anybody can create a text link with a Web-kit-in-a-box HTML editor. But you're better than that; otherwise, you wouldn't be reading this chapter.

To make your navigation links and Web pages stand out, you assign *behaviors* to them. Behaviors add pizzazz and interactivity to your designs. In this chapter, I show you how to use behaviors to spice up your Web designs and also show you how to create pop-up menus, a task that used to be quite difficult for even the most experienced Web developers.

Creating Buttons

Use buttons as navigation devices in your Web designs. A link is assigned to a button that when clicked, transports the viewer to another page in the site, or maybe even another site. The buttons you create in Fireworks are quite sophisticated. In other programs, you'd have to know how to write JavaScript to create the same effects, but good old Fireworks has an editor that leads you through the process and then generates the JavaScript that creates all the button magic when you export the document.

When you create a button in Fireworks, you are creating a symbol, which Fireworks adds to the document Library. You can use the button in different parts of your Fireworks creations by dragging an instance from the Library to the canvas and assigning a link to it. (For more information on symbols and the Library, see Chapter 13.)

The first step in the button creation process is to open up the button editor. To open the Button Editor (shown in Figure 17-1), choose Insert⇨New Button.

You can also open the Button Editor by choosing Insert⇨New Symbol and assigning the Button behavior to the symbol. You can also convert a selected object to a button by choosing Insert⇨Convert to Symbol and assigning the Button behavior to the symbol.

Figure 17-1:
Use the
Button
Editor to
create
rollover
buttons.

Rolling out the rollover state

A button's *rollover state* displays a different graphic (that you create in Fireworks or import) depending upon where the user's mouse is in relation to the button. Each button can have up to four rollover states. The four rollover states are:

- ✔ The **Up** state graphic is displayed when the user's mouse is not interacting with the button. This is the default state for the button.

- ✔ The **Over** state graphic is displayed when the user's mouse rolls over the button. When visitors to your Web site see a different image, they know they've discovered a button that will do something when clicked.

✔ The **Down** state graphic is displayed when a button is clicked or while the button is depressed.

✔ The **Over While Down** state graphic is displayed after the user has clicked the button. This state is used for navigation menus and not for simple rollovers.

Creating buttons with multiple states

When you create a button, you create different images or variations of the same image for each button state that you use. The simplest button employs the Up and Over states. (All the buttons you create in Fireworks use these two states.) If you neglect to put a graphic in the Over state, the button disappears from view when the user's mouse passes over it. And you wouldn't want a visitor to a Web site created by you wondering where the button went, would you?

Before you rush in and create your first button, I want to take a second to explain the Button Editor. The Button Editor has an individual tab for each button state, plus an additional tab entitled Active Area. The Active Area tab is where you define the target area of the button. By default, a button's active or target area is a rectangle that encompasses an area equal to the perimeter of the graphic images used for each of the button's states. You can increase a button's active area to give the user a larger button target, which is useful when you're using a small graphic or a single line of text for the button. To create a multi-state button:

1. **Choose Insert⇨New Button.**

   Fireworks opens up the Button Editor and the Up tab is displayed.

2. **Use the drawing tools to create the image for the Up state or import an image for the Up state. Figure 17-2 shows the Up tab of the Button Editor with a typical pill shape.**

   Although it's not essential, aligning the button's shape to the center of the Button Editor's Workspace is a good idea. When you align the shape to the center of the Button Editor, the button's registration point is centered, which makes precise alignment on the canvas much easier.

3. **Click the Over tab.**

   Fireworks gives you a blank canvas to create the object that will be displayed for the button's Over state.

4. **To display the same basic shape for the button's Over state, click the Copy Up Graphic button.**

   Fireworks copies the graphic from the Up tab to the Over tab.

You can also create a different object for the button's Over state. If the buttons in your document will be placed close together, make sure the different shapes you use for each state are close in size.

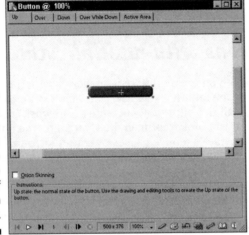

Figure 17-2:
Create the
basic shape
for the
button in the
Up tab of
the Button
Editor.

5. **Modify the object to create a different appearance for the Over state graphic.**

You can use any effect to make the shape appear different — change its color or even skew it. If you're creating a complex button — using many shapes or a text overlay to identify each button state — you can add layers to the button. If you had text displayed on the button's Up state, you can delete it or change the color of the text object. Figure 17-3 shows the graphic from Figure 17-2 as it appears in the button's Over state.

Figure 17-3:
Change the
button's
appearance
in the Over
state.

6. **If you're creating a button with the Down state, click the Down tab.**

   Fireworks opens the Down section of the button editor and gives you a clean sheet of virtual paper to create an object on.

7. **To use the graphic from the Over state, click the Copy Over Graphic Button; otherwise, create or import the graphic you want displayed when the button is clicked.**

   If you're copying up the graphic from the Over state, modify it so the button has a different appearance when someone clicks it.

8. **If you're using the Over While Down state for your button, click the Over While Down tab.**

   Fireworks opens the Over While Down section of the Button Editor, and you have yet another blank canvas before you.

9. **Either click the Copy Down Graphic button or create a new shape for the button's Over While Down state.**

   If you copied up the graphic, modify it to give the button a different look in this state.

10. **To increase a button's active area, click the Active tab.**

    Fireworks opens the Active section of the Button Editor. The button's active area is designated by a light green overlay.

11. **Click the green overlay.**

    Fireworks creates a bounding box with four dots around the active area.

12. **Select the Subselect tool, and click one of the dots and drag to increase the button's target area.**

13. **Close the Button Editor to complete the button.**

    Fireworks creates the button on the canvas and adds a curved arrow in its lower left corner that identifies it as a symbol. Fireworks also adds the word Button followed by the current optimization format.

You can use an imported bitmap image as a button. Select the image and then choose Insert⇨Convert to Symbol. (Be sure to specify Button as the symbol type and remember to copy the image in the Over state or the button will disappear when a user's mouse is over it.)

Using onion skinning

You use onion skinning when you're creating a button with different shapes or combining objects, such as a shape and text to create the button. When you enable onion skinning in the Button Editor, you can see the shapes for each button state and edit them, even if you're in a different section of the Button Editor than the shape. For example, you can edit the shape used for the button's Up state while you're in the Over While Down section of the Button Editor. (The only time you can't select an object from another section of the Button Editor is if it's covered by the shape in the section of the editor you are currently editing. Then you can use the Select Behind tool to select the shape from the section before the section you are currently editing.)

To enable onion skinning in the button editor, click the checkbox to the left of the option. Figure 17-4 shows a button being created in the Button Editor with onion skinning in action.

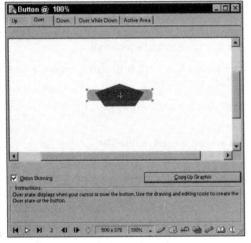

Figure 17-4:
With onion skinning, you can easily edit all shapes used to create a button.

Using the Link Wizard

The Link Wizard is your link to links. That may sound like double-talk, but it isn't. You use the Link Wizard to change export settings for a button, assign URLs to buttons, open a URL in a different target window, and assign a unique filename to a button. The Link Wizard really is a wizard when it comes to linking your buttons.

Changing a button's export settings

When you create a button in a document and then export the document, Fireworks creates a slice (an area of the document that gets exported as a separate image and is reassembled in an HTML document) for the button. By default, Fireworks exports the button with the same settings as the rest of the document. You can, however, use the Link Wizard to change the export settings of the button. This feature comes in handy when your document is being exported in the JPEG format and you want to export the button and its text as GIF images. To change a button's export settings:

1. **Using the Pointer tool to select the button whose export settings you want to change.**

2. **Choose Window⇨Object.**

   Fireworks opens the Object panel.

3. **Click the Link Wizard button at the bottom of the panel.**

   If you have more than one instance of the button in your document, Fireworks opens a dialog box asking you if you want to edit all instances of the button in the document or only the currently selected one.

4. **Click Current to apply the link to the selected button or click All to assign the link to all instances of the button in the document.**

   Fireworks opens the Link Wizard. The Export Settings section is selected by default.

   When you use the Object panel to modify an instance of a button symbol, Fireworks creates a duplicate of the button symbol in the document Library with the new settings applied.

5. **Click the triangle to the right of the Export defaults field and select an export setting.**

   To edit the settings in the Export Preview window, click the Edit button. I show you how to use the Export Preview window in Chapter 18.

6. **Click OK to apply the export settings to the button.**

You can use the Next and Previous buttons to navigate from section to section in the Link Wizard instead of clicking the tabs.

Adding a link to a button

Unless you want to totally dumbfound or flummox people who visit your Web designs, a button should be linked to something — another page in the site or another Web site. If you build it, they will click. To add a link to a button:

1. **Using the Pointer tool, select a button in your document.**

2. **Choose Window⇨Object.**

   The Object panel opens.

3. **Click the Link Wizard button at the bottom of the panel.**

   If you have more than one instance of the button in your document, Fireworks opens a dialog box asking you if you want to edit all instances of the button used in the document or only the currently selected one.

4. **Click Current to apply the link to the selected button or click All to assign the link to all instances of the button in the document.**

   Fireworks opens the Link Wizard.

5. **Click the Link tab.**

   The Link section of the Link Wizard opens.

6. **In the URL field (it has a chain link icon to its left) enter the URL for the page the button will link to.**

   If you already have URLs that you've used in the document or you want to use a URL from the currently loaded URL library, click the triangle to the right of the URL window and select a URL from the drop-down menu. If you're creating a URL from scratch, remember to use proper syntax when entering the URL, for example, `http://www.votingfordummies.com/butterfly_ballot.htm`.

7. **To open a URL in a specified frame or browser window, click the Target tab.**

   Fireworks opens the Target section of the Link Wizard.

8. **Choose one of the following target options:**

   - **_blank** opens the linked document in a brand new, unnamed browser window.

   - **_parent** loads the linked document in the window of the frame that contains the link. If the frame isn't nested, the linked document loads in the full browser window.

   - **_self** loads the linked document in the same frame or window as the link.

   - **_top** loads the document in the full browser window, removing all frames.

9. **Click OK.**

 You can also open the Link Wizard from the Button Editor by clicking the Active Area tab and then clicking the Link Wizard button below the Button Editor's work area window.

Adding messages to browser status bars

You can use the Link Wizard to display a message in a Web browser's status bar when a mouse passes over the button. Add a message to a Web browser's status bar when you want to give viewers a better idea of what they'll see when they click the button. For example, if you're creating a Web site for a photographer, you might add a message to a status bar that says, "Click here to view my portfolio." To add a message to a browser's status bar:

 1. **Use the Pointer tool to select the button that will trigger the message display when clicked.**

2. **Choose Window⇨Object.**

   The Object panel opens.

3. Click the Link Wizard button at the bottom of the panel.

The Link Wizard appears.

4. Click the Link tab.

The Link section of the Link Wizard is open for business. At the bottom of the Link section, away from everything else in the Link section, is a window that says Status Bar Text (Optional).

5. In the Status Bar Text field, enter the message that you want displayed on the status bar when the user's mouse rolls over the button.

6. Click OK.

Creating a Navigation Bar — Without a Compass

A navigation bar is a series of buttons that are used for navigation throughout a Web site. Whether you place the navigation bar vertically or horizontally depends upon the number of buttons you have in the Web site and your personal taste. To create a navigation bar for a Web site with a home page, an About Us page, an Our Services page and a Contact Us page, do the following:

1. Choose Insert⇨New Button.

Fireworks opens the Button Editor.

2. Use the Rectangle tool to create a rectangular button shape.

Choose a tasteful fill color that contrasts well with the document's background. If desired, use the Effect panel to apply an effect such as the Inner Bevel to the rectangle.

3. Select the Text tool.

Fireworks opens the Text Editor.

4. Select your favorite font style, font size, and font color for the button's text.

Choose a color that contrasts well with the button.

5. Type the word Home **and then Click OK.**

Fireworks closes down the Text Editor.

6. Align the text to the left side of the button.

7. Click the Over tab.

Fireworks opens the Over section of the Button Editor.

8. Click the Copy Up Graphic button.

Fireworks copies the button's shape and text to the Over section.

9. **Use the Pointer tool to select the text and then press Delete.**

When the document is published, text won't be displayed in the button's Over state.

10. **Select the rectangular shape; then in the Colors section of the Toolbox, click the Fill Color well.**

The color palette appears.

11. **Select a different color than the one you used for the shape in the Up state.**

12. **Click the Active Area tab.**

Fireworks open the Active Area section of the Button Editor.

13. **Click the Link Wizard button.**

Fireworks summons the Link Wizard.

14. **Click the Link tab.**

Fireworks opens the Link section of the Link Wizard.

15. **Enter the URL for the site's home page.**

Most Web hosting services refer to the home page as index.htm. A typical URL for a site's home page would be something like: `http://www.mywebsite.com/index.htm`.

16. **Click OK.**

Fireworks closes the Link Wizard.

17. **Close the Button Editor.**

Fireworks creates the button. Your button should resemble Figure 17-5.

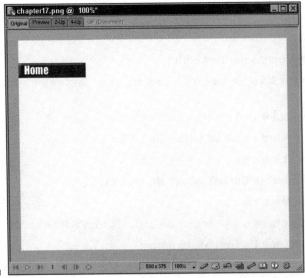

Figure 17-5:
You begin
building a
navigation
bar by
creating a
single
button.

To get an idea of what a button looks in the document window, click the Hide Slices button in the View section of the Toolbox and Fireworks hides the slice overlays and slice lines. You can also preview the button's rollover states in the Preview, 2-Up, and 4-Up tabs.

The first button for the navigation bar is a symbol. To finish creating the navigation bar, you create instances of the button symbol and modify the text. To complete the navigation bar:

1. **Use the Pointer tool to select the button you just created, and while holding down the Alt key (Windows) or Option key (Macintosh) drag the button to the right.**

   Fireworks creates an instance of the button symbol.

   You can also create an instance of a button by choosing Window⮞Library and then dragging the button to the canvas.

2. **Align the instance you just created next to the first button.**

3. **With the second instance still selected, hold down the Alt key (Windows) or Option key (Macintosh) and drag to the right.**

   Fireworks creates a third instance of the symbol.

4. **Position the new button next to the other two.**

5. **Hold down the Alt key (Windows) or Option key (Macintosh) and drag to the right to create a fourth instance of the button.**

6. **Align the last button to the other three. Your partially completed navigation bar should resemble Figure 17-6.**

Figure 17-6:
You create instances of a single button to create a navigation bar.

When you create a navigation bar from scratch, you generally align it with other graphic elements in the site, for example a header with text and perhaps a logo. To properly align the buttons to themselves and the other elements on the page, you'll find it helpful to create a set of guidelines.

Okay, now that you've got your buttons all in a row, it's time to complete the navigation bar. The fact that buttons are symbols means that you can modify each instance without affecting the other buttons. When you apply a modification to the current button instance, Fireworks creates a duplicate of the original button symbol with the new modifications applied. To finish the navigation bar, you modify each button's text and link. Here's how you do it:

1. **Double-click the second button on the navigation bar.**

   Fireworks displays a dialog box asking if you want to edit all instances or just the current one.

2. **Click Current.**

   Fireworks opens the button in the Button Editor.

3. **Double-click the text object.**

   Fireworks opens the Text Editor.

4. **Select the block of text, type** About Us **and click OK.**

   Fireworks closes the Text Editor and displays the new text on the button.

5. **Click the Active Area tab.**

   Fireworks opens the Active Area section of the Button Editor.

6. **Click the Link Wizard.**

   Fireworks opens the Link Wizard.

7. **Click the Link tab.**

   Fireworks opens the Link Wizard's Links section.

8. **Enter the URL for the About Us page.**

   In this hypothetical example, the URL would be: http://www.mywebsite.com/about.htm.

9. **Click OK.**

   Fireworks assigns the new URL to the button.

10. **Close the Button Editor.**

    Fireworks modifies the instance of the button.

11. **To modify the next button, repeat Steps 1–10.**

    Rename this instance of the button to Our Services. Modify the URL to read: http://www.mywebsite.com /services.htm.

12. **To modify the final button, repeat Steps 1–10.**

Rename this instance of the button to Contact Us. Modify the URL to read: `http://www.mywebsite.com /contact.htm`. Figure 17-7 shows the completed navigation bar as it might appear in a Web site, complete with a nifty banner.

Figure 17-7:
Navigation bars can be created quickly by modifying instances of a button symbol.

To create a template for an entire Web site, create the common graphic items that will be shared throughout the site (such as the site's name and perhaps a logo) and then create the navigation bar. Save the document in Fireworks' native .png format. Use the Save As command to save the document under the names of the other pages used in the site, for example, About, Contact, and Services. Then it's a simple matter of adding the text and images to flesh out the individual pages.

Creating a Pop-Up Menu

One of the coolest new effects in Fireworks 4 is the pop-up menu. The old way to create a pop-up menu involved creating a lot of JavaScript. And if you've ever worked with JavaScript, you know how much fun it isn't.

You use *pop-up menus* when you've got a complex site with a lot of links. For example, if you're creating a site for a company that wants a separate page for each of their 20 services, that's 20 links you've got to create. You could create one link for services on the home page and then create a services page with 20 links to each page, or you could create a pop-up menu with all the links in one convenient package. To create a pop-up menu:

1. **Create a hotspot by using one of the hotspot tools or by selecting an existing object and then choosing Insert⇨Hotspot.**

   Fireworks creates an aqua-colored hotspot with a circle in the center.

   You can also use a selected slice as the starting point for a pop-up menu.

2. **Move your cursor towards the circle and click it.**

   As you move your cursor towards the circle, it becomes a hand. After you click the circle, Fireworks opens the Behaviors menu.

3. **Choose Add Pop-up Menu.**

   Fireworks opens the Set Pop-up menu dialog box.

4. **In the Text field, type the text you want to appear for the first item on the pop-up menu.**

5. **In the Link field, enter the URL for the page you want to link to the pop-up menu item.**

   You can enter a URL by typing the address in the field or by clicking the triangle to the right of the field and choosing a URL from the menu.

6. **Click the plus sign (+) button to add the item to the menu.**

   Fireworks adds the text and the link to the menu.

7. **To create another item for the menu, enter the menu name in the Text Field, enter the URL in the link field, and then click the plus sign (+) button.**

   Fireworks adds the new item to the menu. Continue adding text and links for all of the items you want to display on the pop-up menu.

8. **To create a submenu, you indent one or more menu items. To indent a menu item, select it and then click the Indent Menu button (Windows) or the Create Menu button (Macintosh).**

   Indented menu items are shifted over. When a document with indented menu items is exported, the first menu item is displayed when the user's mouse rolls over the hotspot. A small arrow appears to the right of the item with additional indented links. Figure 17-8 shows the Set Pop-Up Menu dialog box with several items and links. Notice the indented menu items.

9. **After adding the desired menu items and links, click the Next button.**

   Fireworks opens the second section of the dialog box. In this section, you choose whether to display the menu cells as text in HTML format cells or text with image cells.

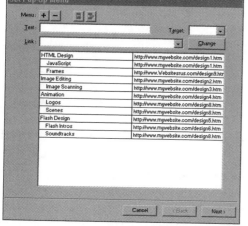

Figure 17-8:
You use the
Set Pop-Up
Menu dialog
box to
create items
and links for
a pop-up
menu.

10. **To display the menu cells in HTML format, enable the HTML option and set the following parameters:**

    • Click the triangle to the right of the **Font** field and select a font style from the drop-down menu.

    • Click the triangle to the right of the **Size** field and select a font size from the drop-down menu.

    • In the **Up State** section, click the Text Color swatch and choose a color from the palette. This is the text color that displays when the cell is dormant.

    • In the **Up State** section, click the Cell Color swatch and choose a color from the palette. This determines the cell's color when the cell is dormant.

    • In the **Over State** section, click the Text Color swatch and choose a color from the palette. This is the text color that displays when the user's mouse rolls over the cell.

    • In the **Over State** section, click the Cell Color swatch and choose a color from the palette. This determines the cell's color when the user's mouse rolls over the cell. Figure 17-9 shows the settings for a pop-up menu using HTML formatting.

11. **To display the cells as images, click the Image option and set the following parameters:**

    • Click the triangle next to the **Font** field and select a font style from the drop-down menu.

- Click the triangle next to the **Size** field and select a font size from the drop-down menu.

- In the **Up State** section, click the Text Color swatch and choose a color from the palette. This is the text color that displays when the cell is dormant.

- In the **Up State** section, click the Cell Color swatch and choose a color from the palette. This determines the cell image's color when the cell is dormant.

- In the **Up State** section, select style for the cell. This is the image that displays when the cell is dormant.

- In the **Over State** section, click the Text Color swatch and choose a color from the palette. This is the text color that displays when the user's mouse rolls over the cell.

- In the **Over State** section, click the Cell Color swatch and choose a color from the palette. This determines the cell image's color when the user's mouse rolls over the cell.

- In the **Over State** section, select a style for the cell. This is the image that displays when the user's mouse rolls over the cell. Figure 17-10 shows the settings for a pop-up menu using Image formatting.

12. **Click Finish.**

     Fireworks creates the JavaScript that exports with the document. Fireworks draws an aqua blue bounding box showing the menu's outline and each cell with a blue line connecting the menu to the hotspot or slice. Figure 17-11 shows the completed pop-up menu as it will appear in a Web browser. The cells in this menu are displayed as images.

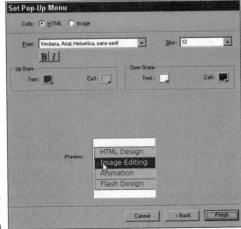

Figure 17-9: You set these parameters to display a pop-up menu with HTML formatting.

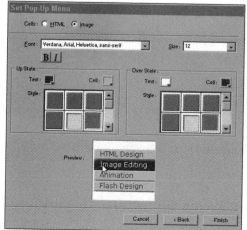

Figure 17-10:
You set these parameters to get a pop-up menu with images.

To apply a behavior to a button, hotspot, or slice, click the white circle in its center to open a drop-down menu of behaviors. Click a behavior to apply it to the item.

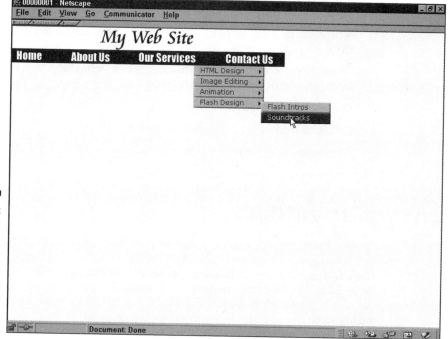

Figure 17-11:
You can create pop-up menus in Fireworks without knowing JavaScript.

You can't preview a pop-up menu in any of the Fireworks preview windows. In order to see the pop-up menu in all its glory, you have to preview it in a Web browser. To preview the pop-up menu in your system's primary Web browser, press F12.

Using the Behaviors panel

You use the Behaviors panel to assign and modify behaviors to hotspots or slices. The Behaviors panel is also used to delete behaviors from a hotpot. To modify an item's behavior:

1. **Use the Pointer tool to select the item whose behavior you want to modify.**

2. **Choose Window➪Behaviors.**

   Fireworks opens the Behaviors panel. If a behavior can be modified, an arrow appears between the Events and Actions columns.

3. **To delete a behavior, select it and click the minus sign (–) button.**

   Or you can click the trash icon at the bottom of the panel.

4. **To add a behavior, click the plus sign (+) button.**

   A drop-down menu of behaviors appears. Select a behavior to add it to the item's behavior list.

5. **To modify the mouse event that triggers a behavior, click the arrow between the event and the action.**

   Fireworks opens a drop-down menu.

6. **Select an option from the drop-down menu.**

   Fireworks applies the new mouse event option to the action.

Swapping Images

One very cool behavior you can add to your Web pages is *image swapping.* When you apply the Swap Image behavior to a slice, another image appears when the user's mouse rolls over the image. For example, you can apply the Swap Image behavior to a picture of a person so that the picture is replaced with a funny face when a user rolls his or her mouse over the image. The following steps show you how to create an image swap.

Image swapping works best if both images are the same size.

1. **Use the Pointer tool to select the image you want to swap.**

2. **Choose Insert➪Slice.**

   Fireworks creates a light green overlay with a white circle in the middle.

3. **Click the white circle.**

   The Behaviors menu appears.

4. **Choose Add Swap Image Behavior.**

   The Swap Image dialog box appears.

5. **Select the External File option and then click the folder icon to the right of the field.**

   The Open dialog box appears.

6. **Navigate to the image on your hard drive that you want to appear when the user's mouse rolls over the slice; then click Open.**

   Fireworks creates the JavaScript to swap the images. Both images pre-load when the page is first loading into the user's browser.

   Make sure the image you are swapping is uploaded to the Web site with the rest of the Fireworks documents and images.

Chapter 18

Exporting Images

● ●

In This Chapter

▶ Using the Export Preview window

▶ Exporting the HTML document

▶ Previewing the image in a Web browser

▶ Using the Export Wizard

● ●

*A*fter you put all of your creative energy — or at least a good bit of it — into creating a Fireworks document, you *export* it. When you export the document, Fireworks saves the document and its associated files in the format you chose when you optimized the image. When you export a document, you can export it as a single image or as a selection of images (sliced and diced so nice), and an HTML document that puts the whole thing back together again in a Web browser. After you export the files (image files and the HTML document) from Fireworks, you can upload them directly to a Web site or incorporate the HTML file with an existing HTML document created with Macromedia's Dreamweaver or a similar HTML editor.

The beauty of Fireworks is that you don't have to have a Ph.D. in HTML to be effective. Fireworks takes care of all the heavy stuff like creating tables and JavaScript for you. After you export the image files and the HTML file, you can edit it in your favorite HTML editor.

Previewing the Export

After looking at the document in the workspace all during its creation, you may feel that you've looked at the document enough. However, you can get one last go-round with your creation before exporting it in the Export Preview window. This gives you one more opportunity to tweak the settings and get the file size as small as possible.

If you've looked at the document so much that the mere sight of it causes anguish, I suggest you save the file, shut off the computer, take a deep breath, and then take a walk or put on some soothing music (heavy metal is not soothing). After your brief respite, you can open the file again and your frame of mind will be better.

Using the Export Preview window

Use the Export Preview window to view your document as optimized before exporting it. You can bypass the Export Preview window and just export the file if you feel your optimization has been spot on. However, if you feel that perhaps your document is not quite as optimized as it could be, you get one final chance to fine-tune the settings before exporting the document. To optimize a document using the Export Preview window:

1. **Choose File⇨Export Preview.**

   Fireworks opens the Export Preview window (see Figure 18-1). When the window first opens, you see your document as a single image with no slices. It's really a scaled-down version of the actual document window with the exception that you don't get to see the original document; you see only the optimized version. The right side of the window shows the document as it will be exported. In Figure 18-1, notice that the optimization file format is displayed along with the download time. You use the left side of the Export Preview Window to tweak export settings.

2. **Change the export settings in the left window to tweak the file size or appearance of the finished document.**

   As you change the settings, Fireworks updates the image in the right-hand window along with the file information and download time.

3. **To preview the document with more than one optimization setting, click the appropriate button to display the export with two windows or four windows.**

   When you display the export with multiple windows, you can change the export settings for each window and choose the one that works best for the intended home of the document.

4. **Click a window to select it.**

5. **Change the settings on the left-hand side of the Export Preview window.**

   As you change the settings, Fireworks updates the image, optimization settings, and file size in the selected window.

6. **If you've selected the four-window preview, optimize the settings in the other two windows and then choose the window that is the best compromise between image quality and file size.**

   Fireworks updates the optimization settings in the left window. These are the new settings that will be applied to the exported file.

7. **To export the document, click the Export button.**

Fireworks opens the Export Dialog box, which I show you how to use in the "Exporting for the Web Made Easy" section of this chapter.

8. **To apply the settings without exporting the document, click OK.**

Fireworks applies the settings to the document and closes the window.

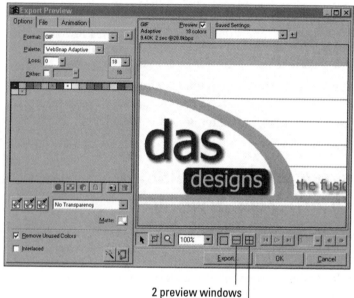

Figure 18-1:
You can change export settings in the Export Preview window.

2 preview windows

4 preview windows

Previewing the export in a Web browser

While you were adjusting all of these cool optimization settings and putting more eye candy into your document than the law allows, did you ever once stop to think what the thing would look like when you had it on the Internet? I mean after all, Fireworks' reason to be is to create images for the Internet.

When you install Fireworks, it detects your system's default Web browser and creates a link to it.

To preview your export in a Web browser:

1. **Choose File➪Preview in Browser, and then select your default browser from the submenu.**

Fireworks opens the document in your system's default browser.

To quickly preview the document in your system's default Web browser, press F12.

2. **Test all the interactive parts of your document such as hotspots, slices, and buttons.**

   If the document you're previewing is part of a Web site you're creating, you won't be able to check out the links until you upload the finished file to the site's Web host. As you run your mouse over a button or hotspot, most browsers display the link in the browser's status window. If the page you're previewing has links to existing Internet Web pages, dial up your Internet connection before choosing the Preview in Browser command. Then when you preview the document in a browser, you can test the links by clicking the buttons or hotspots to see if they work correctly.

3. **After previewing the document, close down the browser.**

   You are once again in the native Fireworks environment and you can tweak anything that didn't perform up to snuff.

Previewing the document with different browsers

There is the well-known platform war, which has been raging for as long as Windows computer users have believed that Intel is swell and for as long as Macintosh has been the apple of other computer user's eyes. After a long and harrowing conflict, the war still rages on. Add to this another skirmish in the computer world, this one between Web browsers. Many people use Netscape to escape to the virtual world of their choice while others use Internet Explorer to discover their virtual worlds. The browser conflict continues unabated, which leaves you, the intrepid Web designer, in a bit of a dilemma because some things you do don't work in all browsers. To safeguard against this, I recommend that you install the two most popular browsers on your system and use both to preview your documents. By doing this, you'll be sure that visitors to Web sites you've designed view your pages as you designed them, no matter which popular Web browser they're using. To link a second Web browser to Fireworks:

1. **Choose File⇨Preview in Browser⇨Set Secondary Browser.**

   The Locate Browser dialog box appears.

2. **Navigate to the location of your secondary browser's program file.**

   What you're looking for is a file that has an .exe extension. For example, Internet Explorer's executable file is called Iexplore.exe.

3. **After locating the proper file, click Open.**

   Fireworks adds the browser as a submenu item to the Preview in Browser command.

Exporting for the Web Made Easy

Fireworks is a very smart computer program, much smarter than the average Web designer. Most Web designers like the bells and whistles they can add to a Web site, but don't necessarily have the time to spend that it takes to decipher the HTML coding necessary to generate them. Most Web designers would rather devote their time and energy to making the site look pretty, myself included. The thought of creating an HTML document with JavaScript for image swapping, rollover buttons, and slices is enough to make me tremble with fear. Luckily for me — and for you, dear reader — Fireworks takes care of all that weird JavaScript hieroglyphics when you export the document. That's why I use Fireworks and I'm pretty sure that's why you're reading this book. To export your image and an HTML document:

1. **Choose File➪Export.**

   The Export dialog box opens, as shown in Figure 18-2.

2. **Enter a name for the document.**

   Fireworks chooses the name you've given the document if it's already been saved; otherwise, you're stuck with the name "untitled" until you title it.

3. **Navigate to the folder where you want to store the HTML document.**

4. **In the Save as Type field, select the HTML and Images option.**

5. **In the HTML field select one of the following options:**

   - **Export HTML File:** Generates an HTML file for the document, complete with JavaScript, tables, and other HTML nasties that would drive you absolutely bonkers if you had to generate the code from scratch.

   - **Copy to Clipboard:** Generates the HTML code and copies it to your operating system's clipboard when you export the document. Use this option when you want to paste the code Fireworks generates in an HTML editor.

6. **In the Slices field, choose one of the following options:**

   - **None:** Exports the image with no slices.

   - **Slices:** Exports the image with separate files for each slice. When you choose this option, Fireworks generates a table in the HTML document that puts all the pieces of the puzzle back together again when the HTML document is viewed in a Web browser.

• **Slice Along Guides:** Slices the document into images defined by the guides that you've created. Fireworks exports each slice as an image file and creates a table in the HTML document to properly align the image slices when the HTML document is opened in a Web browser.

7. **If you choose to export image slices, the Include Areas without Slices option becomes available. This option is enabled by default.**

   If you accept the Include Areas without Slices option, Fireworks exports images for areas without slices and assembles them in an HTML table. If you deselect this option, Fireworks exports only the image slices and the canvas background color.

8. **To save the images in a different folder, click the Put Images in Subfolder checkbox.**

   The Browse button makes its presence known.

9. **If you chose the Put Images in Subfolder option, click the Browse button.**

   Fireworks opens the Select Folder dialog box. If you don't click the Browse button, Fireworks automatically creates a folder called Images that's located inside the folder you're exporting the HTML document to.

10. **Navigate to the folder you want to store the images in.**

   After you select a folder to store the images in, the folder's name is listed next to the Browse button in the Export dialog box.

11. **Click the Select button (the button's name, Select, is appended by the name of the folder you select) or click Open to accept the default images folder Fireworks assigns.**

   The Select Folder dialog box closes.

12. **Click Save.**

   Fireworks exports the image files and if specified, an HTML file to neatly assemble all the slices and hotspots and buttons in a Web browser.

When you export a Fireworks document with a pop-up menu, Fireworks takes care of generating the pesky JavaScript and it also creates a file called fw_menu.js. When you upload the completed HTML document to the Web site's host, be sure to upload the menu.js file in the same directory as the HTML document. If your pop-up menu has submenus, Fireworks generates a file called, arrows.gif, which creates the tiny arrow to the right of the parent menu. Be sure to upload this file as well. If you choose to save the images in another folder, the arrows.gif file will be there as well. In order for the pop-up menu to function properly, be sure to upload the folder you stored the document images in — the same place the arrows.gif file is saved — when you upload the HTML file to your Web server.

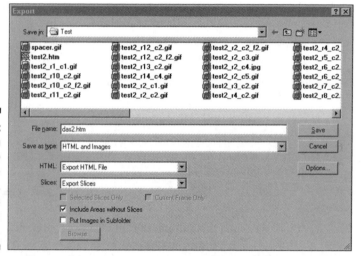

Figure 18-2:
When you
choose to
export the
document,
the end is
almost in
sight.

Setting slicing and HTML options

When you export an image with slices, you can tell Fireworks exactly how you want the slices reassembled in the HTML document. You can even specify how Fireworks names the slices, an option that you use when you edit the HTML document in an HTML editor.

When Fireworks creates the HTML document for a Fireworks document with slices, it uses a table to put the pieces back together. You can choose whether you want Fireworks to create a table with spacers or nested tables.

✔ A **spacer** is an image that causes the image slices to realign properly in the table.

✔ A **nested table** is a table within a table, sort of like those annoying little puzzles where there's a box within a box within a box. . . . Nested tables are slower to load, but are a tad easier to edit.

To specify how Fireworks formats the HTML document:

1. Choose File➪HTML Setup.

Fireworks opens the HTML Setup dialog box (see Figure 18-3). You have three tabs to work with.

You can also open the HTML Setup dialog box by clicking the Options button in the Export dialog box.

2. **In the General tab, click the triangle to the right of the HTML style field and choose one of the following options:**

   • **Dreamweaver** exports the document using an HTML format preferred by Macromedia's Dreamweaver HTML editor.

   • **Front Page** exports the document using Microsoft Front Page's favored HTML format.

   • **Generic** creates an HTML document that is recognized by most HTML editors.

   • **GoLive** creates an HTML document in the preferred style of Adobe's GoLive HTML editor.

3. **Click the triangle to the right of the Extension field and select an option.**

   This option determines the extension that Fireworks appends to the HTML document. The extension you choose is determined by the type of Web site you're uploading the document to. In most cases you'll use the .htm or .html. extension.

   For more information on the different types of HTML documents, pick up a copy of *HTML 4 For Dummies,* 3rd Edition, by Ed Tittle and Natanya Pitts or *HTML 4.01 Weekend Crash Course* by Greg M. Perry, both available from Hungry Minds, Inc. If you use Dreamweaver to edit your HTML documents, you can get the lowdown on the program by reading a copy of *Dreamweaver 4 For Dummies* by Janine Warner and Paul Vachier, also published by Hungry Minds, Inc.

4. **To include useful comments in the exported HTML document, select the Include HTML Comments option.**

   HTML comments are helpful if you're editing the document in an HTML editor. *HTML comments* explain why a certain item was created and provide other pertinent information such as information regarding where to cut and paste HTML and/or JavaScript. Think of HTML comments as a helping hand from Fireworks.

5. **Choose Lowercase File Names and Fireworks will export the document files with lowercase file names.**

6. **Click OK.**

   When the document is exported, Fireworks applies the options you specified.

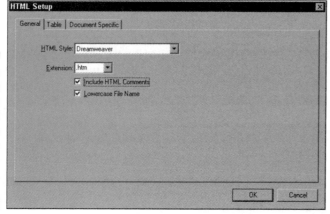

To determine how Fireworks creates the tables and slices in the exported HTML document:

1. Choose File➪HTML Setup.

The HTML Setup dialog box appears.

2. Click the Table tab.

Fireworks opens up the Table section of the dialog box.

3. Click the triangle to the right of the Space With field and then choose one of the following:

- **Nested Tables-No Spacers:** Creates the HTML document with nested tables and no spacers.

- **Single Table-No Spacers:** Creates the HTML document with a single table and no spacers. Note that if you have slices of different sizes the images may not display correctly in a Web browser.

- **1 Pixel Transparent Spacer:** Creates a 1 pixel by 1 pixel (read: tiny) transparent GIF image that resizes as needed to shim the image slices. The shim's sole purpose is to remove any gaps between image slices so everything lines up perfectly.

4. Select a cell color for Text Slices.

The Use Canvas Color default exports text-only slices with the same background color as the document's canvas color. To select a different color for the text slice, deselect the Use Canvas Color option, click the Cell Color swatch and then select a color from the palette.

5. Click the triangle to the right of the Contents field and then choose one of the following options:

- **None:** Empty cells remain blank.

- **Spacer Image:** Fills up empty cells using the single pixel transparent image, spacer.gif, resizing it as needed to correctly align the sliced images.

- **Non Breaking Space:** Places a space HTML tag in empty cells. Empty cells occur only if you deselect the Include Areas without Slices option in the Export dialog box.

6. **Click OK.**

   The next time you export the Fireworks document, Fireworks exports the HTML document just the way you told it to. After all, you are the creator of the document.

You can change the way Fireworks names exported slices by clicking the Document Specific tab (tab number three) in the HTML Setup dialog box and then choosing different options.

Exporting image maps

When you export an image with hotspots, Fireworks creates an *image map,* which is a roadmap to the hotspots in your document. Most popular Web browsers can read the image map Fireworks generates. Fireworks' image maps are client side, which means they are read by the client's (the visitor to the Web site) browser. To export an image map:

1. **Choose File⇨Export.**

   The Export dialog box appears.

2. **Enter a name for the file and locate the folder where you want Fireworks to export the HTML file.**

3. **In the Save as Type field, select the HTML and Images option.**

4. **In the HTML field select Export HTML file.**

5. **In The Slices field, choose None.**

6. **To save the image in a different folder, enable the Put Images in Subfolder option.**

   The Browse button becomes active.

7. **Click the Browse button.**

   Fireworks opens the Select Folder dialog box. If you don't click the Browse button, Fireworks automatically creates a folder called Images, which is located inside the folder you're exporting the HTML document to.

8. **Navigate to the folder you want to store the image in.**

9. **Click the Select button (the button's name, Select, is appended by the name of the folder you select) or click Open to accept the default images folder Fireworks assigns.**

   The Select Folder dialog box closes.

10. **Click Save.**

Fireworks saves the image map's HTML file and the optimized image in the folder(s) you specified.

The folder's name is listed next to the Browse button at the bottom of the Export dialog box.

If you store the images in a different folder, make sure you upload the image folder to the site's Web host when you upload the HTML document.

Exporting images in other formats

You can export your Fireworks image in a number of different formats. Why? Because there's a lot of different places your Fireworks images can end up: in a Flash document, in an Illustrator document, in an image-editing program, and so on. Unfortunately, there's so many different export formats available, if I were to explain each in detail, a number of things would happen: the size of this chapter would increase, you would become listless, put down the book, and turn on the TV, and even though my editor is a dream to work with, she would surely raise one, if not both, of her literary eyebrows, or perhaps furrow her brow, which would in turn create a wrinkled forehead, and she's far too young to have wrinkles of any sort.

In lieu of a detailed treatise of each export option, with figures and vocal accompaniment in four-part harmony, I will give you a gentle nudge in the right direction. To export an image in another format:

1. **Choose File⇨Export.**

Fireworks opens the Export dialog box.

2. **Click the triangle to the right of the Save as Type field and then choose one of the options shown in Figure 18-4.**

3. **After selecting the option of your choice, click the Options button (if it's an option).**

Many of the formats have options specific to the application your exported document will end up in. These are the bits that would bore you, would increase the length of the chapter, and cause my editor a mild bout of discomfort when she had the nasty task of figuring out how to stuff fifty pounds of text in a thirty-pound bag.

4. **After applying the options for the selected format, click OK.**

When you export the document, Fireworks creates files in the specified format with the specified options specified by you.

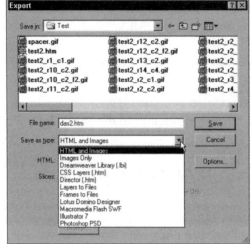

Figure 18-4:
The export
process can
be taxing,
but the file
isn't (taxed,
that is).

Using the Export Wizard

Images that end up on the Internet need to have crisp detail in order to be seen, yet at the same time need to be small files in order to download quickly. That's why you optimize your Fireworks images. Optimizing images can be confusing if you're new at the game. I know the first time I took a look at Fireworks Optimize panels, I shut off the computer and relaxed with a cup of my favorite beverage for several hours. So if optimizing an image mystifies or terrifies you, the Export Wizard knows how to cure your woes. The Export Wizard is also handy when you're pinched for time.

You can use the Export Wizard to help choose an export format that is best for the intended destination of your image. You can also use the Export Wizard to optimize the image to a specific file size. This option comes in handy if you're incorporating the image with an existing HTML document and you have an idea of how many kilobytes you can add to the HTML file without breaking the bandwidth barrier. You can get to the Export Wizard from the canvas, but along the way you will be stopped at a few dialog box checkpoints. To specify a format setting with the Export Wizard:

1. Choose File⇨Export Wizard.

The first Export Wizard dialog box appears.

2. **To select an export format, click Continue.**

   or

   To optimize the image to a specific file size, enable the Target File Export Size option, enter the desired file size in text field, and then click Continue.

   The second Export Wizard dialog box appears.

3. **Choose one of the following destinations:**

   - **The Web** to optimize the image for an Internet Web page.

   - **An Image-editing Application** to prepare the image for use in an image-editing program such as Photoshop.

   - **A Desktop Publishing Application** to prepare the image for use in your desktop publishing software.

   - **Dreamweaver** to optimize the image and HTML for use in Macromedia's Dreamweaver HTML editor.

4. **After selecting a destination, click Continue.**

   The Analysis Results dialog box appears. This is Fireworks' verdict on which format is the best for the intended destination of the image. The dialog begins, "We recommend . . .", which makes me wonder how the choice is made. Does Fireworks dispatch a super-secret modem connection to the Macromedia Web site and beam your image before a panel of robed, gray-haired judges?

5. **Click Exit.**

   The Export Preview window appears, as shown in Figure 18-5. This figure shows an image to be exported for a Web page. Guess what? Sometimes you get two choices. If you're faced with a choice, select the image that looks the best and has the smallest file size. The two choices in this image are a toss up for file size. The text looks a bit better in the .gif format in this case, so that would be my choice. But hey, I'm me, and you're you.

6. **Select the image that looks the best and then click Export.**

   Fireworks exports the document and associated documents depending upon the destination you chose in Step 3.

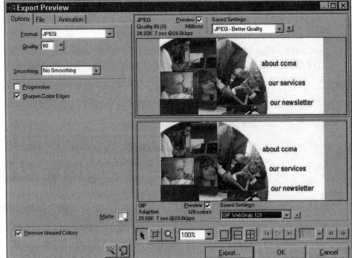

Figure 18-5:
After
answering
the Export
Wizard's
many
questions,
you end up
here.

Part IV
The Part of Tens

The 5th Wave By Rich Tennant

©RICHTENNANT.COM

Jeez—that's impressive! Let's see that airbrush effect again.

In this part . . .

Creating images for your Web pages is challenging but it can also be great fun. With Fireworks, you can let your inner-child run amuck and use the program's features to get creative — you know, draw outside the lines. Creativity is what will set your designs apart from the other drab fodder that people pass off as Web sites. If you've got the time and inclination, you can experiment and create new and unique designs.

In this part there are three chapters that each have ten sections (except for Chapter 21 when the batteries on my abacus quit and I ended up with twelve sections). My editor demanded a recount, but was overruled by the Supreme Court. In Chapter 19, I show you some tips and tricks to streamline your workflow in Fireworks. If you get bored by doing the same thing over and over and over again, read the section on batch processing. In Chapter 20, I show you ten tricks you can use to jazz up your Web designs. In Chapter 21, I show you where to find information on Fireworks and Web design on the Internet.

Chapter 19

Ten Ways to Turbocharge Fireworks

* *

In This Chapter

▶ Creating custom styles

▶ Using batch processing

▶ Writing scripts to save yourself some time

▶ Customizing patterns and palettes

▶ Creating seamless tiles

▶ Using the Find and Replace panel

▶ Managing your project with the Project Log

* *

The images and Web pages you create with Fireworks are creative endeavors. The fact that you're this far back in the book means that you're a creative kind of Fireworks user. In this chapter, I show you ten ways to be more creative and more productive. Speed and creativity in one chapter ought to be illegal, immoral, or at least fattening. But it's neither. In fact, if you spend more time creating with Fireworks and less time in the kitchen, creativity can mean a slimmer, trimmer you.

Creating a Style

Fireworks has style. And Fireworks also has styles, a whole library full of them in fact. The fact that Fireworks Library is full of styles means every other John, Joe, or Mary that uses Fireworks (and there are a lot of Fireworks users) will be using the styles, which means the Internet will be proliferated with the same styles. So how's a Web designer supposed to be original? The answer, my friend, is to create your own styles. And when you do create your own styles, by all means, do it with style. To create a style:

1. **Create an object using one of the drawing tools.**

2. **Choose a fill color for the object.**

   Choose either a solid fill color in the Colors section of the Toolbox or choose Window⇨Fill to open up the Fill panel and apply a gradient or pattern to the object.

3. **Choose Window⇨Effect.**

   Fireworks opens the effects panel.

4. **Apply one of more Effects to the object.**

   Fireworks adds the effects to the object.

5. **When the object is just the way you want it, choose Window⇨Styles.**

   Fireworks opens the Styles library.

6. **Click the triangle near the upper right-hand corner of the panel.**

   Fireworks opens a drop-down menu.

7. **Choose New Style.**

   Fireworks opens the New Style dialog box (see Figure 19-1) and creates a small thumbnail image of the style as it will be saved.

8. **Enter a name for the new style.**

9. **Select the options you want saved with the style.**

   You can choose to save effects applied to the object (Fill Type, Stroke Type, Fill Color, or Stroke Color). You can save any or all of these with the new style. If the object is text, you can specify which text attributes get saved with the style.

10. **Click OK.**

    Fireworks adds the new style to the Styles Library and creates a thumbnail display. To apply the new style to another object, select the object, and then click the style's thumbnail in the Styles Library.

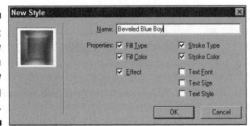

Figure 19-1:
Add new styles with the New Style dialog box.

Making a Batch of Fireworks Goodies

When you've got a task that you have to do over and over again, the whole thing gets a little tedious, not to mention monotonous. After doing the same task over and over several times, your mind begins to wander and you wish you were doing something else, like catching up on your reading or working on your tan. Well lucky for you, the creators of Fireworks have experienced the same monotony and came up with a way to automate repetitive tasks. Enter the *Batch Processor,* a rather clever tool that applies changes to multiple files with one click of the mouse. You can use the Batch Processor to convert selected files to another format; scale selected image files; find and replace text, font styles, URLS and colors; rename files by adding a suffix or prefix; or perform selected commands on the files. To streamline your work with the Batch Processor:

1. **Choose File⇨Batch Process.**

   Fireworks opens the Batch dialog box.

2. **If you use Fireworks on the Windows platform, click the triangle to the right of the Files of Type field. If you use Fireworks on a Macintosh, all readable files are shown in the file list view.**

   Fireworks opens a drop-down menu.

3. **Navigate to the folder where the images you want to batch process are stored.**

4. **In the Files of Type field (Windows), choose the file format for the images you're going to convert. If the images are in more than one format, choose the All Readable Files option.**

   Fireworks displays all the folder's files with the selected format.

5. **Choose the image files you're going to convert.**

   Click an image file to select it. If you're working in Windows, you can select a group of contiguous image files by holding down the Shift key and clicking the last image file you want to select; Fireworks selects all files between the first and last you selected. Also in Windows, you can add non-contiguous image files to the selection, by holding down the Ctrl key and clicking additional image files to add them to the selection. If you're going to batch process all files in the folder, simply click the Add All button.

   If you're working on a Mac, you can add additional files to the selection only by holding down the Shift key and clicking each file you want to add to the selection.

6. **Click Add.**

   Fireworks adds the selected images to the large window at the bottom of the dialog box, as shown in Figure 19-2.

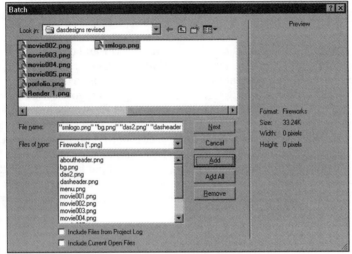

Figure 19-2:
Before
Fireworks
can batch
process,
you've got
to select the
batch.

7. Click Next.

Multi-faceted program that it is, Fireworks opens yet another Batch dialog box. This box consists of two windows: Batch Options and Include in Batch (see Figure 19-3). The window on the left contains the commands you can apply to the selected images. As you choose commands from the left window, they appear in the Include in Batch window.

8. Decide which commands you want to apply to the selected images.

You can choose more than one command.

9. To add a command to the batch, select it and then click the Add button.

Fireworks adds the command to the Include in Batch window.

10. Click a command in the Include in Batch window to select it.

The selected command's options appear in the bottom of the dialog box. Figure 19-3 shows one of the options available with the Scale command. In this case, the files in the batch will all be scaled to 80 percent of their original size.

11. Edit the command, as you will apply it to the batch of files.

If you're applying more than one command to the batch, select each one of the other commands and edit them.

12. To change the order in which a command is applied to the batch, select the command and then click Up or Down arrow to move the command up or down in the list.

The order in which commands are listed is the order in which they will be performed.

To remove a command from the Include in Batch list, click the Remove button.

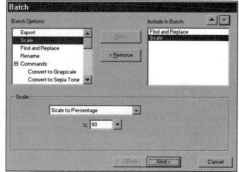

Figure 19-3:
In Batch
dialog box
number 2,
you tell
Fireworks
what you
want it
to do.

13. **Click Next.**

    Fireworks opens yet a third Batch dialog box. This may seem monotonous, but editing each and every file in the batch would be far more monotonous and time consuming.

14. **Choose from the following location options:**

    • **Same Location as Original file** to save the processed files in the same folder as the originals.

    • **Custom Location** and the Select Images Folder dialog box appears. Navigate to the folder you want to store the processed images in and then click Select. You use this option when you want to keep your original files unaltered.

15. **Enable the Backups option to create backups of your original files. This option is selected by default. Choose one of the following options:**

    • **Overwrite Existing Backups** to overwrite the previous file.

    • **Incremental Backup files** to keep existing copies of backup files. If you choose this option, Fireworks creates new backup files with an appended number at the end of the backup file.

If you don't backup your files or store the processed files in a different folder, when you batch process the files with the same file format, the originals will be, like Poe's raven, nevermore.

16. **To save the sequence of commands as a script, click the Save Script button.**

    Fireworks opens the Save As dialog box. Enter a name for the Script, locate to the folder you want to store it in, and then click Save.

17. Click Batch.

Quicker than it took you to read this section, Fireworks batch processes the files with the commands you selected.

Writing a Script

Scripts are another great way to streamline your work in Fireworks. If you've got a set of repetitive tasks that you perform on a regular basis — or irregular if Web design isn't your day job — you can create a *script* to perform the task. For example if you've created a particularly neat navigation menu for a Web page, you can create a script for it and then run the script when you want to create the menu quickly. To create a script, you perform the tasks and then use the History panel to create the script. Here's how:

1. Perform the steps you want to save as a script.

For example, if you're creating a script for a menu, begin at the beginning. Create the buttons and then align them as a navigation menu. As you perform the various steps, they are recorded in the History panel.

2. After you've created the steps you want to save as a command, choose Window⇨History.

Fireworks opens the History panel.

3. Select the steps you want to save.

To add contiguous steps: Click the first step to select it, hold down the Shift, and then click contiguous steps to add them to the selection.

To add non-contiguous steps: Hold down the Ctrl key (Windows) or Command key (Mac) and click non-contiguous steps to add them to the selection.

4. Click the Save button at the bottom of the History panel (see Figure 19-4).

Fireworks opens the Save Command dialog box, also shown in Figure 19-4.

5. Enter a name for the command and then click OK.

Fireworks saves the command to the Commands window and runs the steps you saved next time you choose the command.

Figure 19-4:
You can
command
Fireworks to
create a
special
command
using the
History
panel.

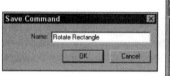

Creating Custom Patterns

If you have an image-editing program or texture generating software capable of creating tiling textures, you can create your own custom patterns. The pattern you create must be a seamless tile, otherwise it won't tile correctly when you apply it to an object in Fireworks. To create a custom pattern:

1. Create a new image in the program you use to create tiling textures.

The image should be sized to 128 pixels by 128 pixels and no larger than 256 pixels by 256 pixels.

2. Generate a seamless texture.

A seamless texture is one that doesn't show a visible seam when you create a pattern that it is tiled upon itself.

3. Choose the program's Save As option.

When the image-editing program's Save As dialog opens, navigate to the Patterns folder, which is a subfolder of the Configuration folder in your Fireworks 4 folder.

4. Name the pattern.

5. Save the pattern as any file type supported by Fireworks (.bmp, .gif, .jpg, .png, and so on).

The tiling pattern is saved into Fireworks Patterns folder. The next time you launch Fireworks and use the Fill panel to apply a pattern to an object, you'll find your custom pattern on the same menu as the Fireworks presets. Figure 19-5 shows an object filled with a pattern I created in a program called Corel Texture. If I can do it, I know you can.

I show you how to create a seamless tile in Fireworks in the "Creating Seamless Tiles" section, which is just a few short sections away. Stay tuned.

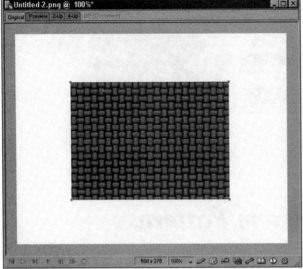

Figure 19-5:
Create your
own custom
patterns and
apply them
to your
Fireworks
creations.

Pasting Attributes

When you create an interesting combination of colors and effects for an object, you can quickly apply the same effects to other objects by applying two menu commands. For example, if you've created a complex fill for an object (which takes a while to do), and then applied a bevel and a drop shadow to it (which takes just a little longer to do), you can apply these same attributes to another object by using the Paste Attributes command instead of recreating them. This will save you loads of time. To paste attributes from one object to another:

 1. **Use the Pointer tool to select the object with the attributes you want to paste.**

   Fireworks creates a bounding box around the object.

2. **Choose Edit⇨Copy.**

   Fireworks copies the selected object to the clipboard.

3. **Select the object you want to paste the attributes to.**

   Fireworks creates a bounding box around the selected object.

4. **Choose Edit⇨Paste Attributes.**

   Fireworks waves its magic wand and the attributes are pasted to the selected shape. Note that when attributes such as color and effects are pasted to the object, the size and shape of the object remain the same except when copying attributes to a text block, in which case the font size attribute increases the size of the text you're pasting attributes to.

Creating Your Own Special Effects

There are effects, and then there are special effects. The difference between effects and special effects is that everyone who owns Fireworks has the effects from the Effect panel available to them, but when you customize an effect and save it, then it's available to only you (or at least until someone finds your handiwork on the Internet and copies it).

When you create an effect that you feel is pretty special, you can save it for future use. To create a special effect:

1. **Create an object.**

2. **Choose Window⇨Effect.**

   Fireworks opens the Effect panel for you.

3. **Choose one of the standard effects that you think will look swell on this particular object.**

   Remember you can apply more than one effect to an object. The effects that you apply can be modified to create something truly unique. If for example you find yourself using the bevel effect in conjunction with a drop shadow, you can combine the two of them into your very own effect.

   I show you how to use the Effect panel in Chapter 11.

4. **Modify the effect to suit your needs.**

5. **After you tweak the effect, click the triangle near the panel's upper right-hand corner.**

   Fireworks opens a drop-down menu of options for the panel.

6. **Choose Save Effect As.**

   The Save Effect As dialog box opens.

7. **Enter a name for your special effect and then click OK.**

   Fireworks christens the new effect and adds your new effect to the Effect presets menu. To use the effect in the future, just choose it from the menu.

Creating Custom Palettes

If you're doing a lot of design work for a particular client or a particular industry, you may find yourself using a limited palette of colors. When you find this happening, rather than wade through all 216 Web-safe colors in the Fireworks palette, you can load your own custom palette with only the colors you need. But before you can load it, you've got to create it. Here's how:

1. **Create a new document and then create some objects.**

   Don't concern yourself with creating a thing of beauty — simply create some shapes and when you choose the color for each shape, select a color that you want to save with the custom palette.

2. **After you've created the objects with the colors you want to save with your custom palette, choose Window⇨Color Table.**

   Fireworks tables all other activities and opens the Color Table panel.

3. **Click the triangle near the upper right-hand corner of the panel and choose Rebuild Color Table from the drop-down menu.**

   Fireworks makes a nice patchwork quilt arrangement of all the colors you've used so far. To add additional colors to the table, create a new object, apply a different color to it, and then choose Rebuild Color Table.

4. **Click the Triangle near the upper right-hand corner of the Table panel and choose Save Palette from the drop-down menu.**

   Fireworks opens the Save As dialog box.

5. **Navigate to the folder you want to store the palette in.**

   If you're creating a number of custom palettes, it's a good idea to create a folder for them. A dash of organization now prevents several ounces of frustration when you're under a deadline and can't locate your lovely palette.

6. **Enter a name for the palette and click Save.**

   Fireworks stores the palette in the folder of your choice.

To load your custom palette:

1. **Choose Window⇨Color Table.**

   Fireworks opens the Color Table panel.

2. **Click the triangle near the panel's upper right-hand corner and choose Load Palette**

   The Open dialog box appears.

3. **Navigate to the folder your custom palette is stored in, select it, and then click Open.**

   Fireworks replaces the current export palette with your custom palette.

4. **Choose Window⇨Swatches.**

   The Swatches panel opens.

5. **Click the triangle near the upper right-hand corner of the panel and choose Current Export Palette from the drop-down menu.**

   The swatches in the panel are replaced with the colors from your custom palette.

   You can also load the custom palette into the Swatches panel by clicking the arrow near the panel's upper right-hand corner and then choosing Replace Swatches from the drop-down menu. When the Open dialog box appears, navigate to the folder your custom palette is stored in, select it, and then click Open to load the palette.

6. **In the Toolbox, click the triangle at the lower right-hand corner of the Fill Color Well.**

   The color palette opens.

7. **Click the triangle at the upper right-hand corner of the palette and choose Swatches Panel from the drop-down menu.**

   The colors from your custom palette are loaded into all of the color wells. After following each of these steps, when you export the document, only the colors from your custom palette will be exported.

You can do lots of other things with the Color Table. To learn more about the Color Table, take a look at Chapter 5.

Creating Seamless Tiles

I know you've seen Web sites with a background image that looks like wallpaper. When you look at the background image, it appears to be one larger image. But looks are deceiving, and beauty is only skin deep. What appears to be one image is actually a small image that is tiled across the background, sort of like the tiles in your shower but without the grout. You can create your own custom tiles easily in Fireworks. Here's how:

1. **Choose File⇨New.**

   The New Document dialog box appears.

2. **Enter a value of 200 in the Width field and 200 in the Height field, choose a background color, and then click OK.**

   Fireworks presents you with a blank canvas, 200 pixels by 200 pixels in the color of your choice.

3. **Select the Rectangle tool and while holding down the Shift key, drag it on the canvas.**

   Your goal is to create a rectangle the same size as the canvas. If you don't get it exact, not to worry, you'll size it and position it with the Info panel.

4. **Release the mouse button to complete creating the rectangle.**

   Fireworks creates a rectangle for you.

5. **With the rectangle still selected, choose Window⇨Info panel.**

   Fireworks displays the Info panel. Make sure the rectangle is exactly 200 pixels by 200 pixels with X and Y coordinates of 0. If not, enter these values in the Info panel to center and size the rectangle.

6. **With the rectangle still selected, choose Window⇨Fill.**

   The Fill panel opens.

7. **Click the triangle to the right of the Fill Category field and choose Pattern from the drop-down menu.**

8. **Click the triangle to the right of the Pattern Name field.**

   Fireworks opens the Pattern menu.

9. **Select a pattern.**

   Fireworks fills the rectangle with the pattern and the pattern eclipses the background color.

10. **To reveal some of the background color choose Window⇨Layers.**

    Fireworks opens the Layers panel.

11. **Click the triangle to the right of the Opacity field and drag the slider down to reveal some of the background color.**

    Drag the slider until you get the effect you're looking for. Remember that when you have a tiling background, it should be decorative, not over-powering, especially if you're putting a lot of text over the background.

12. **Optimize the image using either the Export Wizard or the Optimize panel.**

    Choose the GIF format and optimize for the smallest possible file size.

13. **Choose File⇨Export.**

    Fireworks exports the file. Figure 19-6 shows the seamless tile as displayed on a Web page.

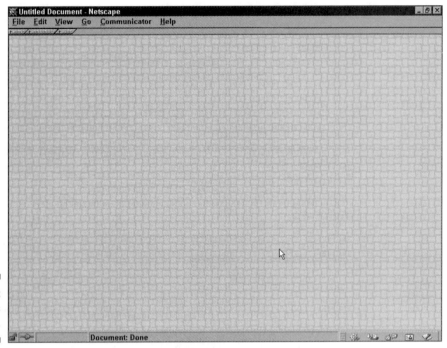

Figure 19-6:
A seamless tile at work.

Finding and Replacing

Another way to streamline your work in Fireworks is to take advantage of all the goodies the program's designers built in for you. If you end up using Fireworks to create images and Web pages for clients, you'll find out very soon that they have the unmitigated gall to change their mind in the middle of a project. If, for example, your client changes the name of the new product you've been diligently creating artwork and Web pages for, you'll have to go back through each and every page and change the name. Fortunately, there's an easy way to do this with Fireworks thanks to the Find and Replace panel. You can use the Find and Replace panel to replace an item in a single document or several documents. To use the Find and Replace panel to quickly find and replace an item:

1. **Choose Window⇨Find and Replace.**

   The Find and Replace panel opens, as shown in Figure 19-7.

2. **Click the triangle to the right of the source field and choose one of the following options:**

   - **Search Selection** to find and replace an element in the current selection of objects.

   - **Search Frame** to find and replace an item in the active frame.

• **Search Document** to find and replace an item in the currently selected document.

• **Search Project Log** to find and replace an element in files listed in the Project Log. (I show you how to use the Project Log to manage multiple files in the next section.)

• **Search Files** to find and replace an element in several files. This option comes in handy when you've created several documents for a project and need to change an item in each file.

3. **Click the triangle to the right of the Type field and select one of the following: Find Text, Find Font, Find Color, Find URL, or Find non-Web 216 (colors).**

4. **After choosing the source, enter the item you want to search for in the Find field.**

5. **In the Change to field, enter the new name for the items Fireworks finds.**

The available options you have to choose from in Steps 4 and 5 will vary depending upon the choice you make in Step 3.

6. **Choose one or more of the available options to fine-tune your search.**

The options you choose determine how Fireworks selects a match for the item you enter in the Find field.

7. **Click the Find button.**

Fireworks locates the next instance of the item you entered in the Find field. To have Fireworks replace the found item with the item you entered in the Change to field, click Replace. The find the next instance of the item, click the Find button. To replace all instances of the item without previewing each instance Fireworks finds, click Replace All.

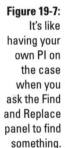

Figure 19-7: It's like having your own PI on the case when you ask the Find and Replace panel to find something.

Using the Project Log

You use the Project Log to keep track of changes to multiple files, which comes in handy if you're creating multiple documents for one Web site and you need to manage them all. Whenever you make a change to a file using the Find and Replace panel, Fireworks adds the file to the Project Log. In addition, Fireworks notes the frame the change was made on as well as the date the change was made. To manage a project with the Project Log:

1. **Choose Window⇨Project Log.**

   Fireworks opens the Project Log (see Figure 19-8). When you initially open the Project Log, it will be as clear as the driven snow if you haven't used the Find and Replace panel.

2. **To add files to the Project Log, click the triangle near the panel's upper-right-hand corner and choose Add Files to Log.**

   Fireworks displays the Open dialog box.

3. **Navigate to the files you want to add, select them and then Click Done (Windows) or Open (Macintosh).**

   Fireworks adds the selected files to the project log. The files listed in the Project Log are saved when you exit Fireworks.

After you have a few files in the Project Log, you can do any of the following tasks.

- ✔ To open a file from the Project Log, double-click its name (Windows) or click Open (Windows & Macintosh).

- ✔ To remove one or more files from the Project Log, select them, click the triangle near the panel's upper right-hand corner, and then choose Clear Selection from the menu.

- ✔ To remove all files from the Project Log, click the triangle near the panel's upper right-hand corner and then choose Clear All from the menu.

- ✔ To export a file from the Project Log using the last export settings you specified, click the file's name, click the triangle near the panel's upper right-hand corner, and then choose Export Again from the menu.

- ✔ To change an item in all files in the Project Log, choose Window⇨Find and Replace, then use the panel to find and replace an item. If you don't know how to use the Find and Replace panel, kindly place your eyes on the prior section before replacing this chapter with the next.

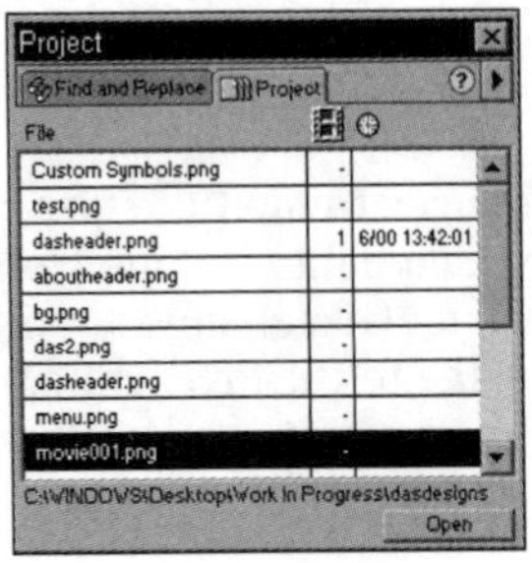

Figure 19-8: You use the Project Log to manage multiple files.

Chapter 20

Ten Fireworks Tips and Tricks

*W*eb sites should be visual feasts for the people who visit them. Unfortunately, many sites fall far short of that goal, using humdrum images that do little to stimulate the viewer's senses. There is, however, a grassroots movement among savvy Web designers to stamp out mediocre Web sites and homegrown sites created with point and click HMTL editors. In this chapter I do my part to add you to that grassroots movement by showing you how put a little sunshine in a Web visitor's day by entertaining them with your spectacular site.

Creating Typewriter Text

Text animations can take on many forms. One very cool and fairly easy to create effect is an animated banner where a message is spelled out one letter at a time, as if it is being typed. The only thing missing is the clicking of the keys. To create animated typewriter text:

1. **Choose File⇨New.**

   Fireworks opens the New Document dialog box.

2. **Choose 468 x 60 for the size of the banner and then choose a background color that matches your design.**

3. **Choose Window⇨Frames.**

   Fireworks opens the Frames panel.

4. **Click the triangle near the panel's upper right-hand corner and choose Add Frames.**

   Fireworks opens the Add Frames dialog box.

5. **Click the triangle to the right of the Number field, drag the slider to add one frame for each letter of the word, and then click OK.**

   Fireworks adds the frames needed to complete your animation.

6. **In the Frames panel, select the final frame of the animation by clicking it.**

   Fireworks transports you to the final frame of the animation.

7. **Select the Text tool and click anywhere on the canvas.**

   Fireworks opens the Text Editor.

8. **Choose a font style, font size, and font color, and then type the message as you want it to appear in the final frame of the animation.**

   As you type, the message also appears on canvas. Remember, in the Text Editor, you can select an individual letter and apply a different color to it, change its baseline, or even change its font size.

   For a refresher course on creating text, mosey on over to Chapter 6.

9. **After typing the text, click OK.**

   Fireworks creates the message on the canvas.

10. **Center the text to the canvas by choosing Commands➪Document➪Center in Document.**

11. **With the text still selected, choose Edit➪Copy.**

    Fireworks copies the text to the clipboard.

12. **In the Frames panel select the preceding frame.**

    Fireworks makes the next frame visible (it's blank).

13. **Choose Edit➪Paste.**

    Fireworks pastes the text to the frame.

14. **Double-click the text.**

    Fireworks opens the Text Editor.

15. **Select the last letter in the message, delete it, and then click OK.**

    You now have one less letter than you did before. Copy the text to the clipboard and then use the Frames panel to move backwards one frame at a time. Paste the text to the new frame and delete one additional letter. Continue in this manner until you're at frame 1 with only the first letter of the message showing.

16. **In the Frames panel, click the frame delay rate to the right of the first frame and then while holding down the Shift key, click the last frame delay rate to select the delay rate for all frames.**

    The frame delay rate for all frames is selected.

17. **Double-click any frame delay.**

    Fireworks opens the Frame Delay dialog box.

18. **Enter a value of 50 or higher for the selected frame's delay rate and then press Enter or Return.**

    The specified frame delay rate is applied to all frames.

19. **Click the Gif Animation Looping button and choose Forever from the drop-down menu.**

20. **Open the Optimize panel, click the triangle to the right of the Export File Format field, and then choose the Animated GIF setting from the drop-down menu.**

21. **Choose File⇨Export.**

    Fireworks exports the document as an Animated GIF. Figure 20-1 shows a seven frame animation in which "Way Cool" is displayed one letter at a time. Each letter is a different color to create viewer interest. Notice the settings in the Frames and Optimize panels.

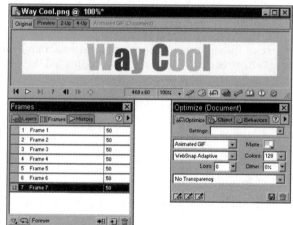

Figure 20-1:
Creating animated text is way cool.

Animating Special Effects

Yet another way to add interest to your animations is to create animated special effects. By animating special effects you can make shadows appear to elongate over time, shapes like rectangles and ovals can bevel before your eyes, or make text glow like a flashing neon light. To animate an effect:

1. **Choose File⇨New.**

    Fireworks opens the New Document dialog box. Enter the desired width and height for your animation and choose a background color.

2. **Choose Window⇨Frames.**

   Fireworks opens the Frames panel.

3. **Click the triangle near the panel's upper-right-hand corner and choose Add Frames from the drop-down menu.**

   Fireworks opens the Add Frames dialog box.

4. **Add the desired number of frames for the animation.**

   You can create as many frames as you want. However, if the animation is going to be part of a Web page, additional frames bloat the file size. Five or six frames is usually enough to animate an effect.

5. **In the Frames panel, click the first frame.**

   Fireworks presents you with a blank canvas on the first frame.

6. **Create an object.**

7. **Choose Window⇨Effect.**

   Fireworks opens the Effect panel.

8. **Apply one or more effects to the object and adjust the parameters of the effect the way you want them to appear at the beginning of the animation.**

   For the purpose of this demonstration, I created a rectangle and applied the Inner Bevel effect to it. In the first frame I adjusted the bevel's width to 0 so the rectangle would be perfectly flat.

9. **After applying the effect, select the object and choose Edit⇨Copy.**

10. **In the Frames panel, click the second frame to select it and then choose Edit⇨Paste.**

    Fireworks pastes the object into the second frame.

11. **Move the object to a different position.**

12. **In the Effect panel, click the icon to the left of the effect's name.**

    Fireworks opens the effect's edit dialog box.

13. **Change the parameters of the effect.**

    For the purpose of this demonstration, I increased the inner bevel's width.

14. **Repeat Steps 10-14 for the remaining frames of the animation.**

    In the remaining frames, move the object and modify the effect's parameters. Figure 20-2 shows the animation I created to illustrate this process. Of course you can't see it in motion because Animated GIFs don't work on book pages, only in Web browsers. In lieu of a full-fledged animation, I've turned on the onion skins so you can see how the object's bevel gets larger in each frame.

Figure 20-2:
Animated
effects
create
visual
interest on
your Web
pages.

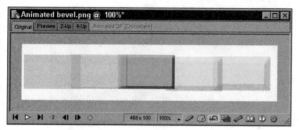

Using the Eye Candy Bevel Boss Filter

Fireworks has some bonus toys for you to use when you create your Fireworks documents. You get three filters from the newest version of Eye Candy, a powerful set of image-editing filters. The first filter in the lot is the Bevel Boss filter, which really is boss. To apply the Bevel Boss filter:

1. **Select a bitmap image in your document.**

   You can apply the Bevel Boss filter to a vector object such as an oval or a rectangle, but Fireworks will convert it to a bitmap if you select the filter from the Xtras menu. However if you apply the filter through the Effect panel, the vector object maintains its vector status.

2. **Choose Xtras⇔Eye Candy 4000 LE⇔Bevel Boss.**

   You can also apply any filter through the Effect panel. When you apply a filter through the Effect panel, it can be edited by reopening the panel. Filters applied through the Xtras menu can't be edited after the fact.

   Fireworks opens the Bevel Boss dialog box for you, boss man or boss lady.

3. **In the Basic section, adjust the basic characteristics of the bevel, such as width, height, and smoothness.**

   This is not rocket science — it's eye candy. Drag the sliders and adjust the parameters until you see a bevel that you like (see Figure 20-3).

4. **Click the Lighting tab.**

   Fireworks opens the filter's lighting section, as shown in Figure 20-4. Click the highlight on the ball in the left window and drag it to adjust the direction of the light. Drag the sliders to adjust the highlight brightness and size. If desired, choose new colors for the highlight by clicking the color swatches to choose a color from a palette or by clicking the eye-dropper and clicking a color in the document to select it. As you make changes, Fireworks updates the image in the right-hand window of the dialog box.

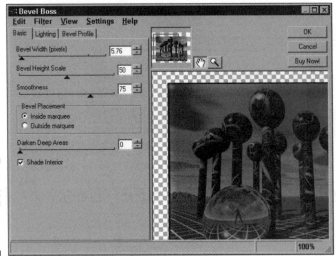

Figure 20-3:
You adjust
the looks of
the bevel in
this section.

Figure 20-4:
In this
section you
adjust the
filter's
lighting
character-
istics.

5. Click the Bevel Profile tab.

Fireworks opens the filter's bevel section. Select a preset from the menu shown in Figure 20-5. To modify the preset shape, in the window below the menu, drag the individual points on the shape's outline.

6. Click OK to apply the bevel.

Fireworks bevels the object.

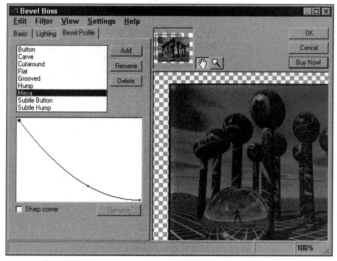

Figure 20-5:
You adjust
the bevel's
shape in this
section.

Using the Eye Candy Marble Filter

If you've ever marveled at marble floors, marble tabletops, or just marbles in general, you'll really like this effect. You can apply marble texture to objects in your Fireworks documents with the Eye Candy Marble filter. Here's how:

1. **Create an object with one of the drawing tools.**

2. **Choose Xtras⇨Eye Candy 4000 LE⇨Marble.**

   Fireworks displays a warning dialog telling you the vector object will be converted to a bitmap. Click OK, and Fireworks opens the Marble filter dialog box (see Figure 20-6).

3. **Drag the sliders to adjust the characteristics of the veins.**

   As you drag the sliders, Fireworks updates the image in the right hand window. Drag the sliders until you get a marble that rivals Michelangelo's famed Carrara marble. To generate a marble pattern without manually adjusting the sliders, click the Random Seed button.

4. **Choose the Bedrock and Vein colors for the marble.**

   Click the color swatches and select a color from the palette. To match a color from the document, click the eyedropper icon and then click a color from the document.

5. **When the marble is just the way you want it, click OK.**

   Fireworks creates a lovely marbled shade on the chosen object.

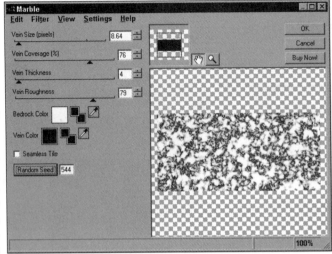

Figure 20-6:
To create
your very
own marble,
choose the
Eye Candy
Marble
filter.

Using the Eye Candy Motion Trail Filter

Use the Eye Candy Motion Trail filter to modify a bitmap image so that it looks has just swooped in from the great beyond. This effect kind of looks like those comic strip images of Superman in flight, with blurs stretching out from his body to simulate speed. To apply the Motion Trail filter to a bitmap:

1. **Using the Pointer tool, select the object you want to apply the filter to.**

2. **Choose Xtras⇨Eye Candy 4000 LE⇨Motion Trail.**

   Fireworks opens the Motion Trail dialog box, as shown in Figure 20-7.

3. **Click the dot on the rotary slider in the Direction window and drag it to adjust the trail's direction.**

   As you drag the dot, Fireworks changes the image in the right-hand window.

4. **Drag the sliders to adjust the trail's width, taper, and opacity.**

   As you drag the sliders, watch the image in the right window. When you see something you like, stop dragging.

5. **Accept the default Smear Color from Edges or choose the Draw Only Outside Section option.**

   • Choose the default option to start the taper by blurring the outside edges of the object.

   • Choose the Draw Only Outside Section option to leave the object untouched and create the motion trail only.

6. **Click OK to apply the filter.**

Figure 20-7:
Look, up in
the sky. Is it
a bird? Is it
a plane?
No! It's
Motion
Trails!

Creating Cut-Out Text

Another way to make text stand out on a Web page is to create a cut-out
effect. Cut-out text looks like it was chiseled out of the background. Here's
an effect that can be created quickly and is bound to get attention. To create
cut-out text:

1. **Choose File⇨New.**

   Fireworks opens the New Document dialog box.

2. **Enter the width and height for the document and then choose a
   canvas color.**

   Fireworks creates a blank canvas in the workspace, all ready for your
   dazzling cut-out text.

3. **Select the Rectangle tool and create a rectangle on the canvas.**

4. **Choose Window⇨Fill.**

   The Fill panel opens.

5. **Click the triangle to the right of the Fill Category field and choose
   Pattern.**

6. **Click the triangle to the right of the Pattern Name field and choose
   one of the wood patterns.**

   Fireworks applies the pattern to the rectangle.

7. **Choose Window⇨Layers.**

   Fireworks opens the Layers panel.

8. **Click the triangle near the upper right-hand corner of the panel and choose New Layer from the drop-down menu.**

    Fireworks adds a new layer to the document.

 9. **Select the Text tool.**

    Fireworks opens the Text Editor.

10. **Choose a font style and font size, and then choose black for the font color.**

    Bold font styles work the best with this technique. Black is used for the text's color because this text serves only as a border for the cut out text.

11. **Type the text you want to apply the effect to and then click OK.**

    Fireworks creates the block of text.

12. **Use the Align commands to center the text to the rectangle.**

13. **Select the text block with the Pointer tool and choose Edit⇨Copy.**

    Fireworks copies the text to the clipboard.

14. **Create a new layer as outlined in Steps 7 and 8.**

15. **Choose Edit⇨Paste.**

    Fireworks pastes a copy of the text to the new layer.

16. **Apply the wood fill to the text object as outlined in Steps 4 through 6.**

    The text now matches the background (you can barely see it).

17. **Choose Window⇨Effect.**

    Fireworks effectively opens the Effect panel.

18. **Click the triangle to the right of the Effects field and choose Inner Shadow from the drop-down menu.**

    Fireworks opens the effect's dialog box.

19. **Accept the default settings.**

    Fireworks creates an inner shadow.

20. **In the Layers panel, click the text object's thumbnail on Layer 2 to select it.**

    Fireworks selects the text object.

21. **Use the computer keyboard's arrow keys to nudge the text object down and to the right.**

    Fireworks moves the text object, which completes the cut-out text effect. Your cut-out text should resemble Figure 20-8.

Figure 20-8:
Fireworks
can create
cut-out text
without a
chisel.

Creating Fading Text

Another animation effect that's easy to create and easy on the eyes is fading text. When you create a fading text animation, you can have text fade in or fade out; the choice is yours. To create a fading text animation:

1. **Choose File⇨New.**

   Fireworks opens the New Document dialog box.

2. **Specify the width and height for your fading text animation, choose a background color, and then click OK.**

   Fireworks creates a new document.

 3. **Select the Text tool.**

   Fireworks opens the Text Editor.

4. **Select a font style, font size, font color, type the fading text, and then click OK.**

   Fireworks creates a block of text. This effect works best with large text.

5. **Choose Window⇨Info.**

   Fireworks opens the Info panel.

6. **Align the text to the center of the document.**

7. **With the text object still selected, choose Modify⇨Animate Selection.**

   The Animate dialog box appears.

8. **Enter the following values in each named field to fade the text:**

   - Frames: 7

   - Movement: 0

- Direction: 0
- Scaling: 100
- Opacity: 100-0
- Rotation: 0

The opacity settings cause the text to fade out. To have the text fade in, reverse the values and the text will be invisible when the animation starts and fully opaque at the end.

9. Click OK.

Fireworks closes the Animate dialog box.

10. Choose Window➪Frames.

Fireworks opens the Frames panel.

11. Adjust the frame delay rate for each frame.

To adjust the frame rate, click the number to the right of the frame's name, and enter a value in the Frame Delay dialog box. (This option determines how long the next frame is delayed from displaying.)

12. Choose Window➪Optimize.

Fireworks opens the Optimize panel.

13. Choose Animated GIF for the export file format.

14. Choose File➪Export.

Fireworks exports your fading text animation.

Creating a Text Image Mask

Another effect that you can create quickly is a text image mask. A text image mask reveals the portion of a bitmap image that is beneath a text object. The end result looks like the letters are constructed from photographs. An image masked with text makes a nice banner for a Web site. To create a text image mask:

1. Choose File➪New.

Fireworks opens the New Document dialog box.

2. Specify the width and height for the document and choose a canvas color.

Fireworks creates a new canvas for you to work with.

3. Choose File➪Import.

Fireworks opens the Import dialog box.

4. **Select the bitmap image you want to mask and then click OK.**

5. **Move your cursor over the canvas.**

   The cursor becomes two lines forming at a right angle.

6. **Click the spot on the canvas where you want to upper-left corner of the bitmap to appear.**

   Fireworks imports the bitmap. The exact placement isn't important at this time. After you mask the image, you can move it to its final position.

 7. **Select the Text tool and click anywhere on the canvas.**

   Fireworks opens the Text Editor.

8. **Choose a font style and font size; then enter the text in the window and click OK.**

   Fireworks creates the text object on the canvas. You needn't concern yourself with a text color, as this is only a mask.

9. **Align the text to the bitmap image using either the Pointer tool or the Align commands.**

10. **Select the text object with the Pointer tool and then choose Edit⇨Cut.**

    Fireworks whisks away the text.

11. **Select the bitmap image with the Pointer tool and then choose Edit⇨Paste as Mask.**

    Fireworks pastes the cut text object to the bitmap image as a mask to create the effect shown in Figure 20-9.

Figure 20-9:
Masked text
strikes
again.

Attaching Text to Both Sides of an Elliptical Path

Fireworks makes short work out of attaching text to a path. However, if you want to attach text to the top and bottom of an ellipse, it involves a bit more work on your part. The results are well worth the effort though. To attach text to both sides of an elliptical path:

For more information on creating and working with paths, check out Chapters 3 and 10.

 1. **Select the Ellipse tool.**

2. **In the Colors section of the toolbox, click the paint bucket icon and then click the No Color button.**

3. **Click the color swatch to the right of the pencil icon and choose black from the color palette.**

    Your goal is to create an elliptical outline with no color.

4. **Drag the tool on the canvas to create an ellipse. When the ellipse is the size and configuration you want, release the mouse button.**

    Fireworks creates an elliptical outline.

 5. **Select the Knife tool. (It's the ninth tool on the left side of the toolbox that looks like a scalpel.)**

6. **Hold down the Shift key and drag the tool across the center of the ellipse.**

    Fireworks cuts the ellipse in two.

 7. **Select the Text tool.**

    Fireworks opens the Text Editor.

8. **Select a font size, font color, and font style; then type the word you want to attach to the top of the ellipse, click the Center Alignment button, and click OK.**

    Fireworks creates the text.

 9. **Select the text with the Pointer tool and while holding down the Shift key, click the top part of the ellipse.**

    Fireworks selects the text and upper ellipse.

10. **Choose Text⇨Attach to Path.**

    Fireworks creates a magnetic bond between the ellipse and the text.

11. **Create another text object as outlined in Steps 7 and 8.**

12. **Select the Text and the bottom part of the Ellipse with the Pointer tool.**

13. **Choose Text⇨Attach to Path.**

    Hmm, something doesn't look quite right here. The text is upside down.

14. **Choose Text⇨Reverse Direction.**

    Fireworks rights the text, but it's on the wrong side of the ellipse.

15. **Double-click the text object.**

    Fireworks opens the Text Editor.

16. **Click the triangle to the left of the Baseline Shift field and drag the slider down.**

    The actual setting for the baseline shift varies depending upon the font's style and size.

17. **Drag the slider down and release it.**

    Fireworks slips the text below the baseline. If the alignment isn't right, drag the slider again.

18. **When the text is aligned to your satisfaction, click OK.**

    Fireworks realigns the text just the way you want it. Figure 20-10 shows text aligned to both sides of an elliptical path. For clarity, the text objects and paths have been selected.

Figure 20-10:
Aligning text to both sides of an elliptical path is a cool effect.

Creating a Shadow Box

Nothing says special like an image with a shadow box around it. If you've got a special image that you want to spice up, you can create a shadow box around it with just a few quick steps. To create a shadow box:

1. **Choose File⇨New.**

   Fireworks opens the New Document dialog box.

2. **Specify the width and height for the document and choose a canvas color.**

   Fireworks creates a new canvas for you to work with.

3. **Choose File⇨Import.**

   Fireworks opens the Import dialog box.

4. **Select the bitmap image you want to create a shadow box around and then click OK.**

5. **Move your cursor over the canvas.**

   The cursor becomes two lines forming at a right angle.

6. **Click the spot on the canvas where you want to upper-left corner of the bitmap to appear.**

   Fireworks imports the bitmap.

7. **Select the Rectangle tool.**

   Accept the default settings for the tool.

8. **Click and drag the tool on the canvas to create a rectangle.**

   Create a rectangle that's slightly larger than the bitmap.

9. **Choose Window⇨Info.**

   Fireworks opens the Info panel.

10. **Resize the rectangle so that both its width and height are 15 pixels larger than the bitmap.**

11. **With the rectangle still selected, choose Modify⇨Arrange⇨Send Backward.**

    Fireworks places the rectangle behind the bitmap.

12. **Use the Align commands to center the rectangle vertically and horizontally to the bitmap.**

13. **Choose Window⇨Effect.**

    Fireworks opens the Effect panel.

14. **Click the triangle to the right of the Effect field and then choose Inner Shadow from the drop-down menu.**

    Fireworks opens the effect's parameters.

15. **Select the Knock Out option, click the triangle to the right of the Softness field and drag the slider to 15.**

    Fireworks creates an inner shadow and your shadow box is done. Figure 20-11 shows what evil lurks in the heart of a shadow box.

Figure 20-11: A shadow box is a nice effect for an image.

Chapter 21

Top Ten Internet Sources for Fireworks

*T*he Internet is a large uncharted sea of `https` with more information than any one person could hope to assimilate in a lifetime. When you're searching for information on the Internet, you can whittle down the sea of possibilities by typing a key word into a search engine. Or someone who's sailed the friendly `https` can direct you to a Web site of known quantity and quality. And that's what this chapter is about. Okay, now that you know you can get there from here, check out some of the Web sites below for information about Fireworks, Web site authoring and other HTML goodies. Oh, there are more than ten sites in this chapter, which makes the chapter title seem rather silly. But this is the Part of Tens.

Macromedia Fireworks Support Center

The Macromedia Fireworks Support Web page (`http://www.macromedia.com/support/fireworks/`) is a storehouse of Fireworks information. Bookmark this site and check it out often for tech notes, tutorials, and downloads. Macromedia has recently created a program called the Extension Manager. There are no extensions for Fireworks yet, but I'm sure they will become available and when they do, you can download them from this site. Extensions have already been created for Macromedia's Flash and Dreamweaver programs. (*Extensions* enhance the usability of the program.)

In addition to finding support from Macromedia here, you'll also find links to other informative Web sites and Fireworks user groups. If you've never experienced a user group before, I suggest you check out the Fireworks user groups. You'll find a group of highly creative individuals who are more than willing to share their gems of wisdom with you.

Playing With Fire

Playing With Fire (http://www.playingwithfire.com/) is a Web site devoted to Fireworks tutorials. Here you'll find detailed instructions that show you how to create interesting effects with text and buttons. Many of the tutorials were written for Fireworks 3, but work equally well for Fireworks 4. As time goes on, I'm sure you can expect to see tutorials for effects that can be created with the enhanced tools of Fireworks 4.

Id Est

Id Est is Joseph Lowery's Web site. Joseph Lowery is the author of the *Fireworks 3 Bible* and has a section devoted to Web design with Macromedia's Dreamweaver. This site is a must if you're using Fireworks in conjunction with Dreamweaver. You can find it at: http://www.idest.com/dreamweaver/. Check out the link to the Objects section. Here you'll find some extensions to streamline your work in Dreamweaver. As I write this chapter, Joseph is working on his *Fireworks 4 Bible* so I'm sure you'll find lots of new stuff for Fireworks 4 after the book is published.

Web Monkey

Web Monkey (http://hotwired.lycos.com/webmonkey/) is a daily Internet newsletter devoted to Web design. The site is not Fireworks specific, but has a wealth of information on Web design. You'll find articles by Web design gurus that keep you abreast of the latest trends in Web design. There are individual sections devoted to authoring html, design, multimedia, e-business, programming, and there's even a job section.

If you find Web Monkey is useful, you can arrange to have it delivered to you daily via e-mail. After you subscribe, the page will be attached to an e-mail with links to each article in the issue and the rest of the Web Monkey site.

Matt's Script Archives

When you start creating bigger and better Web sites and start incorporating your Fireworks images and documents in more complex Web pages, you may be tempted to dabble with CGI *(Common Gateway Interface)* scripts. CGI scripts are used to run Web page items like counters, guestbooks, and real-time clocks. They are also used to forward the results of Web site forms to e-mail addresses.

It takes quite a while to master the art of creating a functional CGI script. I know that the first time I examined a CGI script in detail, I got lost after the first few lines of the script. Fortunately, you can get some very powerful CGI scripts for free at Matt's site. Point your Web browser to `http://worldwidemart.com/scripts/` to check out the latest and greatest that Matt has to offer.

Lynda.com

This author's Web site (`http://www.Lynda.com`) features information about many different aspects of HTML authoring. You'll find information on image formats, Web-safe colors, and Web site authoring. Check out the Inspiration section for some excellent examples of creative Web site design.

Project Fireworks

Project Fireworks (`http://www.projectfireworks.com/`) is a site that is devoted to none other than the subject of this book, Fireworks. Here you'll find a wealth of information about Fireworks including detailed tutorials that show you get stuff done with Fireworks. In this site, you get material that is specific to Fireworks 4. There's also a section called Gadgets that has some patterns and textures you can download for free. Such a deal. Please note that you'll need Netscape 6 to view this site, as it will not function properly in earlier versions of Netscape's browser. (I tested the site with Internet Explorer 5.5 and the site worked fine with that browser.)

Gif Foundry

The GIF Foundry (`http://www.digital-foundry.com/index_gif.html`) was created by a very talented Web design duo from Great Britain. This site features information about how to create images and animations with the GIF format. You'll find information about color palettes, transparency, and animation. The workshop section is a must.

BrowserWatch

Go to BrowserWatch (`http://browserwatch.internet.com/`) when you want to find out the latest information on Web browsers. If you know what platform and browser the intended audience of your Web design prefers, you can get any browser specific information you need here. The Browser Boulevard section features information on platform specific browsers. The Plug-In Plaza section shows you which plug-ins are available for a particular browser. This information comes in handy when you edit your Fireworks documents in an HTML editing program and incorporate different media that require specific plug ins.

Pretty Lady

Here's a site devoted to Web design and all things HTML. Visit the main site (`http://nirvana.media3.net/pretty_lady/#`) and click the Pretty Lady button. The page that loads is an extensive Fireworks and Dreamweaver resource center. In the Fireworks section, you'll find a section on tutorials, interfaces, styles, and commands. As of this writing, the material is all Fireworks 3 specific, but I'm sure by the time this book is in your hands, there will be Fireworks 4 material available.

The JavaScript Source

Fireworks takes care of creating the JavaScript needed to create the program's behaviors such as image swapping, rollover buttons, and pop-up menus. If you have the need for other JavaScript effects in your work, you have no choice other than to create the JavaScript yourself or download it from a site like the JavaScript Source (`http://javascript.internet.com/`). The JavaScript source has an extensive database of ready to use JavaScripts that you can download and paste into your HTML documents. Most of the scripts come complete with instructions on how to paste them into the HTML document and, if necessary, configure them for the intended application they will perform.

Fireworks FAQ and Extension Database

Point your Web browser to `http://comharsa.com/firefaq/index.htm` and prepare yourself for a wealth of information about Fireworks. There's a list of FAQ (*Frequently Asked Questions* for the acronym challenged) that may answer a question that's been troubling you. There's also a command section that links to command scripts that have been created for Fireworks.

Index

●●

• *O* •

Notes

Notes

Notes

Notes

YOUR ONLINE RESOURCE

WWW.DUMMIES.COM

Discover Dummies Online!

The Dummies Web Site is your fun and friendly online resource for the latest information about *For Dummies* books and your favorite topics. The Web site is the place to communicate with us, exchange ideas with other *For Dummies* readers, chat with authors, and have fun!

Ten Fun and Useful Things You Can Do at www.dummies.com

1. Win free *For Dummies* books and more!
2. Register your book and be entered in a prize drawing.
3. Meet your favorite authors through the Hungry Minds Author Chat Series.
4. Exchange helpful information with other *For Dummies* readers.
5. Discover other great *For Dummies* books you must have!
6. Purchase Dummieswear exclusively from our Web site.
7. Buy *For Dummies* books online.
8. Talk to us. Make comments, ask questions, get answers!
9. Download free software.
10. Find additional useful resources from authors.

Link directly to these ten fun and useful things at **www.dummies.com/10useful**

For other technology titles from Hungry Minds, go to
www.hungryminds.com

Not on the Web yet? It's easy to get started with *Dummies 101: The Internet For Windows 98* or *The Internet For Dummies* at local retailers everywhere.

Find other *For Dummies* books on these topics:
Business • Career • Databases • Food & Beverage • Games • Gardening
Graphics • Hardware • Health & Fitness • Internet and the World Wide Web
Networking • Office Suites • Operating Systems • Personal Finance • Pets
Programming • Recreation • Sports • Spreadsheets • Teacher Resources
Test Prep • Word Processing

Hungry Minds™

FOR DUMMIES
BOOK REGISTRATION

We want to hear from you!

Visit **dummies.com** to register this book and tell us how you liked it!

- Get entered in our monthly prize giveaway.

- Give us feedback about this book — tell us what you like best, what you like least, or maybe what you'd like to ask the author and us to change!

- Let us know any other *For Dummies* topics that interest you.

Your feedback helps us determine what books to publish, tells us what coverage to add as we revise our books, and lets us know whether we're meeting your needs as a *For Dummies* reader. You're our most valuable resource, and what you have to say is important to us!

Not on the Web yet? It's easy to get started with *Dummies 101: The Internet For Windows 98* or *The Internet For Dummies* at local retailers everywhere.

Or let us know what you think by sending us a letter at the following address:

For Dummies Book Registration
Dummies Press
10475 Crosspoint Blvd.
Indianapolis, IN 46256

BESTSELLING BOOK SERIES